PARAMAHANSA YOGANANDA
(1893–1952)

"Mejda"

The Family and the Early Life of

Paramahansa Yogananda

BY
Sananda Lal Ghosh

SELF-REALIZATION FELLOWSHIP
Founded by Paramahansa Yogananda

Second printing, 1992

Authorized by the International Publications Council of Self-Realization Fellowship

Self-Realization Fellowship was founded in 1920 by Paramahansa Yogananda as the instrument for the worldwide dissemination of his teachings. The reader may be certain of the authenticity of publications by or about Paramahansa Yogananda and his teachings if the registered Self-Realization emblem, and/or the statement of authorization (shown together above), appears on those works.

Library of Congress Catalog Number: 80–54206
ISBN 0–87612–265–9
Printed in the United States of America
11112–54321

DEDICATION

To my father, Bhagabati Charan Ghosh

Father,

You filled our home
With the radiance of your piety.
Your fathomless affection
Helped us to suffer less
For want of the mother we lost.
O dispassionate stoic,
Renunciant of desire and attachment,
Initiate of love divine,
Your life, like the sacred homa,
Was a sacrificial fire, pure and true,
Dedicated to God.
Though tied to a hundredfold duties,
Yet ever were you free,
Serving tirelessly; seeking no reward.
Like an ancient banyan tree, your nature was—
How many distressed hearts found solace
In the sheltering shade of your wisdom
And the soothing breeze of your kindness.
As a great river nourishes its shores,
So did you transform the barrenness of life
Into a fertile land of fruits and flowers.
You have departed.
Bless us from heaven; strengthen our hearts.
May the vestige of your life
Be our viaticum.

Your ever affectionate
Sananda (Gora)

CONTENTS

ADDENDA

ILLUSTRATIONS

Photo section, following page 266

FOREWORD

By Dr. Ashutosh Das, M.A. (Double), Ph.D., D.Litt. (Calcutta), Vidya-Vachaspati, Sahitya-Shastri, Tantrayoga-Siddhantabagish, F.R.A.S. (London), Prachavidya-Maharnava, Professor, Calcutta University

*"Mejda": The Family and the Early Life of Paramahansa Yogananda,** written by Paramahansaji's younger brother, Sri Sananda Lal Ghosh, is a valuable biography of the great Guru. An excellent supplement to Paramahansaji's *Autobiography of a Yogi,* it presents many incidents about Paramahansa Yogananda's family and early life in India not included in his autobiography.

Autobiography of a Yogi is regarded as an *Upanishad*† of the new age. Published in sixteen languages, it has satisfied the spiritual thirst of hundreds of thousands of truth-seekers throughout the world. We in India have watched with wonder and fascination the phenomenal spread of the popularity of this book about India's saints and philosophy. We have felt great satisfaction and pride that the immortal nectar of India's *Sanatan Dharma,* the eternal laws of truth, has been stored in the golden chalice of *Autobiography of a Yogi.*

Paramahansa Yogananda's life and work are captivating. As a true propagator of the Hindu religion, and as the spiritual pioneer who was divinely chosen to dis-

* *Mejda* means "second eldest brother," which was Paramahansa Yogananda's relationship to the author, Sananda Lal Ghosh. *(Publisher's Note)*

† Historically, there are 108 *Upanishads,* which contain the essence of the four Vedas. The *Upanishads* were designated as "wisdom scriptures."

seminate *Kriya Yoga* worldwide, Paramahansaji's fame has spread like a fragrance from the Calcutta home at 4 Garpar Road, from the Serampore hermitage of his preceptor, Swami Sri Yukteswar Giri, and from the Brahmacharya Vidyalaya* in Ranchi to America and the farthermost horizons of the globe. Under the banner of Yogoda Satsanga Society of India/Self-Realization Fellowship, he established numerous meditation centers in many lands. The ashrams, temples, and centers of his work are holy places for the practice of India's great science of Yoga.

Devotees of Paramahansaji from many countries have visited their gurudeva's home in Calcutta, and have thrilled to hear from his brother stories of Paramahansaji's childhood and early life in India. "*Mejda*" is a grand accomplishment that will share with a wider audience these stories of an uncommonly spiritually powerful ascetic. Many of these were not included by Paramahansa Yogananda in his autobiography because of his natural reticence about calling attention to himself.

It was quite unexpected that I should be asked by the author to write the foreword to this book. Though the question of my competency arises in my mind, I have acceded to the request because I feel it a great privilege. While on summer vacation in 1938, in the hermitage of an ascetic on a hill in Chotanagpore, I heard about the glorious life of Paramahansa Yogananda. I was overwhelmed. Later, when I was in the Chakrebaria area of Bhawanipore seeking out a manuscript of "Padma Puran," by Jiwan Moitra, in the course of my work I went to the house of a devout person to see a highly regarded white statue of Lord Krishna. I was

* School for boys established by Paramahansa Yogananda.

surprised to meet there two American disciples of Paramahansa Yogananda who had come from his ashram in Ranchi to view the beautiful image.

Then one day, Sri Sananda Lal Ghosh invited me to visit him. I learned during our conversation that Paramahansaji had found God in this house at 4 Garpar Road. I went to the attic room, made sacred by the great yogi's *sadhana,* bowed down and sat for some time in meditation. In one of Paramahansaji's letters to his brother he had said, "This is my holy *pith* [seat, place] where I found God." It was my good fortune to have the opportunity to pay my respects at this sacred shrine—a precious moment in my ordinary life. I cannot but wonder if through his divine power Paramahansaji had accepted my humble obeisance in the hermitage of the ascetic on the hill of Chotanagpore, and blessed me with his grace that I could visit his attic room where he pursued his *sadhana;* and that, as a result of that visit, I was given the opportunity to write the foreword to this book.

In this modern age, it is wonderful that in spite of the materialism of the West, innumerable persons there have shown such interest in the spiritual accomplishments of Paramahansa Yogananda, a yogi from the East. The divine power of Sri Ramakrishna Paramahansa is widely known; he is worshipfully venerated by all spiritually minded people throughout India, and by many abroad. The mysticism of great saints has a deep appeal and promise of hope for the troubled human mind. Thus, many have been similarly inspired by the life of Paramahansa Yogananda, and Yogoda/Self-Realization members from all over the world have come to his childhood home to hear firsthand accounts of his early life from his brother, Sananda Lal Ghosh. He was Paramahansaji's follower, devotee, and companion during the great yogi's childhood. And now, in the closing years of his life, Sananda Lal Ghosh has undertaken the task of writing this book to share with all seekers these spiritually rich incidents in the life of Paramahansa Deva. The effort crowns the author with glory. His work has significant historic value, since many of the incidents he has recorded took place in his presence.

Paramahansa Yogananda was born in a family of virtuous yogis. His father was a true ascetic, while at the same time he fulfilled admirably his family responsibilities. His mother was like a goddess. Paramahansaji's parents were initiated by Yogiraj* Lahiri Mahasaya. Born Mukunda Lal Ghosh, Paramahansa Yogananda had three brothers and four sisters, all of whom were reared in a spiritual environment.

Each brother achieved a high degree of success in his own field. The eldest, Ananta Lal, was well established in his work in accountancy, and greatly respected. He achieved the position of a high-ranking officer,† earning a large salary while still a young man. His affectionate concern for his brothers and sisters was exemplary. He was frugal, moderate in his habits, kind and benevolent. Initially, he had not much faith in religion. Through the spiritual influence of his younger brother Mukunda, Ananta's whole outlook changed, and he received initiation from Mukunda. Ananta Lal died at the age of thirty-one. Paramahansaji has lovingly described his life in *Autobiography of a Yogi*.

Sri Sananda Lal Ghosh is himself an accomplished

* A "royal" or "kingly" yogi; one who has achieved the highest mastery of the yoga science. *(Publisher's Note)*

† A supervising accountant for the Government Department of Public Works.

yogi. In his full life he has combined the qualities of artist, musician, architect, mechanic, and devotee of God. The paintings of Paramahansa Yogananda by Sananda Lal Ghosh have been widely acclaimed. His painting of Rabindranath Tagore, chief among India's poets, has received worldwide recognition. This picture hangs in many of the schools and colleges of India. Rabindranath himself felt it was the best standing-pose of him ever painted. He personally complimented Sananda by sending him a certificate to this effect. A marble statue of Tagore installed in the Assembly Hall in New Delhi is patterned after Sananda's painting.

The late Bishnu Ghosh, youngest child of the family, gained national and international fame as a physical culturist. He was the first and only Indian judge in a Mr. Universe contest held in London. He was the first Indian of contemporary times to introduce and make popular a system of *Hatha Yoga* that appealed greatly to the general public. He brought the ancient science of *Hatha Yoga* out of the hermitages and into the courtyards of homes and the fields of villages. I was charmed to meet Bishnu. He exuded a warm personality, strength, courage, sincerity, and highmindedness. He was a devotee of God, as well as a genius in the field of *Hatha Yoga* and physical culture. He was a pride of India, and will ever be remembered for introducing yoga exercises to the masses.

Paramahansa Yogananda was a *Yogeshwar* (Lord of Yogis). His mastery of yoga came to him as a natural inheritance. The renowned Lahiri Mahasaya was the guru of Paramahansaji's parents, and of his guru, Swami Sri Yukteswar Giri. In the historic and traditional lines of illumined masters who bring truth to the world, Paramahansaji was the fourth of the Yogoda/Self-

Realization line of great Gurus.* Paramahansaji's mission led him to preach the art and science of yoga-living in America, Europe, and throughout the world.

It was commonly thought that the practice of a soul science like *Kriya Yoga* was restricted to secluded ascetics in forests and mountain caves. Paramahansa Yogananda's mission was to show that a person in ordinary family life anywhere in the world could receive and practice *Kriya Yoga* with highest spiritual benefit. He has rendered a supreme service to mankind by bringing the science of Yoga, and the technique of *Kriya Yoga,* into practical everyday application in life. Persons in India and worldwide will receive beneficent effects by learning the *Kriya Yoga* as taught by Paramahansa Yogananda.

"*Mejda*" is a great light of oblation to the worldwide spread of *Kriya Yoga.*

* Mahavatar Babaji, Lahiri Mahasaya, Swami Sri Yukteswar, and Paramahansa Yogananda. Paramahansaji's work, Self-Realization Fellowship/Yogoda Satsanga Society of India, is carried on by his line of spiritual successors. The first was Sri Rajarsi Janakananda, who served from 1952 to 1955. He was succeeded by Sri Daya Mata, who, like Rajarsi, was personally trained and appointed to this position by Paramahansa Yogananda. *(Publisher's Note)*

PUBLISHER'S NOTE

It is with sadness that we record here the death of the author of *"Mejda."* Sri Sananda Lal Ghosh passed away in Calcutta on October 10, 1979, at the age of eighty-one. We are indeed grateful to him for setting down these memoirs of the family and early life of his elder brother, whom he called "Mejda," known to the world today as Paramahansa Yogananda, author of *Autobiography of a Yogi* and founder of Self-Realization Fellowship/Yogoda Satsanga Society of India. Sri Ghosh also furnished many of the photographs in the work; others are from the files of Self-Realization Fellowship.

It was our good fortune to be able to consult with the author in clarifying and confirming many points in the manuscript, a service to which he gave himself unstintingly to his last days. Though he was not able to complete this task, invaluable assistance came from other family members and friends. It is a remarkable account, and we deeply regret that Sri Ghosh did not live to see its publication. He has left with us a worthy contribution to the lore of one of the world's greatest spiritual teachers.

SELF-REALIZATION FELLOWSHIP

Los Angeles, California
October 27, 1980

INTRODUCTION

In writing *Autobiography of a Yogi,* Paramahansa Yogananda—whom I respectfully call "Mejda," second eldest brother—omitted several revealing incidents of his early life. I believe he did so purposely. Had he fully disclosed himself, he would have surpassed many of the contemporaries he extolled. Some might have thought the Yogi Maharaj* was given to praising himself. On the contrary, it was always his way to place himself in the background and push others to the fore. So I have long felt that *Autobiography of a Yogi,* to be complete insofar as Mejda's life story is concerned, needed a sequel to make public many of the incidents of his early life. For several years I have labored to this end. The plant of my desire has now matured. Had I not received timely inspiration and help, the seedling of my wish would have been destroyed by circumstances; I would have exited this world with a heavy debt unpaid. Mejda was my childhood companion and friend, and the guiding light of my youth. The most prized treasures among my memories are of those incidents that were a part of the early years spent with my wise preceptor, Yogeshwar† Yogananda.

Inspired by *Autobiography of a Yogi,* many Yogoda Satsanga/Self-Realization Fellowship devotees from all parts of the world have come on pilgrimage to their guru's beloved India. Many were persons of ordinary means who had to save for years in order to make the

* King among yogis.

† A title given to both Shiva and Krishna, meaning Lord of Yogis; also, one who has attained oneness with God, Ishwara, through yoga.

journey. During every season of the year, they have visited Mejda's childhood home, the holy place of his early *sadhana,** 4 Garpar Road, Calcutta. Out of reverence for the Yogeshwar, they have regarded his home as a special place of pilgrimage, and have bowed their heads in devotion as they entered. Ofttimes, when ascending the staircase to the upper floors, they have reverently placed the dust of the steps on their heads,† recalling that Paramahansaji climbed these stairs many times. The pilgrims visit the room where he slept and the front room where he conversed with Mahavatar Babaji. They especially request permission to meditate in the small attic room where their guru meditated daily, and which was witness to the early dawn of his spiritual awakening.

They have been deeply gratified to meet members of Mejda's immediate family, and to hear stories of his boyhood. All have earnestly requested that I publish these stories, since I was a companion to him, being only five years younger than he, and an eyewitness to many of his early-life experiences.

In narrating these stories, some references to myself have been unavoidable. It is not my desire to give myself any prominence. I have made mention of myself only to give testimony to the verity of these unusual incidents in the life of Mejda.

It is one thing to write a book, quite another to publish it. The intricacies of printing are unknown to me, and my time and energy are limited. Several friends offered help and encouragement; it was through their aid that this book became a reality. I thank them all

* Spiritual quest.

† A gesture of devotion in which one touches the floor and then one's head, symbolically taking the blessing of the illumined soul who has walked there.

sincerely from the deepest core of my heart, and with gratitude mention here their names:

Dr. Ashutosh Das, M.A. (Double), Ph.D., D.Litt. (Calcutta), F.R.A.S. (London), Professor of Philosophy and Literature at Calcutta University, particularly encouraged and supported the publication of this book. His two sons, Sri Prem Sundar Das, M.A. (Double), B.S., L.L.B., and Sri Dibya Sundar Das, M.Comm., L.L.B., assisted valuably with the writing of this book. It would not have been possible to complete my work without their help. My neighbor, Sri Binay Das, assisted me gratuitously. My grandson, Somnath Ghosh, was an able, enthusiastic helper. My wife, Parul, contributed greatly; it was one of her last offerings in this mortal world. I was bereft of her faithful companionship of many years when she died on September 3, 1978. I here express my heartfelt appreciation to each of them.

"MEJDA"

CHAPTER I

Father's Humble Beginnings

Our Ancestral Home in Ichapur

Paramahansa Yogananda's family name was Mukunda Lal Ghosh. Our elders called him Mukun or Moko, but we youngsters addressed him as Mejda, "second eldest brother."*

We were four brothers and four sisters. The eldest was our brother, Ananta Lal, nicknamed Nantu. The second was our eldest sister, Roma Shashi, nicknamed Tuni. The third child was our second sister, Uma Shashi, whom our elders called Muni. The fourth was Mejda. Fifth was our third sister, Nalini Sundari, nicknamed Nali. Sixth was myself, Sananda Lal, called Gora. The seventh child was our youngest sister, Purnamoyee, nicknamed Thamu. And the eighth and last child was our youngest brother, Bishnu Charan, nicknamed Bistu. From among the four brothers and four sisters, I alone am still living.†

* In Bengali, the terminology to designate the order of brothers in a family is *Bara* (eldest), *Meja* (second), *Seja* (third), etc. *Dada* means elder brother. Therefore, Meja-dada or Mejda, as shortened in common usage, would be one's second eldest brother. The eldest brother would be called Bara-dada or Barda, and so forth. In referring to an elder sister, one would add *didi,* meaning elder sister, e.g.: Bara-didi or Bardi, Meja-didi or Mejdi, Seja-didi or Sejdi.

† Since writing this, Sri Sananda Lal Ghosh has left his body, on October 10, 1979, in Calcutta (see p. xix). *(Publisher's Note)*

To understand the spiritual environment of Mejda's childhood, it is necessary to know something of the ideal lives of our saintly father and mother, unto whom such an exalted yogi was born. The scriptures state that "he who has acquired wisdom may be born in a family of enlightened yogis." Our parents were *Kriya* Yogis,* initiated by the Yogavatar Sri Sri Lahiri Mahasaya. Mother was a strong spiritual force in Mejda's life, and long after her death Father continued to help Mejda fulfill his spiritual destiny. For ten years he gave Mejda financial assistance to aid him in his mission in America, spreading *Kriya Yoga* and divinity throughout the world.

Father's family home was in Ichapur, a village in the Barrackpore Subdivision of District 24-Parganas in Bengal. Here settled our ancestor Dayaram Ghosh. We are *Kayasthas*† from western Bengal. Our ancestry is traceable back to Makaranda Ghosh, who settled in Bengal in the eleventh century at the request of King Adisur of Bengal.‡ In the twelfth century, Makaranda's great-great-great-grandson, Nishapati Ghosh, settled in Bali Village in the Arambagh Subdivision of District Hooghly, Bengal, on land gifted by King Ballal Sen, with the mission of social service in the name of the king. The move of our ancestral family to Ichapur by Dayaram

* A meditation technique whereby the sensory tumult is stilled and the consciousness raised to a state of God-awareness. Of ancient origin, *Kriya Yoga* was reintroduced in modern times through the lineage of Gurus of Self-Realization/Yogoda Satsanga Society of India: Mahavatar Babaji, Lahiri Mahasaya, Swami Sri Yukteswar, and Paramahansa Yogananda. An introduction to this sacred science is given in Paramahansaji's *Autobiography of a Yogi.*

† A section of the *Kshatriyas:* traditionally the class of rulers and warriors.

‡ For more information on the ancestry of the Ghosh family, see the Genealogical Chart in the Appendix. *(Publisher's Note)*

Ghosh took place in the eighteenth century during a period of turmoil caused by the *Bargis,* outlaws from Maharashtra. They periodically swept across the subcontinent to plunder villages. But as it was difficult for them to cross the Ganges, they would turn back when they got that far. Since the Ghosh family was living on the west side of the Ganges, they were vulnerable to these invasions. Thus Dayaram Ghosh decided to move the family across the Ganges to Ichapur and safety on the east side of the river. For this move, he acquired a large plot of land with many valuable trees.

In Ichapur, our place was known as the "house of Ghosh under the *gab* tree," as there was an old *gab* (mangosteen) tree—whose age none could conjecture—in front of our home.

Grandfather, Ishan Chandra Ghosh, was a schoolteacher in the village. He had two daughters and three sons. His daughters, our aunts, were named Beni Nandi and Harimati. Grandfather's eldest son was our father, Bhagabati Charan. The second son was named Sarada Prasad; and the youngest son, Satish Chandra.

In addition to teaching, Ishan Chandra supported his family by selling vegetables from his garden and milk from his cow. On one occasion, he borrowed fifty rupees from a distant relative to purchase a brick kiln for the purpose of building a house. But Grandfather passed away before construction of the house could begin.

Grandfather had felt deep affection for a small child in a neighboring house. The child was also fond of him. When the little girl contracted smallpox, Grandfather prepared a special medicine that eventually cured her. During her illness, he sat with the stricken child whenever he had time. On the evening of the tenth day of the disease, the child was frightened in her sleep by a bad dream. Upon awakening, she jumped up and threw herself into Grandfather's protective arms. The disease was still in a highly contagious stage, but Grandfather could not resist comforting her. He then went straightway to the Ganges River to bathe in its sacred waters; but the next morning he fell ill with the dread disease. He was too weak and feverish to leave his bed in order to prepare for himself more of the medicine that had saved his young friend, and none else knew the formula. Within a few days he was dead.

Upon our father, Bhagabati Charan Ghosh, fell the heavy responsibility of caring for his widowed mother and younger brothers and sisters. The loan of fifty rupees could not be repaid. The creditor-relative took the bricks from the kiln, but claimed they were insufficient to repay the loan. Grandmother's only possession of value was a pair of silver bangles, but these, too, were inadequate to cancel the debt. Our relative then took cruel advantage of the family's destitution to humiliate our widowed grandmother. Her weeping and the look of despair on her face left our father, and his brothers and sisters, with a deep sense of helplessness and fear.

Years later, when Father's financial condition improved, he repaid the entire loan, with interest, to the deceased creditor's surviving relatives. But he never forgot this tragic episode in his life. Thereafter, when any unnecessary expenditure was proposed, Father reminded us of the hardship he had endured as a youth.

Through diligent effort and personal merit, Father received a full-tuition scholarship at Hooghly Collegiate School. Daily he walked to his classes from Ichapur.

Father's elder cousin was well-to-do, but not overly charitable. From time to time he gave Father one paisa for midday refreshment. With this coin Father could buy eight small plantains (bananas). He made this fruit last the whole day. When his cousin did not offer the paisa, Father searched the roadside trees for guavas. If no fruit was to be found, he fasted.

The tales of distress that surrounded Father's childhood are innumerable. One day, the stitching in the sole of one of his shoes broke on the way to school. Without money even for food, how could he get it sewn? He improvised with string, binding the sole as tightly as he could to the top of his shoe. To spare himself embarrassment at school, he would remove his shoes and hide them behind a bush near the gatekeeper's room, and attend classes barefooted.

Lacking funds to purchase school books, he borrowed the texts from teachers and classmates and copied them by hand. Even though this arduous task took a great deal of time, he achieved the highest scholastic marks in his class through his painstaking efforts. The daily study period at home found Father sitting under the *gab* tree in front of his house, writing his lessons on dried plantain leaves with a reed. Using soot from the oil lamp, he prepared ink in an earthen pot. His blotter, a little sand or fine dust from the ground.

From time to time an English newspaper would find its way to our remote village. Father studied every page intently, in an effort to learn the English language. At school he asked his teachers the meanings of words he did not understand, and he never forgot the definitions. Many of his friends and teachers were astonished at his command of the language. They pondered how he, a poor village boy, could master the foreign vocabulary and syntax. On one occasion Father won first place in an all-India letter-writing contest in English. By the time he was an adult, his use of English was flawless. He had committed to memory the entire English dictionary he had long had in his possession! When asked, he could give the correct definition of any word, as well as the number of the page and place on the page where the definition appeared.

Students in Father's day had to purchase their own paper for annual examinations. Since Father had no money, he could not obtain the necessary paper. His mathematics teacher noticed his plight and gave him an outdated pad of printed letterheads. Father carefully tore the printed portion from each sheet and worked out the examination problems on both sides of the portions that were left. He obtained a perfect score in mathematics. Though his tools were limited and his difficulties many, he meritoriously passed his college entrance exams.*

In college, Father's urgent desire was to complete his higher education, but he had no money to pay the tuition. He requested financial assistance — literally begged it — from many, but only a few persons could spare even a little money. When he put his resources together, he was short of the required sum. He asked a wealthy judge for a grant of one rupee per month; the judge refused. He hopefully approached others, but to no avail. Finally, he accepted the devastating fact that he could not continue his education. He vowed then and

* Final exams in high school were referred to as entrance exams, because they had to be passed before a student could apply for entry to a college or university.

there that he would do everything in his power to see that his younger brothers were not similarly denied.

It was then that Father sought work as a tutor. With the small sums he earned in that service, he managed to finance the education of his younger brothers and to meet family expenses.

A Family to Support

Father moved to Calcutta when he was eighteen. A kind neighbor tried to obtain employment for him in the office where he worked. But ironically, when Father met the English superintendent and applied for a job, the latter replied, "You are too young, son. You should be in college." In vain Father tried to convince the man of his capabilities and his desperate need for work.

This refusal aggravated the deterioration of Father's health resulting from his feeling of utter helplessness. His goals seemed distant mirages that he would never reach. He sadly considered returning to Ichapur, but that prospect held no future for him. He rekindled his inner resolve, and with indomitable will determined to remain in Calcutta.

Through the effort of the kindly neighbor and the favor of another gentleman, Father was given shelter in a tiny room in the upper story of a stable, in a lane near Beadon Street in the Chitpur area. The room was so small that Father could not stretch out straight when he was lying down, even though he was short of stature. He slept on a torn mat, and covered himself with a cheap, patched rug; he had no blanket. A small tin case served as a pillow.

Searching diligently for some kind of work, Father finally obtained employment as a tutor. In one home he received only a meal each day as payment for two sessions of teaching. No matter what his circumstances, Father would not acknowledge defeat. In fact, one day he felt such enthusiasm and invincible courage that he acted upon an impulse and brought his second brother, Sarada Prasad, to Calcutta to enroll him in college.

The road to Chitpur from Calcutta, over which Father had to walk daily, was not paved. During the rainy season its usually dusty surface became mud bogs and puddles. For three rupees Father bought a pair of rejected military boots at Fort William to tramp through the mud during the long monsoon season.

Tap water had not yet been introduced into the area, so Father had to walk daily a half-mile to Hedua* to obtain drinking water. He carried it home in a pottery jug.

In time, Father obtained better employment in government service. He joined the Public Works Department, Government of India, as Assistant Accountant, and was posted at Baidyanath Dham in Deoghar, east-central Bihar, December 31, 1873.†

Father's brother (our Uncle Sarada, whom we called *Nakaka*‡) wanted to go on to law college after obtaining his bachelor's degree. Father was deeply saddened because he could not afford the tuition fee. Just at that time Father struck up an acquaintance with a Bengali gentleman whose residence was in Rangoon. The man encouraged Father to accept a posting in the British

* Now known as Azad Hind Bagh.

† This and subsequent dates and places of Father's postings during his government service years until 1907 have been drawn from the "*History of Services of the Officers of the Engineer and Accounts Establishment,*" *Government of India, Public Works Department.*

‡ An affectionate term for one's *kaka,* or paternal uncle.

Gyana Prabha Ghosh (1868–1904)
Our Mother

Bhagabati Charan Ghosh (1853–1942)
Our Father

Sarada Prasad Ghosh
Father's younger brother

Satish Chandra Ghosh
Father's youngest brother

Sri and Srimati Govinda Chandra Bose
Our maternal grandparents

Burma Central Office of the Public Works Department, in Rangoon.* Because the job there paid enough to put Sarada Prasad through law school, Father agreed to move to Burma. But knowing that the family would strongly object to his going, he left Calcutta almost surreptitiously.† In Rangoon, he spent very frugally from his salary for his own food and lodging, and sent most of the money to Sarada Prasad, and to his youngest brother, Satish Chandra, in Ichapur. But because of poor health, Satish Chandra could not proceed far in his education.

Father's Marriage and Service Years in Rangoon

When Father went to Rangoon, there were only four Bengalis in the city. Father, the youngest, made five. The older four often drank when together. One of them, while drunk, struck Father in an attempt to force him to drink, but Father held firmly to his principles. Another man in the group was sympathetic, and took Father's side in the altercation; soon the four agreed to cease teasing and trying to coerce their younger companion.

While in Rangoon, Father received the bitter news that his beloved mother had passed away. The following year, he returned to Calcutta. There he married Gyana Prabha, the third daughter of Govinda Chandra Bose, a deputy magistrate of Rajibpur (near Barasat, in District 24-Parganas). As was the custom, the family of the bride had examined the prospective groom's health, the work

* At that time, and up until 1935, Burma was a province of India, ruled by its own British Governor.

† Father began his service in Burma April 16, 1875, and worked there for ten years.

he was engaged in, and his family position. Father had easily fulfilled all conditions.

After his marriage, Father returned to Rangoon. His bride stayed for a time with the family in Ichapur, and later joined Father in Rangoon. Their first child, a son—Ananta—was born there.

Sarada Prasad wrote to Father in Rangoon asking for more money to pay for his law examination fees. But Father, who was sending his entire salary home after deducting a meager amount for his own subsistence, had not a single rupee left. So he sent to his brother the woolen shawl he had received from his father-in-law as a wedding gift. Uncle sold the shawl to pay the examination fees.

Father's colleagues knew of his plight. Mouthfuls of well-intentioned advice were courteously received and quietly discarded by Father. But in one practical offering, Father saw the basic warp and woof of his situation: "Bhagabati, it isn't right for you to send your entire salary home. You are in a foreign land. Who will help you in an emergency? You should save something to take care of medical expenses should you fall ill." Father took this advice to heart; his dependents would suffer if anything happened to him so that he could not work. He began to save a little money out of each paycheck. He adhered to this practice throughout life. With his savings he was able to cope with emergencies and to provide well for all his children. He helped his sons establish themselves, and was able to offer his daughters in marriage to highly respected families. He assisted Mejda by paying for his journey to America, and for ten years he sent funds to help with his living expenses there. He also aided many of his relatives in the education and marriages of their children. He never turned down anyone who asked for his help.

Father passed his examination in accounting during the time he was in Rangoon. Shortly thereafter, he was transferred to the PWD Office of the Government Examiner of Railway Accounts in Saharanpur in the United Provinces of India (now Uttar Pradesh; U.P.), serving the Shahdara-Saharanpur Railway. Father moved his family with him to Saharanpur. His posting there began April 7, 1885. After about a year and a half there, he was transferred to Muzaffarpur, in Bihar.* Here our two elder sisters, Roma and Uma, were born.

My Parents' Initiation by Lahiri Mahasaya

After four years at Muzaffarpur, Father was transferred to Gorakhpur in the United Provinces, where he served in the Office of the Government Examiner of Railway Accounts, Bengal and North-Western Railway and Tirhoot Railway Section from October 16, 1890.†

Abinash was Father's subordinate officer in Gorakhpur. One day Abinash applied for a week's leave. Because he had previously taken several leaves of five to seven days, Father refused. Work could not be kept current if employees took unnecessary time off. Talking

* In Muzaffarpur, Father served in the Office of the Government Examiner of Railway Accounts, Tirhoot and Nalhati State Railway, from October 10, 1886.

† Father began his service in Gorakhpur as Accountant 2nd Grade. He was promoted to Accountant 1st Grade, Deputy Examiner of Railway Accounts, and for several extended periods between September 10, 1899 and October 1902 he held charge of the Office of the Government Examiner of Railway Accounts, Bengal and North-Western Railway and Tirhoot Railway; and of the Bengal-Nagpur Railway (with head office in Calcutta) from April 9 to July 7, 1900.

the matter over with Abinash, Father asked him where he went on these leaves.

"I go to Banaras to see my guru," Abinash replied.

Father upbraided Abinash: "So you are trying to acquire piety. Can you tell me what religion really is? Our nation is being ruined in the name of religion. My dear man, there is nothing in it. Don't be a fanatic. If you want to get ahead in life, work. Work, and you will surely profit in the long run."

Father hadn't intended to be rude. His sarcasm reflected an undercurrent of sensitive frustration about his own unsatisfactory relationship with religion. He soon repented of having spoken so harshly. "After all," he reasoned to himself, "each one has to make his own choices in life. Only then can he say for certain whether the decisions were good or bad. In any case, roughness is unbecoming." Father decided to talk further with Abinash.

That afternoon he met Abinash on his way home from the office. Dismissing his palanquin, he walked with Abinash and tried to explain his reasoning. Abinash remained silent. Father could see that he was grieving, and also embarrassed because of the difference in their official positions at work. A junior officer would never contest an issue with his superior. At the time, Father didn't know that Abinash was fervently praying to his guru!

The roadway was lined with large, shady trees, their leafy branches intertwined overhead to form a natural caravansary. In this peaceful setting it was not difficult to feel the presence of the Divine Architect. Passing beyond the line of stately trees, they came upon a large field, waves of rippling grass turned auburn in the flaming rays of the setting sun. Such a supernal scene they had never witnessed before. A thrill of joy filled their hearts, and both felt an overpowering desire to become one with that beauty.

Father was silent, motionless, absorbed in this grand display of nature. Then, just a few yards ahead, a person of tranquil visage suddenly appeared. Abinash exclaimed: "He is Lahiri Mahasaya, my guru!"

Both Father and Abinash were astonished to hear Lahiri Mahasaya's gentle remonstrance: "Bhagabati Babu, you are too hard on your employee." In an instant Lahiri Mahasaya disappeared. Though they searched the area, the master was nowhere to be found. With a rush of tears, Abinash threw himself to the ground.

Father was awestruck. Kneeling down, he tenderly touched Abinash and said affectionately, "Abinash, I will surely grant you leave; and I, too, want to go to Banaras. Will you take me to your guru? He who can appear at will to help his devotee is surely a great being—one with the Preceptor of the Universe! My wife and I will take initiation from him, and seek his guidance for our *sadhana.*" Abinash was beside himself with joy.

Father and Mother, who was expecting her fourth child, Mejda, departed for Banaras the next evening, accompanied by Abinash. They arrived the following morning and made their way to Lahiri Mahasaya's simple dwelling in a narrow lane. The Guru was in the drawing room, seated in the lotus posture in meditation. They bowed before him.

Opening his half-closed eyes, Lahiri Mahasaya looked at Father with penetrating gaze and said, in the same tone they had heard in the field two days before, "Bhagabati Babu, you are too hard on your employee."

Father was thrilled to the very core of his heart. He hung his head humbly. No one had ever chastised him before.

After a vibrant pause, the great yogi said, "But you have made me very happy today. Not only have you granted Abinash leave to come here, you also have come with your wife to receive initiation." Needless to say, Father was startled to hear Lahiri Mahasaya speak the thoughts in his mind.

In receiving *Kriya Yoga* initiation, Father and Abinash became brother disciples and intimate friends. As long as they lived, they were loyally devoted to one another.

Lahiri Mahasaya showed keen interest in Mejda's impending birth. After initiating Mother he said, "My daughter, through the grace of God your son will be a prophet. He will show mankind the way to God-realization. Through his life and teachings, many people will slough off the delusions of this world and find salvation. You traveled here by train. Verily you saw how the engine pulled the cars. In the same manner your son will draw souls from the ordinary to the divine spheres."* Mejda's life was linked with that of the great guru, and bore witness to the truth of Lahiri Mahasaya's prediction.

* It was perhaps in reference to this incident that Paramahansaji's mother had told him, "Shortly before your birth he [Lahiri Mahasaya] told me you would follow his path." The prediction about Paramahansaji's divine mission was repeated when Lahiri Mahasaya blessed him when but an infant. In the words of Paramahansaji's mother as recorded in *Autobiography of a Yogi:* "I first knew your destined path when you were a babe in my arms. I carried you then to the home of my guru in Banaras.... Lahiri Mahasaya seated you on his lap, placing his hand on your forehead by way of spiritually baptizing you. 'Little mother, thy son will be a yogi. As a spiritual engine, he will carry many souls to God's kingdom.'" See Chapter 4, "An Auspicious Message for Mejda." *(Publisher's Note)*

Our Ancestral Deities

After our parents' auspicious meeting with Lahiri Mahasaya in Banaras, they went for a short visit to our ancestral home in Ichapur. One night Mother dreamt that the Goddess Mother Chandi appeared in the *puja** room. It was a strange dream, as Chandi was not customarily worshipped there. Rather, an image of the family deity, Lord Narayan,† had been installed on the altar for our daily *puja.* It was a small Narayan Shila, a special black stone on which symbolic facial features of Narayan had been carved.

Mother arose immediately. Taking a lantern, she rushed to the *puja* room. There she saw a crack in the northern wall, and in the crevice she beheld the face of a statue of Goddess Chandi. Ecstatic with joy, Mother called to Father. Together they reverently removed the image from its erstwhile hidden sanctuary. The statue was made of eight metals: gold, silver, copper, tin, lead, iron, zinc, and mercury. The next day they consecrated the deity and made arrangements with the family priest, Thakur-da‡— whom we called Anukul, "one who believes"—to perform daily worship. And so for many years Chandi was worshipped with Narayan in our home at Ichapur.

* *Puja,* Hindu ritual worship.

† Another name for Vishnu, the Lord as preserver and upholder of the cosmos; one of the Hindu triumvirate that includes also Brahma, the creator, and Shiva, the destroyer who renews creation through his divine power of dissolution, removing the old to make room for the new. In Hinduism there are traditionally 108 names for God, each designating a particular aspect of the one Eternal Spirit. Thus Chandi, for example, is one name for the aspect of God as the Cosmic Mother of all creation. *(Publisher's Note)*

‡As a respectful form of address, *da* (from *dada,* elder brother) is often added at the end of the name of one who is regarded as an elder brother. *(Publisher's Note)*

There were only two bedrooms in our original ancestral house. The family lived in very crowded circumstances, since at that time our home was shared with Father's youngest brother and two sisters. So Mother arranged for the construction of a new double-storied dwelling adjacent to the western side of the old house. Father supervised the construction. For the base of the foundation he raised the level of the land with earth taken from a pond on the northwest corner of the compound. In the process, the pond was enlarged and deepened. The new house was completed shortly. Mother had taken special interest in the planning and decorating of the *puja* room. We always loved to come to Ichapur. We could lie in our beds and look out of the windows of the large house and watch the play of light and shadow on the rippling waters of the pond. How beautiful it was!

The northwest corner of the village of Ichapur, in which Father's family home was located, had never been under the jurisdiction of a *zamindar.** When Father became a successful man, many people in that area became envious. Their agitation awakened the avarice of an unscrupulous landlord. Falsely claiming ownership of Father's property, he instituted a lawsuit. Father received a court summons, charging unlawful possession of the land. The *zamindar,* however, could not produce any document to support his claim. The court ruling required him to ask Father's forgiveness for the unjust harassment.

In 1918, the British Government purchased Father's land for an extension of the Ichapur Ordnance

* A landlord. The *zamindars* were owners of large parcels of land—sometimes whole villages. Families living on those lands paid rent or sharecropped for benefit of the owner. *(Publisher's Note)*

Factory. The money received as compensation Father divided equally between his youngest brother and sister —who were living in the home at that time—keeping nothing for himself. He purchased a piece of property east of the railroad, and had a small thatched temple erected on the land to house the family religious shrine. The images of the deities, Ma Chandi and Narayan, were moved from the old homestead to the new site.*

When our family priest, Anukul Thakur, passed away, Father generously arranged for construction of a small house for his widow and children. He asked them to engage another priest to perform daily worship in the family shrine, and provided the priest with a monthly stipend for his services and the *puja* expenses.

Not long after the new priest had been engaged, he sold Father's land and the temple without notifying us and went to stay with a friend of his in Kashi,† taking with him our family deities. The priest wrote to Father from Kashi asking that the monthly allowance be sent to him there. Realizing that something was amiss, Father inquired and learned that his land had been sold illicitly, and that the allowance he had been sending for *puja* had been misused by the priest. In addition, he had left his wife and children without any means of sustenance.

Father felt that the derelict should be severely punished, but relatives persuaded Father to let him go with only a reprimand. A short time later, we were informed by the friend with whom he had been staying that the

* According to an account kindly offered by Dr. Prakash Ghosh, youngest son of Sarada Ghosh, this move took place under the direct supervision of Prabhas Chandra Ghosh, second son of Sarada Ghosh, and cousin Jatinda Ghosh, who generously contributed financially to the construction of the temple. *(Publisher's Note)*

† Banaras.

priest had died. The family deities were retrieved from Kashi and installed in the home of Prabhas Chandra Ghosh, the elder son of our Uncle Sarada, on Allenby Road in Calcutta. Prabhasda's wife, in particular, was overjoyed to have the family shrine in her home. After Prabhasda retired, he moved from Allenby Road to his late father's house in Serampore, sharing the home with his younger brother Dr. Prakash Ghosh, and Prakash's family. The images of Ma Chandi and Narayan were enshrined in the *puja* room on the second floor of the home. All the family contributed toward the yearly expenses for regular performance of *puja*.*

* Prabhas Chandra Ghosh passed away in 1975. The family deities are now with Dr. Prakash Ghosh and his family in Madras. *(Publisher's Note)*

CHAPTER 2

Mejda's Birth and Boyhood in Gorakhpur

Mejda's Birth Is Blessed

The city of Gorakhpur is quite historic. It is located a hundred miles north of Banaras in Uttar Pradesh. Gorakhnath,* a great devotee of God, lived here centuries ago. The temple in which he worshipped and attained liberation is still standing today. Within, a sacred fire is kept perpetually burning by devotees of the saint. Pilgrims come from afar to receive *vibhuti,* the sacred ash of the fire ceremony. More recently, his devotees have constructed an ashram and a large temple adjacent to the original one.

The birth of Yogiraj Gorakhnath inaugurated a new era in Hinduism. Not since Adi Shankaracharya† had such a great soul been incarnate in India. Gorakhnath is regarded as the foremost religious teacher among all those of the tenth and eleventh centuries. According to many, he surpassed even his preceptor, Matsyendranath.

Tradition tells us that Gorakhnath's mother prayed to have a son as holy as Lord Shiva. One day the Lord appeared to her and directed her to eat *vibhuti* from a

* The account of Gorakhnath's life told here is drawn from *Bharater Sadhak,* Vol. II, in Bengali, by Sri Shankar Nath Roy.

† India's greatest philosopher; a rare combination of saint and scholar. The ancient monastic Swami Order exists today in the form in which he reorganized it. Western historians assign Shankara to the late eighth century A.D.

bel leaf. A year later this faithful devotee of Lord Shiva gave birth to a godlike child, Gorakhnath.

Gorakhnath's mother was poor, often in distress. Many were the days that they had little to eat. One day, when Gorakhnath was twelve years old, he was helping his mother make cow-dung cakes for use as fuel in cooking fires. The cakes were to be sold the next day in the bazaar so that the mother could buy meager provisions for their own sustenance. A religious mendicant with gray matted hair came by and stopped in front of her.

"Soon your son will leave home to become a *sannyasi,*"* he said. "The boy you now see playing is an exalted ascetic. Mother, do not weep! Great blessings of God are upon you. Qualities of the Divine Mother Herself are incarnate in you. You will be proud of your son, for he shall acquire immense fame as a result of his holy works."

The very next day, while his mother was still asleep, Gorakhnath left home to begin his search for God. Before becoming enmeshed in the fascination of things of this world, he had severed himself from all desire and attachment. Little did his mother dream that the saint's words were to come true so soon, for she had not fully perceived the spiritual stature of her young son.

Gorakhnath taught new methods of prayer and worship. He spoke out against distinctions of caste and creed. Any devotee, he said, could follow his teaching and become a saint, a master over life and death. Gorakhnath was the founder of a group of ascetics known as *Gorakh Panthis,* who, along with other ascetics following a similar path, are also known as *Kankata*† *Yogis.*

* Renunciant.

† *Kankata,* from *kan,* ear; *kata,* cut: the right ear is pierced with a small brass ring which is worn as a sign of their sect.

Thus, Gorakhpur is named after Gorakhnath. Hallowed by the memory of the divine sage, this city is still considered one of the holiest in India.

Mejda was born in Gorakhpur. Our home was near the police station on Police Office Road, near the Nakhasi crossing at Main Bazar. A well in the area between our house and the police station provided water for our family, the police, and other neighbors. Our playground was a vacant field in front of our house.

Mejda was born on January 5, 1893. A room on the second floor of our home served as a lying-in room. It was here that Mejda's birth took place. I also was delivered in this same room, five years later, on March 13, 1898. Mejda was named Mukunda, a name by which the child Krishna is known. I was named after the sage Gorakhnath; my elders called me Gora.

Those present at the time of Mejda's birth said Mother was having severe labor pains. She fervently cried out to Lahiri Mahasaya. Suddenly a celestial light filled the room, and from the concentrated rays in the center emerged the form of Lahiri Mahasaya. Mother's pain vanished instantly. The divine light continued to illumine the room till Mejda was born.

The Devout Little Mejda

From infancy, Mejda was attracted to quiet and solitary places. His behavior from day to day was obviously changing from that of an ordinary child. Whenever he had an opportunity, he sat in a secluded spot and, with half-closed eyes, assumed the yogic posture of meditation. At times he was overheard murmuring something, as though in prayer or conversation.

Mother paid homage to Lahiri Mahasaya by performing *puja* before his photograph, which was mounted in a lovely frame and placed in the prayer room. Mejda often sat with her as she made the traditional offerings of flowers, sandalwood paste, incense, camphor, and *arati* (the rotation of burning lamps before the image).

Customarily, our parents took Mejda with them to the temple of Gorakhnath to worship every Sunday and on holy days. However, on one Sunday they didn't go to the temple because a religious festival was being held at our house. Many people came, and the celebration lasted far into the night. As guests were departing, Mother realized that she had not seen Mejda for several hours. The house and neighborhood were searched, but he couldn't be found. Knowing well her son's nature, and at last taking this into account, Mother said to Father, "Since we go to the temple of Gorakhnath every Sunday for worship, but have not gone today, perhaps Mukun is there."

Father and some of the guests went directly to the temple. As Mother had surmised, there was Mejda, sitting like a little sage, absorbed in meditation. While the family was enjoying the festivity, he had quietly slipped out of the house to make his customary Sunday visit to the temple—more than a kilometer* away; a great distance for such a young child.

One of the guests accompanying Father was about to call to Mejda, but Father motioned for silence. All waited; inevitably, some became impatient, talking in whispers among themselves:

"Why this leniency?"

* About two-thirds of a mile.

"If this disobedient child is not punished, what will become of him?"

"He is not getting proper training."

The child of whom they were speaking remained blissfully oblivious to them all.

Dawn was approaching, and many of those with Father wanted to leave for their homes. Mejda at long last opened his eyes, and was at first surprised to see so many people gathered around him. Then he realized where he was and why everyone was so anxious about him. With a sweet little smile he gazed at Father, then bowed his head in recognition of the trouble he had caused. Father addressed him in a grave voice: "Come home now. It is late. We were so worried about you."

In every way she could, Mother encouraged Mejda's spiritual inclinations. With her own hands, she made for Mejda a perfect image of the Divine Mother Kali,* one and a half feet high. He placed it on a low stool as an altar and daily offered flowers, fruits, and incense in ceremonial worship; then he meditated before the sacred image. During his periods of worship, he screened himself from the rest of the family by hanging an ochre-colored curtain around the altar. The entire daily allotment of milk, sweets, and fruits for Mejda, Sejdi, and me was ritually offered to the Divine Mother.

From behind the curtain, Sejdi and I would watch Mejda perform the *puja.* When the offering was completed, and he had finished his meditation, we all partook of the *prasad.*† Though I was only an infant at that time, these scenes made a permanent impression on my mind, and I can recall the happiness of those days.

* See Chapter 4.

† Food that has been ritually offered to God.

Shyama Puja, worship of Mother Kali, is one of the most important festivals of the Bengali Hindu community. According to custom, in some places arrangements are made for the sacrifice of animals. Buffalo or goats are sometimes used in the ritual, according to the means of the devotee. Those opposed to killing animals offer fruits as symbolic sacrifice. Many arguments have been advanced in favor of, or against, the purpose of these sacrifices, and their meaning. The premise that seems to me the most reasonable and universally acceptable is that in the mind of every person the animal instinct works in one form or another. Ritual sacrifice symbolizes sacrificing, or destroying, these base instincts in the human mind. The corollary is that if a person seriously thinks or prays something, that desire will bear fruit.

Every year Mejda performed his worship of the Mother Kali in great splendor. Cucumber was sacrificed in place of an animal. And his prayer to the Divine Mother was: "O Mother, make us sinless. Destroy our evil desires."

The Goldfish Tragedy

A very sweet Bengali woman lived next door to us; we called her "Auntie." She loved us all and often demonstrated her affection. We used to go over to her house and play with many of her household articles. We gave her cause for worry, because we unintentionally broke some of them. She never scolded. Rather, she disciplined us by saying, "You see, this is now broken and lost. You will not have it to play with any longer." Sometimes, because of having broken something of value, we would not go over to her house for several days. Mother would become suspicious and ask our neighbor what had happened. She would reply: "What can I say? I have seen very few such loving, peaceful, and happy children. Don't put me to shame by making me say they have done something wrong."

We always felt she loved Mejda most. Once she gave him a red-colored goldfish, which he carefully placed in the cistern of our house. Maidservant, servant, and cook drew their water from this cistern for household work. Mejda worried that his little fish might be killed when their buckets scooped water out, so he kept a close vigil to see that his pet was not harmed. He loved to watch his little fish play in the cistern, and at times Ananta and Roma would watch with him. We all loved Mejda's red fish.

One night, Roma had a nightmare and awakened early. There is an old Bengali proverb that if one soliloquizes on a bad dream in a place near water, that dream will then not come true. Distressed by her nightmare, Roma arose and went to the cistern to soliloquize her dream—just in case there might be truth in the superstition. Distracted for a moment, she looked down into the cistern for Mejda's fish. It was gone! To make certain, she rubbed her sleepy eyes. Then she looked about on the floor, and there she saw the little red fish, lying very still. She looked more closely and saw that it was dead.

She called loudly: "Mother! Mother! Moko's fish has been killed!"

Roma's outcry awakened the household, and we all came running downstairs. Father asked the servants if they knew how the accident had happened. Nitu finally admitted, "While lifting water from the cistern I didn't see the fish caught in the bucket. When the water was thrown on the floor of the courtyard for washing, the fish was killed by the shock. I didn't try to pick it up because I was afraid."

In the midst of the commotion, no one had noticed that Mejda had come into the room. With tears in his eyes he grabbed Nitu with both hands, and shaking him, cried, "Why have you killed my goldfish? Why?" Everyone tried to console Mejda, but he kept crying, "Why did he kill the fish? Was it nothing because it was only a fish?" Saying this, he looked at Nitu for some moments, then at each of us; and turned and ran upstairs sobbing.

Mejda wept all morning long. Sitting on the stairs near the door to the terrace, he leaned his head against the wall and cried. The sounds of his sobs were so loud he could be heard from the first floor. Father told us to leave him alone. But before going to his office, he called Nitu, and within hearing distance of Mejda, said in a loud voice, "Nitu, take your money. You are relieved of your services as of today." But the dismissal of the careless servant was of no consolation to Mejda. He wept until his eyes were red and swollen. He steadfastly refused to take his bath or come down for food. After Ananta left for school, Roma went to see if she could persuade Mejda to come downstairs, but he refused to yield to her urging.

The day passed; his grief still unassuaged, Mejda would not come downstairs. Even Mother did not go near him because she knew he would only cry harder. In the late afternoon, Roma sought out her teary-eyed little brother and asked him to eat. But he still refused to budge. When she attempted to pick him up, he ran from her and hid. She chased him, and finally caught him.

Lifting Mejda up gently, she kissed his forehead and said, "Listen to me." But he tried to pull away.

"Moko! You love Mother so much. Is this the way you show your love to her, by giving her pain?"

Mejda looked at Roma with his swollen eyes and said, "I haven't given any pain to Mother."

"Are you not causing her pain by keeping her from eating all day? She won't touch food unless you do." Mejda stopped his crying as Roma continued, "Come quickly with me and ask Mother to eat. Catch hold of my neck with both your arms."

Mejda put only one arm around Roma's neck. "Use both your arms," she repeated. "You don't want us to fall down the stairs, do you?"

When Mejda still hesitated, Roma saw that he was clutching something tightly in one fist. He quickly hid his hand behind his back. She caught hold of his hand and pried his fist open with her fingers. He was clasping a small pencil and a tiny notebook in which he had written, in English:

"my
red fish is die."

Mejda's first poem!

A Letter to God

Mejda's school life began in Gorakhpur. He was enrolled at St. Andrew's School (later converted into a college). St. Andrew's was about a half-mile from our home. Father took Mejda there in his palanquin on the way to his office, and Mejda returned home in the palanquin after school, accompanied by a servant.

It was about this time that Mejda became involved in

a tussle with God. Letters addressed to Father or Mother often came to our home. Friends of our eldest brother Ananta corresponded with him from time to time. Ofttimes, while our parents or eldest brother read their letters, Mejda stood nearby, and at an opportune moment would ask who had written, where the letter had come from, and why the person had written. Our parents patiently answered his questions, but Ananta would tease Mejda by saying: "See how many friends I have? They write to me from far and near. Does anyone write to you? Alas! you have no friends, and so you don't get any letters." Mejda was hurt by Ananta's taunting remarks.

Mejda's unhappiness increased as time went by. Sadly he would climb onto Mother's lap, touch her chin to get her attention, and then ask why no one ever wrote to him. Mother would smile and say to Father, "Do you hear your son? Tell him why nobody sends him letters." This would bring forth a laugh from our habitually reserved father. Then in mock gravity he would scratch his head and reply: "How strange! No one writes to Mukunda."

Mejda would stare intently at Father and Mother, trying to understand. And then Mother would say: "First you must grow up, and then you will see how many people will send you letters. You won't be able to find time to read them all. Now go and play with your sisters."

But Mejda was not satisfied, and no one could make him understand. At times he became depressed. He wondered if his elder brother were more special than he. Did everyone consider him too small for anything worthwhile? God, too, seemed cruelly silent. Mejda asked God why He did not send him a letter. If God had created him, could He not understand his heart and his longing for a letter? He decided to write to God and ask Him to send him a letter. On a sheet of plain paper he carefully wrote:

> To Your beautiful lotus feet, my Bhagavan.
>
> How are You? Are You ill? I talk to You every day and ask You to send me a letter. Probably You have forgotten my request? I am very hurt. You know that many letters come to my father and mother and eldest brother; but no one sends a letter to me. Certainly You will send me a letter. Please write quickly. Don't forget about it. What else shall I write? Father and Mother are well.
>
> Thus bowed,
> Mukunda

The letter was carefully folded and put into an envelope and pasted shut. He addressed it: "To Splendid God, Heaven," and posted it.

Ten days passed, and no reply came from God. Mejda began to worry. "Perhaps God did not receive my letter," he thought. Every day, when the postman arrived at our door, Mejda inquired if there was a letter for him. The postman would reply: "No, my little one, no letter has yet come. If one does, I will give it to you and to no one else. And for that you'll have to give me a big tip."

The days passed, and still no reply came from God. Mejda did not know that workers at the post office, noting the address on his letter, had thrown it away, thinking it had been written by a lunatic. Impatiently Mejda prayed: "Is it so difficult to run the world that You cannot find time to write a few words to me?" In childish anger Mejda resolved he would write no more letters to God. But he continued his fervent prayers: "Why are You so cruelly silent? I talk to You every day and sent You a letter, but You do not reply."

Even though many more days passed without response, Mejda never ceased his onesided argument with God. One night, Mejda was awakened suddenly by a great light in his room. God replied to his letter in that divine light! Mejda was overjoyed. He called to Mother and told her the wondrous experience. Mother hugged him and said, "I knew it, Mukunda; God cannot remain far from a devotee like you. His reply to your letter was sure to come."

God's Judgment of a Wrathful Man

After their morning exercises, wrestlers often came to wash at the well near our house. One day, for some unknown reason, one of them got into an argument with a hawker. In the midst of the altercation, the wrestler threw the hawker to the ground, sat on his chest, and began to pummel his face and neck with heavy blows. The incident took place so quickly, the hawker at first didn't realize what was happening. Then he began to cry out desperately for help. His clothes were torn, and his face began to swell from the ceaseless rain of blows; blood gushed from his mouth.

People who gathered at the scene shouted to the wrestler's companions to stop the beating, but the wrestler kept striking his victim. Soon the hawker lay still, his head rolling from side to side with each successive blow. The enraged wrestler was blinded by the instinct to kill, and none had the courage to pull him off the hapless man. It seemed their hearts were in their boots with fear.

Mejda, standing nearby, could not contain himself. He cried out in a loud voice: "God will judge you! God will judge you because you have greater strength and are beating a helpless man! If he dies, you will also die a cruel death."

Just then, three or four husky constables came running from the police station and began striking at the wrestler with their batons. Many of the wrestler's companions fled, but some were caught and put under arrest. The police took the unconscious form of the hawker to the hospital in a palanquin.

I believe the hawker's life was saved; but when we saw the wrestler six months later, his tall frame was bent, his stout health broken. He was attacked with gout and could walk only if someone took pity on him and gave assistance. Otherwise, he lay helplessly in bed. Flies hummed around him in the humid, stale air of his small room; often he cried out in pain and muttered repentance for what he had done. He fervently wished he could meet the hawker again to ask his forgiveness, but I don't know if he ever had the opportunity. A part of Father's legacy of wisdom was etched in our minds when he said to Mejda: "Behold God's punishment for the oppression of the weak by the strong."

A Muslim Doctor's Miraculous Cures

Mejda suffered an attack of malaria and jaundice during a visit to Ichapur. His liver became inflamed. Though he recovered briefly, he had a serious relapse. We were compelled to return to Gorakhpur, where Father had remained to attend to his work. In the right-hand corner of the field in front of our house was a hut in which a *hakim*, or Muslim doctor, lived. The success of his method of diagnosing and curing patients was miraculous. By feeling the pulse, he could accurately tell not only what the patient was suffering from, but also how long the patient had been ill. His natural herbal medicines, in the form of a blackish pill, worked without fail. Mejda's case was no exception; he was soon cured of his malaria and jaundice.

A medical hospital had been constructed in Gorakhpur a few years earlier and was situated near the Muslim doctor's humble dwelling. However, few patients ever went to the hospital. They crowded around the *hakim's* quarters instead, even though he never solicited. To diagnose their illnesses, he simply opened the blind of the window and reached out to touch the pulse of each patient.

The English Civil Surgeon of the hospital could not tolerate this situation. He sent for the Muslim doctor to try to reason with him:

"You cannot treat all diseases this way; if your method were scientific, I would not interfere. Please stop your treatments. You have no right to play with human life. I admit that your pills have cured many people, but I believe the relief may be only temporary. Can you say you successfully cure every patient? Who's to say that the disease may not recur when you have passed away and are no longer able to help. My hospital is about to be closed for lack of patients. After your death, what would be the fate of your patients, with no hospital to go to?"

The *hakim* replied humbly: "Is there any doctor

greater than God?" To this the English doctor had no reply.

The Muslim continued: "I promise you that I will not see a single patient during daylight hours, so that I will not interfere with your hospital."

But this didn't stop the flow of patients that came to the Muslim doctor; they simply came at night instead. They arrived from distant places on palanquins, in bullock carts, on the shoulders of others. Sometimes the area in front of our house was crowded with patients. At four o'clock each morning, without fail, the doctor opened the blind of his window. Though he had no watch or clock of any kind, he was never late. His fees were a mere token: ten paise for those who came to his hut; fifty paise for a house call.

One day the son of the English doctor fell seriously ill. Though the Englishman tried every prescription his skill and knowledge could conjure, he could not heal his son. Day by day his son grew worse. An old, trusted servant of the doctor loved the boy as though he were his own. He pleaded with his master: "Sir, many healings have been effected through the *hakim*. Kindly consider my request and consult him. Please give him a chance to cure your son."

The English Civil Surgeon was shocked at the servant's impudence. In an annoyed tone of voice he said, "What did you say? Do you want me to go to that quack? Remember your place; you have no right to advise me. It is because of the ignorance of people like you that we English had no difficulty conquering your country; nor do we have trouble maintaining control. Your quack physician is a cheat; he is making money by deceiving others."

This outburst surprised the servant. Why was his master so angry, hurling abuses when he had simply offered the best advice he could? The enraged English doctor went on: "If you mention this matter again, I will be compelled to dismiss you."

As the child's condition deteriorated, the servant could no longer bear to see his suffering. He went to his master and, humbly touching his feet, said: "Sir, please dismiss me. This boy is as dear to me as my own son; it is intolerable to see him die a slow, painful death. You may be his father, but I have brought him up. Doesn't this have meaning? I cannot stay near a father who, for unreasonable obstinacy, allows his son to die. Please discharge me. I also am a father; I too have a son."

The Englishman had never before encountered such affection for another who was not one's own: he had not thought of his Indian servants as possessing minds of integrity that could resist injustice without anger or concern for self. His servant's sincerity moved him deeply. Tears welled up in his eyes and, forgetting his station, he embraced the servant and at once sent for the Muslim doctor.

The *hakim's* tiny black pill cured the child. The English Civil Surgeon was fully ready to admit that all knowledge comes from God, and that He alone is the power that sustains life.

The Muslim doctor did not pass on to anyone, not even his own son, his mystical knowledge of healing. He told his son frankly, "No, I will not give you the knowledge of my medicine because you may sacrifice the welfare of your patients in your greed for money." He knew the power of greed once it possessed men's hearts, and felt his son would not be able to resist the temptation to use this unique healing power to acquire wealth.

The Power of Mejda's Words

One day our elder sister Uma was teaching Mejda in our courtyard in Gorakhpur, under a neem tree. Parrots in the branches above them were squabbling. A boil had erupted on Uma's leg. Our family doctor had advised an ointment as a cure. She interrupted her tutoring to fetch the phial of medicine. As she tended her boil, Mejda also rubbed some ointment on his forearm. Uma was annoyed. "What are you doing, Moko? Why do you apply ointment where there is no boil?"

Mejda replied, "I think that tomorrow morning a boil will erupt exactly on this spot, and so I am applying the medicine in advance."

Sister laughed. Rebuking him, she said, "Moko, you are not only a rogue, but a liar as well."

Indignantly, Mejda said, "Don't call me a liar unless you don't see a boil on my arm tomorrow morning."

Uma continued the argument lightheartedly. Finally Mejda spoke slowly and forcibly, "There is divine power in words. I say that by that power in me, tomorrow morning you will see a boil in this spot on my arm, and the boil on your leg will be *twice* its present size!"

When Uma awoke the next morning, she saw that the boil on her leg had indeed doubled its size. She awakened Mejda and examined his arm; the promised abscess was there! She ran to Mother, crying, "Moko is a magician!"

After hearing her story, Mother spoke gravely to Mejda. "Mukunda, never use the power of words to harm others. The evil of such deeds always returns to the doer."

Strangely enough, no medicine or ointment could reduce the size of Mejda's boil; finally it had to be lanced. To the last day of his life, Mejda carried a scar on his right forearm as testimony to the power of man's word.

CHAPTER 3

Mejda at Lahore

Two Kites from Divine Mother

Father was transferred from Gorakhpur to Lahore.* Alighting from our carriage on arrival, everyone hastened to inspect the rooms and verandas of the large house. Mejda's interest had one purpose: to find a suitable place to install the image of Mother Kali. I followed him about the house. Finally, after much deliberation, he placed the statue lovingly in a corner of an upstairs veranda. A screen was hung for privacy. During our stay in Lahore, Mejda faithfully worshipped the Divine Mother in this simple, improvised temple.

Roma loved Mejda and expressed a deep affection for him; but she also teased him mercilessly. Sometimes when she would find him rapt in thought instead of his studies, she would tiptoe close and then shout into his ear: "You! Moko!" Startled, he would stare at her, and then she would say, "I'm going to tell Mother you are not studying, but daydreaming." With mock gravity she would add, "Oh, see what a sovereign has come into our house. He looks as if the troubles of the whole world are crowded into his mind." Then, back to reality: "Take your books and read quickly! Otherwise I will twist your ear." Sometimes after teasing him, or for no special rea-

* The head office of the North-Western Railway was in Lahore, Punjab. Father's service with the Railway, as Deputy Examiner in the Office of the Government Examiner of Railway Accounts, was from November 24, 1902 until April 1904.

son, she would hug him affectionately. It used to annoy me when Roma did this because she never caressed me as she did Mejda.

Uma was similarly both playful and affectionate toward Mejda. One morning, standing near the sanctified recess in the wall of the veranda upstairs, Mejda was lost in thought. He felt that if in this simple temple a prayer to the Divine Mother were spoken with all his heart and mind, it would surely be fulfilled. Just then, Uma came upon Mejda, touched his cheek affectionately, and said, "Our quiet little brother, you are so still. What plan is hatching in your mind?"

Mejda replied, "Do you know, Mejdi,* what I am thinking?"

"Doubtless to say you are thinking of how you could teach me a good lesson so that I won't annoy you anymore. Is that right?"

Mejda said, "I was thinking that whatever I want from the Divine Mother, She will give it to me."

Uma mockingly retorted, "Do you know what I want?" Pointing to the kites being flown by two boys in a lane some distance from our house, she said, "I would like to have you get me both those kites through the grace of the Mother."

Mejda was disappointed. "Only this? You should ask for something of greater value. You have read to me from all our books that this world is Her creation. Why then don't. . . ."

But Uma interrupted Mejda brusquely, "I didn't come here to listen to your preachings!"

Without replying, Mejda looked at those two kites,

* One's second eldest sister.

praying silently to Divine Mother. Suddenly both kites struck each other, and the string of one was cut. It came flying toward our veranda. The current of wind stopped just as the kite flew over the house next door. The kite's string became entangled in a cactus on the roof of the adjoining house in such a manner that Mejda had only to stretch out his hand to catch it. But Uma believed it to be a coincidence. "Do you think that your prayers brought you that kite? Oh, no! It was only by chance that the wind blew it this way."

Again, Mejda said nothing. He looked at the second kite and continued his prayers to the Mother. In a few moments the other kite also blew his way and became entangled in the cactus plant, presenting its string to Mejda's outstretched hand. Mejda caught hold of it, and turned to give both kites to Uma. But she ran into the house like a startled deer.

A Will That Couldn't Be Thwarted

In our youth, Tikkar Singh and Kalu were famous wrestlers. Drum beaters and posters along the road announced their forthcoming program. Mejda asked Father to take him to the wrestling match, but naturally our parents did not want us to see the barbarous contest, which often had a rowdy aftermath. Mejda was adamant. Finally Mother agreed, but Father and Ananta would not consent. Mejda ran to Father's room and bolted the door from inside, and refused to come out or let anyone in. "I want to see the wrestlers," he demanded.

Father could not go to work because his office clothes were in that room. All his appointments had to be postponed. Mejda refused to leave the room for twenty-four hours, even though he went without his meals. But that didn't bother him. At last, Father was compelled to give his consent. Mejda unbolted the door and came out of the room as though he had conquered the world! He showed no signs of fatigue. Though Father was very grave, we children were overjoyed. Mejda was criticized for his obstinacy, but this little incident showed his indomitable spirit and determination—early signs of the great man he was to become.

Our Baby Brother and the Skylight Incident

The nights in Lahore were as hot as the days. During the summer months, we slept outside on the roof of our house on cots of woven fabric strips. Every evening water was poured across the roof to cool it. Mejda and I helped our servants with this task.

Our youngest brother, Bishnu, was born in Lahore on the 24th of June, 1903. I was asleep on the roof when Mejda awakened me. "Gora, get up. Come see our new baby brother." I opened my eyes and saw that the sun was already high in the sky. It was very hot. Everyone else had long since left his roof-bed. I jumped up and ran downstairs.

In the hallway outside our mother's room I met Sejdi, our third sister Nalini. She and I danced in circles, crying: "Our brother is born! Our brother is born!"

Suddenly Ananta caught us by the ears, putting an abrupt halt to our raucous merriment. He hustled us into an adjoining room and closed the door. "You're making too much noise. Mother is unwell after her delivery," he said. How vividly I recall that severe ear-twisting.

A few days later, Mother was sitting in the hall with our new baby brother Bishnu on her lap. Mejda, nearby,

Partially reconstructed building that had been our Gorakhpur home—Mejda's birthplace—on Police Office Road

Well, between Police Station and our home, from which we and neighboring families drew household water

Entrance to Police Station compound

Gorakhnath, tenth-century saint after whom the city of Gorakhpur was named

(Above) Ancient temple in Gorakhpur at which Gorakhnath worshipped

(Right) Temple of more recent date dedicated to Gorakhnath

Mejda at age of six

St. Andrew's in Gorakhpur; the first school attended by Mejda

The Divine Mother as Kali, who symbolizes both the benign and the fearsome aspects of cosmic nature *(see p. 139)*

was asking for an orange. His persistence was annoying. Mother asked Mejda to get the orange himself, but Mejda insisted she must get it for him, *now*! Exasperated, Mother got up to fetch the orange. At that moment, pieces of broken glass from the skylight above rained down upon the spot where she had been sitting with Bishnu. Because of Mejda's insistence that Mother get the orange for him, she and Bishnu were saved from a serious accident.

Capricious and naughty as I was, I had gone to the roof to test my daring and dexterity by walking on top of the glass skylight. It gave way. Being afraid, like a goat meant for sacrifice, I hid myself in a concealed corner. Ananta rushed up to the roof and found blood near the skylight. He soon found my hiding place. I hadn't noticed that my leg was badly cut, with a piece of glass still lodged in the wound. The scar on my leg is permanent evidence of the skylight incident.

CHAPTER 4

Our Mother

Her Love, Artistry, and Charity

We all felt that Mother was, in Mejda's words, a "queen of hearts." We can never forget her simple, beautiful qualities. Through her love and affection she never failed to inspire us to be good and to live honestly. She gave us our first schooling, and taught us manners and virtues from stories in our ancient scriptural epics, the *Ramayana* and *Mahabharata*. She brought their timeless spiritual principles into our daily affairs; and with them, affection and discipline went hand in hand.

Mother was an artist. I remember the image of Kali she made for Mejda when we lived in Gorakhpur. Its creation so occupied her mind that she didn't feel my presence one day when I came up to her. It was only when I softly called, "Mother!" that she realized I was standing next to her. Patiently she admonished me, "I am making this statue of Mother Kali for Moko, who is so persistent in asking for it; now sit quietly and watch."

The image was beautiful. I can still see it in my mind's eye: one and a half feet high, of flawless quality, like those made by the professional statue-makers. Statues Mother made of other deities were equally perfect; they could have been placed alongside the world-famous earthen deities made at Krishnanagar.

Her artistry was also evident in culinary crafts. The many confectioners we see nowadays were not so common during our childhood. The women of the household prepared at home the delicious juicy sweetmeats so highly relished by family and guests. The confections were shaped in delicately carved molds of clay.

Mother loved to prepare food for the family. She never allowed us to eat the sweets sold in the marketplace. After taking a little rest following lunch, she would cook many varieties of sweetmeats for us. For patterns, she herself had carved flawless earthen molds. I still have in my possession a few of those molds. As I look at them today, I am wonderstruck by the artistry of their designs. At the time of Mother's death, many of the molds were taken by relatives, but in later years I managed to collect and save a few. I marvel at her craftsmanship, which so richly illustrates her knowledge of art. She was matchless. I know for certain that Mother's delicate hands and her artistic perceptions were the great influences that, in my later years, guided my choice of vocation as an artist.

While giving primary education to her children, Mother did not hesitate to teach us the proper relationship between husband and wife. Once she mentioned to our eldest sister that she and Father lived as husband and wife only once a year, for the purpose of having children.

In Gorakhpur, hot winds blow during the summer. As the season progresses, the heat and winds increase. Toward noon on a sweltering Sunday, Father was working in his room. A poor *Brahmin* came to our house. Roma talked with him and learned that he was burdened with the responsibility of financing a marriage for his daughter, and wanted pecuniary assistance from us. Mother asked Roma to bring ten rupees from Father, and invited the *Brahmin* to come into the house. Then Mother went into the kitchen to prepare a cool beverage for him.

On hearing of the matter, Father called Mother and told her: "Why ten rupees? Give him one rupee, and ask him to go." Mother was not satisfied. Finally, Father gave the ten rupees.

Mother's charities were on a par with family expenses. But once she spent in a fortnight more than Father's monthly income. Father told her, "Please keep your charities within reasonable limits, lest you land our family in financial difficulties."

This hurt Mother very deeply. Without replying, she arranged for a carriage and told us, "I am going to the house of your maternal uncle." At the portent of Mother's words, our throats constricted; we began to cry. Our maternal uncle arrived opportunely. He immediately saw the situation and said something to Father privately. Father's face lit with a tiny smile that flashed and faded like lightning. He went over to Mother and said something to her. Even to this day I cannot describe the sweet smile that came to Mother's face. We children were overjoyed when we heard her dismiss the carriage.

A short while after this incident, Father was transferred to Lahore, where a similar situation arose. Mother came to Father one morning and said: "A hapless girl in the drawing room downstairs is in great distress. Can you spare her ten rupees?" Father had not said anything more about charity since the episode in Gorakhpur. But today, his natural instinct for thrift came to the fore. "Why ten rupees? Is not one sufficient? You know how destitute my childhood and early life were. I attended school almost without food, walking miles on foot. I could not appear in the Intermediate Arts Examination for the want of only one rupee. So I ask you, is not one rupee sufficient?"

Mother wept. "The remembrance of that single rupee has kept alive the painful experiences of your childhood. Do you want to force this girl also to remember forever her destitution because you refuse her ten rupees? You now earn a high salary, and in spite of your success you still cling to the unbearable nightmare of your former poverty. Will compassion, love, and sympathy perish from our society because true concern for the poor and suffering is lacking?"

Father had no argument. With a gesture of defeat he opened his wallet and took out a ten-rupee note. "You win!" he said. "Take this with my blessing, and give it to her yourself. But remember, don't put into your own bag that portion of the girl's blessings and good wishes that are meant for me!" Father smiled. Mother returned his smile and left the room with the ten rupees.

Loving Discipline

I recall an incident of Mother's training of us children. It happened during our stay in Lahore. Our family was invited for tea at the home of a Bengali. A little girl sitting near me was playing with attractive colored picture cards that one could get only from cigarette packages. I stared intently at the bright cards, contriving how I could obtain them for myself. Mother sensed my intention and looked askance at me over the heads of the guests. I had been discovered! Immediately I controlled myself. But luckily I did get a card quite by chance. When the little girl left, she unknowingly dropped one of the picture cards, and I hastily picked it up and put it in my pocket.

After we returned home, I was getting ready for bed while Mother brushed and arranged the clothes we had worn. I suddenly remembered the picture in my pocket and knew Mother was bound to find it. "Mother!" I cried. But it was too late. She removed the picture from the pocket, but said nothing at that moment, because Father was in the room. I quickly jumped into bed and shut my eyes tightly, pretending to be asleep. Of course Mother knew better, and softly spoke my name. But I was so fearful I could say nothing.

Then she said: "Have I not read to you from the scriptures that to take something without the owner's permission is stealing? Why did you bring the picture home without asking? So many things in this world are lying about momentarily unattended; will you also pick them up? Never do this again. Will you remember this?"

With my eyes still shut tight, I nodded. I felt a strange tingling current pass through my spine.

The next morning, Mother sent the picture and some sweets to the mother of the girl. She enclosed a letter to beg forgiveness for what I had done. She had humbly written: "My son has committed a great offense. Please forgive me for his behavior."

On another occasion we had gone over to the house of Uncle Sarada Prasad in Serampore. Our room was upstairs, in front of the staircase. Uncle's room was on the right side. However, being a child, I was permitted to roam freely through all the rooms of the house. Out of curiosity, I touched everything my hands could reach; and soon knocked over and broke a phial in Uncle's room. I ran from the scene of the crime.

As Uncle was a well-known and successful government lawyer in Serampore, I could see myself being unceremoniously hauled into his court. When Uncle discovered pieces of broken glass scattered on the floor, he started shouting.

Mother heard this from another part of the house and quickly sought me out. Fearfully, I had hidden behind the door of our room, but Mother found me immediately. She looked at me steadfastly and said, quietly but firmly, "Your hiding like this indicates you have done something wrong. I will say no more now, but never do this again." Her words sank deep. It was wrong to have broken the phial; but doubly so, not to have bravely owned up to it. I would not have remembered this incident and its lesson if Mother had merely spanked me.

Death Takes Mother from Us

About the time Mejda was eleven, Father was transferred from Lahore to Bareilly.* En route, we halted at Delhi before going on to Calcutta to make final arrangements for the marriage of our eldest brother, Ananta. Father and Mejda, in the meantime, continued on to Bareilly. At Delhi, our aunt (wife of our second maternal uncle) came with her children to the railway station to welcome us. Her eldest son, Jnanada, was the same age as Ananta. He insisted on coming with us to Calcutta, as he had never been there.

Upon our arrival in Calcutta, extensive wedding preparations were begun. Relatives came from distant places. We had rented a house at 50 Amherst Street, now the site of the Hindu Academy. When we first entered

* Father's service in Bareilly, U.P., as Deputy Examiner in the Office of the Government Superintendent of Accounts, Establishment Department, Rohilkund and Kumaon Railway, began officially April 26, 1904. This is also the date on which our beloved mother died.

the gateway to the house, Mother sensed an ill omen and remarked that it seemed as if the building would devour us. However, out of consideration for all who were planning the marriage festival, she said nothing further. Arrangements were made for a palanquin, strings of colored lights, elephants and camels made of paper, and Indian, English, and Scottish bands.

Mother was accompanied to the house of the bride by her fourth sister. Attired in a plain handloomed sari with a black border, Mother wore no ornaments, having loaned hers to her sister. Our aunt, a lifelong resident of the city, was stylishly dressed and was wearing Mother's jewelry. Understandably, the bride's relatives mistook her to be the mother of the bridegroom, and devoted most of their attention to her rather than to Mother. When they realized their error, they were acutely embarrassed not to have immediately recognized the simple, polite, and reserved woman with our aunt as the mother of the groom.

The next day, Ananta and Jnanada went to the market to make purchases for the wedding. By the time they returned, Jnanada was deathly ill. He was carried upstairs, where Mother diligently and lovingly nursed him. But Jnanada could not be saved; he died of the dreaded Asiatic cholera.

Since Mother had come in close contact with Jnanada during her constant care of him, she too contracted cholera. Ananta sent an urgent telegram to Father. But that night, before the telegram reached Father in Bareilly, Mejda dreamt that Mother was calling him: "Mukunda! Get up! Arouse your father and come to Calcutta if you wish to see me alive. Come at once!" Still asleep, Mejda burst into tears. The sound of his crying awakened Father, and he asked Mejda why he was crying. Mejda told him of the ominous dream, but Father brushed it aside. "It is only your imagination. Your mother is well."

In grief and anguish Mejda retorted: "If my dream is true, Father, I will not forgive you."

The next morning Ananta's telegram arrived. "Mother seriously ill. Marriage postponed. Come at once." Father and Mejda left Bareilly for Calcutta immediately. Father deeply reflected on the strange coincidence of Mejda's dream and the arrival of Ananta's telegram.

Father and Mejda did not reach Calcutta before Mother died. Mejda had a strange premonition when he came into the house on Amherst Street. He called out, "Mother, Mother, we have come!" and frantically asked, "Where is she?" Those in the hallway broke down and began to wail. In a frenzy Mejda turned to dash out of the house, shouting, "I will get her. I will bring her back!" Ananta caught him and held him to his breast. Mejda cried, "Release me! Release me!" and collapsed, unconscious.

Mutely, Father stood watching Mejda, stunned by Mother's death and Mejda's foreknowledge of this tragedy.

Mother's death on Tuesday, the 26th of April, 1904, was an irreparable loss to us. She was our most beloved companion. Throughout our childhood, her two affectionate, calm, and beautiful eyes were our shelter from every agony. Even years after her death, many of our relatives wept at the mention of her name. She was not only an educated and pious woman, she was compassionate and understanding. Whenever we went to Ichapur to visit our relatives, she saw to it that we first went to see those of low income, lest they be in need of something or other. She always seemed to know beforehand what each one required, and took with her the needed aid. How she had such foreknowledge I do not know.

An Auspicious Message for Mejda

Fourteen months after Mother's death, Ananta gave a small box to Mejda. He had written down on a piece of paper Mother's last words to Mejda and had kept the paper in it. Mother had asked that Mejda be given the box and her message within a year of her death, but Ananta feared Mother's words would send Mejda flying to the Himalayas. He therefore held back, thinking that as Mejda grew older, his ideas of renunciation might change. But because Ananta's marriage was again being arranged in Calcutta, he was compelled to tell Mejda of the box and of Mother's last words. Since it was Ananta who was at Mother's side during her last moments, it was to him that she entrusted the sacred message for Mejda:

"Let these words be my final blessing, my beloved son Mukunda! I first knew your destined path when you were but a babe in my arms. I carried you then to the home of my guru in Banaras.

"Lahiri Mahasaya seated you on his lap, placing his hand on your forehead by way of spiritually baptizing you.

"'Little mother, thy son will be a yogi. As a spiritual engine, he will carry many souls to God's kingdom.'

"Shortly before your birth, he had told me you would follow his path.

"Later, my son, your vision of the Great Light was known to me and your sister Roma, as from the next room we observed you motionless on the bed. Your little face was illuminated; your voice rang with iron resolve as you spoke of going to the Himalayas in quest of the Divine.

"In these ways, dear son, I came to know that your road lies far from worldly ambitions. The most singular event in my life brought further confirmation—an event which now impels my deathbed message.

"It was an interview with a sage in the Punjab. While our family was living in Lahore, one morning the servant came into my room.

"'Mistress, a strange sadhu is here. He insists that he "see the mother of Mukunda."'

"These simple words struck a profound chord within me; I went at once to greet the visitor. Bowing at his feet, I sensed that before me was a true man of God.

"'Mother,' he said, 'the great masters wish you to know that your stay on earth shall not be long. Your next illness shall prove to be your last.' There was a silence, during which I felt no alarm but only a vibration of great peace. Finally he addressed me again:

"'You are to be the custodian of a certain silver amulet. I will not give it to you today; to demonstrate the truth in my words, the talisman shall materialize in your hands tomorrow as you meditate. On your deathbed, you must instruct your eldest son Ananta to keep the amulet for one year and then to hand it over to your second son. Mukunda will understand the meaning of the talisman from the great ones. He should receive it about the time he is ready to renounce all worldly hopes and to start his vital search for God. When he has retained the amulet for some years, and when it has served its purpose, it shall vanish. Even if kept in the most secret spot, it shall return whence it came.'

"I proffered alms to the saint, and bowed before him in great reverence. Not taking the offering, he departed with a blessing. The next evening, as I sat with folded hands in meditation, a silver amulet materialized between my palms, even as the sadhu had promised. It made itself known by a cold, smooth touch. I have jealously guarded it for more than two years, and now leave it in Ananta's keeping. Do not grieve for me, as I shall have been ushered by my great guru into the arms of the Infinite. Farewell, my child; the Cosmic Mother will protect you."

The amulet was inscribed with Sanskrit symbols, probably an indication of the supernal power that was guiding Mejda's destiny. The amulet eventually did disappear from Mejda's carefully selected hiding place, after it had served its divine purpose.

On learning how Lahiri Mahasaya had blessed Mejda and predicted his spiritual destiny, I understood why Mother had so carefully made for him the image of the Mother Kali when we were living in Gorakhpur. She felt it her divine duty to nurture his every spiritual inclination.

CHAPTER 5

Family Life After Mother's Death

Jhima—Our Faithful Maid-Ma

Jhima was like a guardian of our family. She joined the household after Grandfather's death, when Father's family suffered not only from dire financial difficulties, but also for want of an experienced person to help manage family affairs. Though all of Father's relatives knew of his circumstances, none came forward to help. It was at this critical time that Jhima, a poor widow—alone in the world—joined the family as a maidservant. She was like a fresh wind in the tattered sails of the battered family boat. For the remainder of her life, she faithfully cared for Father and our uncles with motherly affection. And in the same manner, she looked after us children when our mother passed away.

Jhima came to work for the family at a monthly salary of three rupees. Unhesitatingly she performed every type of household chore—and more. During Father's childhood in Ichapur, Jhima helped to supplement their income by going from house to house selling fruit and vegetables from the family's garden, and milk from their cow. As Father could not meet all the family expenses, our maternal uncle made arrangements to give them ten rupees a month along with eighty kilos of rice from his home in the village of Jasara. Father didn't have enough money to hire a cart to collect the rice from the village each month, so Jhima carried it on her back —a little at a time—making several trips. It was in large part through Jhima's sacrifices that Father was able to meet expenses for six people.

In later years, after our mother's death, Jhima took on the household tasks of our home. The touch of her loving, untiring hands was everywhere. This is how we came to call her "Jhima,"* or "Maid-Ma." Although Mejda often got his own way with others, whenever Jhima gave an order he had to follow it.

Thus Jhima served faithfully as the family guardian for many, many years. Whenever Father's work took him to another area, and the family moved, Jhima moved too. Because of her dedication she became like a member of the family.

Jhima passed away while we were living at 4 Garpar Road in Calcutta. From the time Father had been able to earn enough to cover all family needs, he saw to Jhima's needs also, taking care of her expenses for food and clothing. In addition, he gave her a pocket allowance. She saved almost the entire amount each month. At the time of her passing a sizeable sum had accumulated. Though she and Mejda fought a lot because of his independent nature, she loved him deeply; and when she died, a note was found in which she expressed her wish that her savings be given to Mukunda for his spiritual activities.

Father's Dedication to Service

After Mother's death in Calcutta, we returned to our home in Bareilly. Some friends and relatives advised

* *Jhi,* maidservant; *ma,* mother.

Ananta not to marry the girl to whom he was betrothed, since the marriage had been so tragically and inauspiciously obstructed. But Ananta said that since Mother had selected his bride, he would marry her and no other. So, not long after observing the set time of one year for mourning and customary religious rites for our mother, Ananta went with Father and Mejda to Uncle Sarada's house in Serampore to arrange for the wedding. The rest of the family remained in Bareilly.

The marriage ceremony was performed in a rented house near Shyambazar Crossing in Calcutta; the post-marriage feast was held in Uncle Sarada's house in Serampore. After the festivities, Ananta and his bride returned to Bareilly to live. In April 1906, Father was transferred to Chittagong, and the whole family moved there. Two months later, Father was transferred from Chittagong to Calcutta, where he settled permanently.*

We had been in Calcutta only a few days when Father—serving as Examiner of Railway Accounts—noted serious discrepancies in the Bengal-Nagpur Railway books. These had caused substantial yearly losses to the company. He brought the matter to his supervisor's attention. Father's report was verified. The Agent and General Manager of the company, noting Father's ex-

* According to an entry in Ananta's diary, the family left Bareilly on April 3, 1906, settled in Chittagong on May 3, 1906, and arrived in Calcutta on July 2, 1906. Father served in the Office of the Government Examiner of Railway Accounts, Bengal-Nagpur Railway, at Calcutta from July 1906 until June 19, 1907, when he officially retired from Government of India service as an officer in the Accounts Establishment of the Public Works Department. After a period of retirement, however, he took employment as a private citizen in the Bengal-Nagpur Railway, as Personal Assistant to the Agent, at the company's head office in Calcutta, and served there for eleven-and-a-half years, until December 23, 1920.

traordinary ability and dedication, obtained from the Railway Board in London an order appointing Father as his Second Personal Assistant.

Though Father retired from government service on a pension in 1907, he later joined the Bengal-Nagpur Railway again, but this time as a private citizen. In addition to filling his railway post, Father, working with a few other senior railway officers, established the Urban Bank* of Calcutta. The bank was started at the instance of the Railway Board to encourage middle-class workers to regularly save a portion of their income. Father guided the establishment of the charter, writing all the rules and regulations, which provided equal opportunities and banking service to all. He served as Chairman of the Board, but took no remuneration from the bank.

Father worked continuously for eleven-and-a-half years, serving both his railway office and the bank; but he never appeared tired. His strength came from his meditations and the spiritual techniques taught him by Lahiri Mahasaya. Also, the austerity and simplicity of his daily living gave him fortitude for his work.

Father abhorred flattery, and shunned praise. He officially retired from the Bengal-Nagpur Railway on December 23, 1920. Inevitably, to commemorate his retirement, the railroad authorities arranged a splendid farewell function in his honor. He was presented with a large silver plate and silver glass, and a silver-plated bamboo roller in which was a copy of the farewell address praising him. Father was appreciative, but frankly saw absolutely no point in making so much ado about his years of service. In a few words of humble acceptance he said: "My reward has been the joy of working with devo-

* The Bengal-Nagpur Railway Employees Urban Bank.

tion, loyalty, and honesty. It has given the fullest satisfaction to my heart and earned the good wishes of all of you. Tomorrow I will no longer be in your midst. Please do not deprive yourselves of the happiness, satisfaction, and good wishes you too can receive from work well done."

At the time of Father's retirement from the Bengal-Nagpur Railway, the Agent and General Manager, Mr. Godfrey, told Father: "Bhagabati, since you are now retiring, your income will naturally be reduced. Bring your son; I will appoint him Assistant Traffic Superintendent for the Railroad." Father's early struggles had deeply embedded in him a sense of independence and the principle of working for gain. This made him reluctant to accept favors from others. But Mr. Godfrey, who had great love for Father, persisted for several weeks. Finally Father made the proposal to Mejda, who rejected the offer for a higher destiny. The post was given to our cousin; a story in itself, which is recounted in a subsequent chapter.

Father's Inherent Knowledge of Natural Medicines

When I was still a young child, I once became very ill. That day none of our relatives visited, and no one noticed that for the entire day I didn't leave my room, even to eat. Father had gone to his office as usual, and when he returned, still no one knew that I was bedridden with fever.

About midnight I got up to take a little fresh air on the veranda. As I was returning to my room, my legs trembled with weakness; I felt giddy; and in a moment I collapsed, unconscious. I don't know how Father learned of my predicament, but it was he who aroused me and asked, "Have you eaten anything today?" I told him I had not.

"Don't move," he said, "I'll be right back." Soon I smelled a fire burning and saw that Father was preparing sago. An intuitive feeling and knowledge were inherent in Father. He was soon feeding me half-boiled sago, and as he did so, I felt the life returning to my body. I fell into a deep sleep.

Ordinarily a doctor would have been called, and a hue and cry would have been raised. But Father had diagnosed my illness and the reason for my fainting with the quiet efficiency that characterized all his actions.

On another occasion, Dr. Panchanon Bose, the husband of our sister Nalini, was taken seriously ill. He had a high fever, and was racked with pain. Parts of his body became as though paralyzed. Well-known physicians of Calcutta examined him, but no cure or relief could be found. I often went with Father to Dr. Bose's house. While there one day, I happened to overhear the doctors discussing his case. Because I was so young, they paid no attention to my presence. They had given up hope of saving Dr. Bose, and were saying: "An invaluable life is slipping away from us, and we can do nothing."

Upset, I ran to Father and told him. Father asked the doctors, "If you then can do nothing further, may I prepare an herbal medicine for him?" Although reluctant, under the circumstances the doctors could not refuse. We returned home, and Father prepared a medicine he had learned about from Lahiri Mahasaya. Sister's husband was cured within a few days after Father administered the herbal potion.

Dr. Bose had once been very skeptical of the use of natural medicine; he even made jokes about it. But after he was cured by Father, he became a proponent, and learned from Father to prepare many herbal medicines himself, including a very good one for dysentery. He was able to cure even chronic diseases with them.

When I was reading in Intermediate Arts classes, I was weak from an illness and caught cold in my chest and head. My tonsils swelled, and I had a great deal of pain throughout my body—it seemed to me that even the hair on my head hurt! A doctor was called; he prescribed medicine and an injection of vaccine.

Suddenly Father asked me, "Are you having regular evacuation of the bowels?"

"No," I replied. "For some days I have passed only mucus."

"Why? What have you eaten?"

"My throat was hoarse and sore, and so I drank a lot of tea purchased at the teastalls, and gargled with hot water."

Father's inherent knowledge was at work again. He said to the physician, "It isn't necessary to give him medicine. His cold is almost over. Old clarified butter, beaten into a froth in water and rubbed on his head, and a tonic of rock sugar and aniseed, will cure him. Since he is unaccustomed to tea, his excessive intake of this has inflamed the bowels and caused the dysentery." Father's remedy worked. I was completely well within a week.

Mejda suffered from acute indigestion, aggravated by his irregular hours and eating habits, and by drinking too much tea, which he used to get on the way to his daily visit with Sri Yukteswarji. On one occasion, he was bedridden with pain for two days. Father cured him by massaging his abdomen with a mixture of coconut oil and water, beaten into a froth. Drinking tea was only occasional in our house; after Mejda's illness, it was completely forbidden.

On another occasion, our second sister, Uma, was ill. Father and I went to her home to see her. We were shocked to find she had been in a coma for two days. The doctors could not restore her to consciousness. Father placed his hand on her abdomen and diagnosed flatulence. He rubbed coconut oil and cold water alternately on her abdomen for half an hour. Slowly her stomach cleared of gas, and she opened her eyes. Father explained that the pressure in her abdomen had caused a reaction in certain nerves, which triggered the unconsciousness. Through the massaging of her abdomen, the stomach was freed of gas and consciousness was restored. In later years I, too, used this method to aid many people similarly affected.

Once Father suffered from itching and swelling all over his body. Dr. Bose tried many medicines, but all to no avail. Father then sought the services of a well-known Ayurvedic practitioner, Shital Kaviraj. I went with Father to his house, and thereafter was sent regularly for medicines. Ultimately Sri Kaviraj told Father that there was no particular cause of the problem, that it was just old age drying the cells of his body, thus causing the swelling and itching. Father wouldn't accept this diagnosis. He returned home and prepared a prescription he had learned from Lahiri Mahasaya. In a few days the itching and swelling abated; Father was cured.

Naturally, I stopped going to Sri Kaviraj's home for the Ayurvedic medicines. One day as Father and I were walking along the street in front of his house, we saw the practitioner sitting on his veranda smoking a hubble-bubble. Seeing Father out for a walk he asked him: "Are you rid of your ailment?"

"Yes," Father replied.

After a pause Sri Kaviraj asked: "How were you cured?"

Father replied, "By eating a preparation of *bel* fruit."

The practitioner had no further comment. Perhaps he was disinclined to show, by further questioning, his ignorance of a remedy that had obviously worked when all his prescriptions had failed.

Gleanings from Father's Wisdom

Father asked us to commit to memory all the *slokas* of the *Moha Mudgar,** and particularly to remember the following:

"Who is your wife? Who is your son? The world is full of mysteries. Reflect on who you are and whence you have come."

"Do not take pride in wealth, power, or youth—for Lord Shiva (the ruler of time) can take away all these in the twinkling of an eye."

"Life is always unsafe and unstable, like a drop of water on a lotus leaf. The company of a divine personage, even for a moment, can save and redeem us."

Father had three more favorite maxims:

1) Waste not; want not.
2) A man is known by the company he keeps.
3) The ancient *rishis*† compared man's body to a chariot. The soul is the passenger. Pure intellect

* *Moha,* worldliness, delusion; *Mudgar,* mace. A treatise by Swami Shankara (see footnote on page 21) on the world's delusions, which hammer man incarnation after incarnation.

† Illumined sages.

> (discrimination) is the charioteer. The ten senses (five of perception and five of action) are the stallions that pull the chariot; and will power is the reins that control the stallions. Uncontrolled, the senses will run astray. But under the firm guidance of intelligence, the sense-steeds will pull the chariot safely along the right road in life.

Stoic Nonattachment

Father was a widower for thirty-eight years. Though there were many opportunities for another match for him he would not even consider such a proposal. His first concern after Mother's death had been to bring happiness back into our grieving family through Ananta's marriage. Intuitively, he always correctly assessed the family situation and quietly and firmly moved us along the right course. Reflecting on his wisdom, I am lovingly wonderstruck.

I observed that Father went directly to his room when he returned home from the office. In those hours of seclusion, he meditated and practiced *Kriya Yoga pranayama* as taught by his guru, Lahiri Mahasaya. Mejda was concerned that Father's rigorous schedule and austere life might prove a strain on his health. One day, long after Mother's death, he attempted to engage an English nurse who could take care of Father, look after his personal effects, and shield him when necessary from the maelstrom of family activity. But Father refused. Gazing lovingly at Mother's photograph, he said, "How could I accept the services of another woman after the many years of your mother's care and affection? I still live by the holy marriage vows of love and fidelity we spoke to each other; these cannot be nullified by any argument of necessity. For me there will never be another woman, not even to serve my simple needs." Father's deep sentiment revealed how very much the memory of our mother filled his heart.

We remember how it was Mother's custom to dress us each day for Father's return from the office, and to have us stand primly on the veranda to welcome him home—one of the many ways she found to express her wifely reverence and devotion to Father. She passed away at the height of his material success and just at the time of his promotion. Though the burden of Father's mental distress could not be measured, it is certain that Mother's death brought about the quickening of his spiritual advancement.

Father was meticulously efficient in the performance of all work, and his duty to family was no exception. He did his best to fill the void left by Mother's death. He bathed and fed us; sewed buttons on our coats and trousers; clipped our nails; stitched the torn cloth (though not too skillfully) on our umbrellas; and helped us gather up our books for school each day. He looked after us so devotedly that we often felt in him our mother's presence. Like Mother, Father always sensed our needs and wants, and how best to satisfy them. To this day I marvel at his sensitivity in understanding us children.

Simplicity was natural to Father, but his austerity in regard to material accumulations and his indifference to money were astonishing to his family and friends.

After Father's retirement, Mr. Winney, a director of the Railroad Board in England, came from the Home Office in London to examine the Bengal-Nagpur Railway accounts in Calcutta. He examined the service records of employees in minute detail. He noted Father's laudable contribution to the establishment of the large Bengal-

Nagpur Railway Urban Bank. He was much impressed by Father's conscientious dedication to duty; he had not taken so much as a day's leave during his eleven-and-a-half years of employment with the Railway. He had even gone to his office as usual on the day of Ananta's death.

Though Father's position was that of Second Personal Assistant to the Agent, he had received a salary less than that of a Third Personal Assistant, because he was an Indian. Mr. Winney was astonished when his audit revealed the amount and quality of Father's work, and that Father had taken no salary nor benefit from his position as a founder and chairman of the Urban Bank. The bonuses due Father from the Bengal-Nagpur Railway, which he had never attempted to claim, were awarded to him by Mr. Winney. The compensation amounted to one hundred twenty-five thousand rupees —in the economy of those days, a very substantial sum. Even so, we did not see the slightest change in Father's manner. In fact, he didn't mention the matter.

Our youngest brother, Bishnu, learned of the large deposit from a bank statement some time later. Bishnu questioned Father, but Father only philosophized in reply:

"Don't let worldly gain or loss influence you. There is much more to the purpose of this life than the excitations of happiness and sorrow, gain and loss. The quality of man's character is what really matters. One should be evenminded, anchored in the changelessness of Spirit. In His bliss there are no relativities of *maya,* delusion. In the pursuit of God, all longing for material possessions is destroyed. Just as a man has nothing when he is born, so does he take not even a paisa with him from this earth when he dies. Let your goal be the attainment of unshakable joy in knowing God. Wealth, poverty, family, friends, enemies: all are temporary in His ever-changing drama; and you are here only to witness His cosmic *lila* (play). Because of ignorance, men fail to see the skill with which the Lord accomplishes His will through His players."

We finally learned the whole story of Father's back compensation through Sri Arindam Sarkar, M.Sc., the husband of our youngest sister, Thamu. We could not have known this if Arindam had not been in charge of Establishment, dealing with the B.N. Railway accounts and payroll, as personal assistant to the railway's Agent and General Manager.

On one occasion I saw Father looking over the household accounts and smiling. Since such smiles were rare, I asked him why he was smiling so. He said, "You see, fifty thousand rupees have been spent. How nice! When God shows his favor to anyone, He relieves him from the worry of worldly accounting. I have been freed of the responsibility of this money by the purchase of our house and the Packard car that Bishnu wanted. Money spent is money that I no longer have to devote my time to worrying about!"

Father's health was not good at the time. One of our relatives came to see him, and during their conversation the purchase of Bishnu's car came up for discussion. The relative criticized Bishnu, for we already had two cars and three motorcycles. (Even so, Father himself never used any of them.) Father said to the relative, "Do you think Bishnu could have purchased the car if I had not given him the money? What if I died today? Bishnu would quickly have purchased the car from his inheritance. What can I gain from worry about money? I had to earn a salary to care for the children and to educate and establish them in life. This I have accomplished. If the children do not value money now, they will have that opportunity in the future! I will not be alive then; they will have to manage their own affairs. So, for now, I let them do what they wish, provided it does not harm anyone. From their happiness I also get some pleasure." The lesson from these words of Father's became an important part of our expanding library of understanding. The value of that wisdom has been our viaticum* on our journey through life.

Even Ananta's death did not pull Father into the flux of human emotion. Although I had remained at Barda's† bedside throughout his illness, I was unaware of the moment of his passing. I had gone to the kitchen to get ice to help reduce Barda's fever, and had just returned to his bedside when Father, who had been in his own quarters, opened the door of Barda's room and said, "It is ended." It was about two o'clock in the morning.

Father stood silently near Ananta's lifeless form for a moment, then said, "The body should now be taken from the cot and placed on a covering on the floor." Unnoticed, I followed Father from the room and saw him return to his own room and sit in meditation to practice *Kriya Yoga.*

Later that day, before the body was taken to the cremation grounds, it was placed on a cot on the footpath outside the house near the front entrance, so all could view it for the last time. From above, Father leaned over the veranda and said, "Wait." He came down and asked us to remove the cover from Ananta's face.

* Travel allowance.

† A respectful title for one's eldest brother, from the Bengali *Bara* (first or eldest brother) and *dada* (see p. 17 n.).

He gazed long upon the child whom he had raised to manhood, and to whom he had given so much love and affection.

Father relied greatly on Ananta, and often consulted him before making decisions. So we naturally expected Father to show some deep emotional reaction to Ananta's death; but in fact we saw no change in his demeanor. He went to the office as usual, and returned to his daily routine at home in his normal, quiet manner. He was as calm and unperturbed that day as always. We could not comprehend the power he had mastered that gave him the ability to remain serene amidst the climactic changes of life. This much I came to understand: In the deaths of Mother and Ananta, Father realized more poignantly the impermanence of this world; and that his responsibility in life was merely to perform his God-given duties to the best of his ability.

There was no mirror in Father's room. He often said: "If you continually look at your body—give it too much attention—attachment to it will increase. In as easy a manner, if attachment to the body is removed, the deliverance of the spirit comes quickly. Otherwise, before death frees you, delusion will cause you much suffering."

Father's preference for seclusion and his aloofness from the excitement of day-to-day activity were never more apparent than at the time of Bishnu's marriage, a festive occasion in which normally all family members would joyously participate. Friends and relatives had come from near and far. The excited chatter of so many people in the house was disturbing. Finally, Father came out of his room to ask for quiet, but seeing the festive mood he withheld comment and unobtrusively returned to his solitude. He had not become involved in the arrangements for Bishnu's marriage, nor would he participate in the celebrations; he remained in his room in meditation. Only on the day of the marriage, and upon the request of all the family members, did he come out of his seclusion—and then only for a moment—to bestow his paternal blessing on Bishnu and to greet the guests.

As with Ananta, Father showed the same stoicism when, some years later, our eldest sister, Roma, passed away suddenly one night.* Her husband called to tell us the sad news. Bishnu and I went to their house. Our brother-in-law said he would not allow the body to be taken to the cremation grounds until Father could view Roma's physical form for the last time. By the time we left Roma's home, it was nearly dawn. We stopped by the house of Sejdi, our third sister Nalini, and asked her to come with us to break the news to Father.

Knowing Father always arose early, we decided not to disturb him, but wait until he came out of his room. Shortly, he opened his door, and when he saw Nalini weeping, he asked, "What has happened?"

As gently as we could, we told him of Roma's passing. With characteristic calmness he asked us what time she had died. We told him it had happened at 11:30, during the night. "Then has the body been cremated yet?" We told him of our brother-in-law's wish that he be able to see the body first.

"Call Satish and tell him to take the body to the

* That morning she had dressed herself in her bridal finery and told her husband, "This is my last day of service to you on earth." When later in the day she suffered a heart attack she refused to permit her son to go for a doctor. She died some minutes later. (See biographical notes on Roma in Appendix. See also account in *Autobiography of a Yogi*, in the chapter, "The Heart of a Stone Image."—*Publisher's Note)*

crematory grounds at once," Father replied. "That body is nothing to me now, nothing to Roma." With this, he walked away.

We were astonished. Father—who had always worried when we were ill and never rested until we were well—was as stoically unemotional as he had been when Ananta died: in both instances, there were no words of grief nor any expression of mourning. To him death was as expected and natural as any other normal event of life.

The Austerity of an Ascetic

Father continued to live on a diet that was as simple as the one that had sustained him during his impoverished years. He told us he had been accustomed since childhood to this fare, and there was no reason now to change. His tiffin at the office consisted only of tapioca and a piece of rock candy. We cannot recall Father's ever accepting an invitation to eat out. He would politely excuse himself as being unwell or too weary after his work at the office.

Father's salary was sufficient for him to purchase a car and ride to work, but his iron habit was to avoid luxury; he considered a car unnecessary. To get to his office from our Garpar Road home, Father walked along Upper Circular Road (now Acharya Prafulla Chandra Road)* to Sukia Street (now Mahendra Srimani Street and Kailash Bose Street), and then along Cornwallis Street (now Bidhan Sarani), where he boarded a tram for the High Court. From the High Court he went on the

* After independence from England, many streets were renamed for famous Indian nationals, such as statesmen, saints, and poets.

Bengal-Nagpur Railway river launch to his office in Garden Reach. He returned home by the same route, in reverse.

During the summer months, Father's wardrobe consisted of two shirts of ordinary coarse cotton, two high-necked cotton jackets, two pairs of trousers, and a round Hindustani cap. In the winter he added a high-necked coat of striped navy blue. He wore Meerut shoes that cost three rupees; but in the office he donned a cheaper pair of slippers, since he felt that the constant use of laced shoes was unhealthful.

Mother had once given Father a pair of gold-rimmed glasses to be worn in place of his plain steel-rimmed ones. "A person of Father's position should wear such glasses," she had said. But Father refused to wear them. He preferred the plain ones. When we asked him why, he told us, "When your youngest uncle was temporarily employed in the Ichapur Post Office, he purchased for himself some gold-rimmed glasses because he had seen mine. One day he left them on his desk and went into another office. When he returned, the glasses were gone. He felt great pain over their loss, and self-recrimination at his carelessness. Loss of a cheaper pair of glasses would have mattered little. Expensive possessions are merely for show, and caring for them increases man's worry. Why add unnecessary anxiety to the burdens one already carries?" I still have Father's unused gold-rimmed glasses.

Father would not even allow us to put an electrical line in his room. He preferred using natural implements, such as a castor oil lamp. He never went into a theater or saw a movie, on the grounds that movies strained the eyes, caused undue restlessness of mind, and were harmful to health because of the lack of proper ventilation in the close, crowded rooms.

Father preferred solitude during his leisure hours, and nothing could influence him to change his ways. After finishing work, he went to his room to read from the scriptures and to meditate as Lahiri Mahasaya had taught him.

Father never borrowed from anyone; the childhood experience of his father's debt was a lifelong memory. But though his own ways were Spartan, he was large-hearted toward others. Mother's generosity had greatly influenced him. After her passing, neither friends, nor relatives, nor anyone else who approached Father for help ever left empty-handed.

Our beloved father, born on April 12, 1853, passed away on August 1, 1942, at the age of eighty-nine. After Mother's death, he had never accepted the services of anyone else. Though the rest of us in the family had the assistance of servants, Father did everything for himself until the end of his life.

CHAPTER 6

Our Days in Bareilly

Mejda's Grief Over Mother's Death

Long after Mother's death, Mejda remained inconsolable. A large *sheoli* tree stood in the middle of a field next to our bungalow in Bareilly. Mejda often sat under this tree, lost in thoughts of our mother and of the Divine Mother. He continually prayed: "When can I be near You as our mother is now?"

Father was worried about Mejda's melancholy. To distract him from his brooding, he had Mejda admitted to a school in Bareilly. It was at this time that our cousin, Dhirajda, came to live with us. He was older than Ananta and had seen many hermits, sages, and ascetics during treks in the Himalayas. Hearing his stories of the saints' lives and the spiritual atmosphere of the holy mountains, Mejda felt a strong desire to go to the Himalayas. He secretly decided to run away and join the Himalayan yogis to obtain spiritual instruction on how to find God. One day, in an excess of enthusiasm, he revealed his plans to Dwarka Prasad, the son of our landlord, a family friend. Dwarka tried to dissuade Mejda; and he also told Ananta about Mejda's plans. Thereafter Ananta kept a close watch on Mejda. He taunted him mercilessly, often calling him a "Lilliputian" amongst the towering giants of India's sages. Dwarka Prasad, too, teased Mejda. But their jibes only fanned the smoldering embers of Mejda's desire to seek God in

Father in yoga posture, during his later years

Jhima ("Maid-Ma"), Father, and Father's sister

the solitudes of the Himalayas. The ocher cloth, garb of India's mendicants since ancient times, became to Mejda the symbol of his life's longing.

Ananta knew that one day Mejda would try to run away from home, so he was always on the alert. When Mejda did attempt such a flight one afternoon, Ananta followed him at a distance. He intercepted Mejda in Nainital and made him return home.

Dejected, Mejda sat morning and evening under the *sheoli* tree. I often saw him immersed in meditation, forgetful of his surroundings, his mind soaring upward to mingle with the Infinite. In such states, tears of longing for the Divine Mother would spill from his eyes. Other times, he would weep and pray: "Oh Mother, my dear Mother, they will not allow me to come to You." Seeing him this way brought tears to my eyes and kindled in me an anger toward Ananta. Why? Why did our Barda treat Mejda so?

Adherence to Ahimsa*

Madho Prasad, second brother of Dwarka Prasad, was a great hunter. We loved his hunting dress. My admiration was such that I, too, wanted to become a great

* Harmlessness; nonviolence. In the *Yoga Sutras* (II:35), the great sage Patanjali has written: "In the presence of a man perfected in *ahimsa* (nonviolence), enmity [in any creature] does not arise." In *Autobiography of a Yogi,* Swami Sri Yukteswar explains, "By *ahimsa* Patanjali meant removal of the *desire* to kill. This world is inconveniently arranged for a literal practice of *ahimsa.* Man may be compelled to exterminate harmful creatures. He is not under a similar compulsion to feel anger or animosity. All forms of life have an equal right to the air of *maya.* The saint who uncovers the secret of creation will be in harmony with Nature's countless bewildering expressions. All men may understand this truth by overcoming the passion for destruction." —*Autobiography of a Yogi,* "Years in My Master's Hermitage," by Paramahansa Yogananda. *(Publisher's Note)*

hunter when I grew up—even greater than Madho. The whole world would know of me! The wild animals would run when they caught my scent! Because Ananta and Madho were close friends, our family was often the recipient of some of the game birds Madho killed. The meat was cooked and eaten with relish. But Mejda would not touch it. Although we all sat down together at mealtime, Mejda ate only rice and vegetables. Ananta would make me sit next to Mejda with my plate of savory fowl just to tease him. But, taking no notice, Mejda would eat his own food quickly and silently, and then excuse himself and leave the room.

When Mejda got me alone after these occasions he would scold me: "You are greedy to partake of such food," he would say. "It is a sin to shoot innocent birds. Those who eat the meat share in that sin. It is so easy to accumulate sin, but very hard to earn virtue. All people must answer for their deeds in their life after death. So you must *think* before you do anything. He who cannot distinguish between right and wrong, justice and injustice, violence and nonviolence, may be called anything—but not a man!"

Unshakable Dedication to Truth

Our eldest brother Ananta—or Barda, as we called him—was a strict disciplinarian. Because he himself was so principled, he would not tolerate misbehavior in others. Of course, he erred at times in his judgments, and on occasion his opinions were extremely biased. Even so, his strong-principled character made an impression on us all, especially Mejda. But although Mejda respected Barda, if Barda (or anyone else) was wrong, Mejda could not be swayed from upholding the truth.

Manudi,* a widowed relative who had joined our household to look after us, tried to discipline and control us by many means—some were unjust. She harassed us unnecessarily about our behavior, even in such matters as bathing, eating, and sleeping. Our stouthearted Mejda refused to follow many of her unreasonable directions, but his refusals only made Manudi more determined to exercise her authority. Mejda's outspoken protests were not uncommon; and often he did just the opposite of what she requested. Finally, when she saw she could not subdue him, she brought a false allegation about Mejda to Ananta. He accepted the untrue report in good faith and told Mejda to beg her apology. Mejda refused. "Why? I have done no wrong. Why should I belittle God in me by asking forgiveness for something I didn't do? Such an act would belittle me, too!"

Ananta felt Mejda's words were impertinent. "You *must* apologize! You can't claim to be the only truthful person in this house. Do as I say," he commanded. "You must learn to respect the word of your elders."

Mejda refused to bend. Ananta then became very angry; he picked up a wooden ruler and began to beat Mejda on his arms and body. Wherever the ruler struck, red welts began to rise. Soon Mejda's entire body was swollen. I was crying and trembling in fear. "Mejda is acting like a fool," I thought. "It would have been so simple to ask forgiveness. Then this matter could have been settled without a beating!" Try as he would, Ananta could not make Mejda apologize. The more Barda beat him, the stronger became Mejda's will not to yield. His tearless, silent protest was like steel. Finally the ruler

* Manudi was the eldest sister of our cousin Jatinda. Their father was Sri Phanindra Nath Ghosh, one of our father's cousins.

broke. Ananta cried out in anger and left the room. Mejda was still standing as straight as a deodar tree.

Later that night Ananta spoke to our sister Nalini and learned that the allegation was false. He was overcome by remorse and realized that Mejda's silent and determined resistance was the greatest possible witness to truth. Barda went to Mejda's room, hugged him, and asked forgiveness for the violence he had done against him. He took Mejda to Manudi's room and sternly reprimanded her.

The old widow was shocked by Ananta's severe punishment of Mejda, and later openly wept before Mejda. "Brother," she pleaded, "please forgive this hateful woman. I have greatly erred in my estimation of you. There is no escape from the sins I have committed. I will have no salvation if you do not pardon me. Please tell me, brother, do you forgive me?" Saying this, she wept bitterly. Mejda and I tried to console her. Finally, she stopped crying and Mejda looked at her with a compassionate smile.

"I am not the one to excuse you," he said gently. "Ask forgiveness from God. He will surely pardon you."

While we were in Bareilly, Mejda told me he would immerse the idol of the Goddess Kali made by Mother.* I protested. At first Mejda would not disclose his rea-

* Images are only representations of the Infinite Spirit. Symbolically, the devotee invokes the Divine to manifest in that image so that the Absolute can be worshipped in a form conceivable by the devotee. The images are often made of clay, so that after worship they may be immersed in water, such as in a river or a pond. The form of the image returns to the elements from which it was made, symbolizing the return of Spirit from the finite to the Infinite. Thus God is perceived as both Personal and Impersonal, Immanent and Transcendent. *(Publisher's Note)*

sons for this decision. Finally, to quiet my objections, he told me, "I received a divine command in a dream. I must immerse the statue." Though this explanation was somewhat enigmatic, I did not question a "divine command." That image of Kali was the last one made by our mother.

CHAPTER 7

Chittagong

A Remarkable Encounter

According to Ananta's diary, it was on May 3, 1906, that we moved from Bareilly to Chittagong. Here Mejda used to take me with him to pick fruit from trees in the yards of neighboring homes. One of the homes had some beautiful large swans. Mejda decided he wanted to make a quill pen, so he plucked a feather from one of the graceful birds. The owner found out and complained to Ananta. Barda sought to put an end to Mejda's naughtiness, and decided the best way was to confine him during the day. So he personally took Mejda and me to the local school and enrolled us. Mejda did very well on his papers; mine just barely passed.

Ananta's way was to restrict our movements with prohibitive orders: "Don't do this! Don't do that! Don't go there! People won't like you if you don't behave!" Our days in Chittagong were filled with endless restrictions. But this only made Mejda more obstinate; in the face of unreasonable curtailment, he became more determined to do what he wanted.

One day, Mejda and I were told: "Don't go toward the harbor. Stay away from the mouth of the river."

I thought: "Mejda will never obey this. This is exactly what he rebels against." Of course, it wasn't long before he took me with him to the mouth of the river.

Ananta had directed all of us children to be home by early evening every day, to wash, and to begin our homework by six o'clock. The harbor at Chittagong was about four kilometers from home. Thus, after returning from school and taking tiffin, we couldn't walk the round-trip distance of eight kilometers and be back at the specified time. So we used to run all the way to the harbor, watch the ships for a short while, then run home. From all this sprinting, Mejda became an excellent athlete. I, too, became a pretty good one; but not nearly so much so as Mejda.

The road to the mouth of the river followed several low hills. Fruit hung in abundance in the trees along our way. One day Mejda said, "Listen, when we return this evening we'll pick some *lichis*. No one will see us in the twilight."

So said, so done! Mejda was picking some of the luscious, sweet *lichis* when he heard someone call his name. Startled, Mejda stood stock still. All sense of adventure ended abruptly! Cautiously we moved in the direction from which the voice had come. The twilight was fast fading and we could not see far ahead in the shadows, but we soon discerned a man dressed in white. Seeing that we were somewhat afraid, he beckoned us closer in a friendly manner. If he were the watchman here, how would he have known Mejda's name?

Slowly we advanced toward the gently smiling person. His form seemed lustrous with a wonderful light. I looked around to see where the light was coming from. Suddenly Mejda bowed before the saint and touched his feet. The saint embraced Mejda and kissed him on the head. I also bowed before the saintly figure. With a gesture of blessing, he said to us, "Jaiastu!"* And then he spoke to Mejda:

* "Victory be with you!"

"Mukunda, it is God's wish that I come to you today. Remember what I say to you. You have come on earth as God's representative to fulfill His wishes. Your body is His temple, sanctified by prayer and meditation. Do not run after material pleasures or satisfaction. You will show the way that leads to true happiness; and by your spiritual knowledge you will deliver those who are suffering in ignorance. Never forget that you are one with *Maha Purusha,** attained only by those who are supremely successful in meditation. Your body, mind, and life must never deviate from the thought of God, even for a moment. The blessings of the Infinite Father are upon you. Your faith in Him must be absolute. He will protect you from all dangers. In this world only He is eternal; all else is transient and unreliable. One day your ideals of Yoga will inspire all mankind. Mukunda, march onward!"

I was fidgeting, for time was passing and darkness was upon us. We had a long way to go to reach home. A scolding by Father and a beating from Ananta were inevitable. The saint perceived my thought and said, "Do not be troubled. Go home freely; no one will notice that you are late."

We started for home. After walking a short distance, we looked back and saw the saint blessing us with upraised hands. Then he vanished. I turned to Mejda and spoke, but he wasn't listening. He was walking, head down, in a thoughtful mood. When we reached home, Mejda went directly to his prayer room. I inquired where Father and Ananta were. I learned that Barda had been invited to a friend's home, and that Father had not yet returned from an important meeting at the of-

* "The Great Soul," a title of the supreme Spirit.

fice. What joy! they did not know of our belated return. I ran to the prayer room to tell Mejda.

But Mejda was coming to get me. He took hold of my hand and led me to a photograph that hung on the wall. We stood a moment before it, then he said, "Do you recognize him? Was it not he who spoke to us?"

I was astonished. It *was* he—that very smile. But he had died long ago. How could he have come to us now? How could we have talked with someone who had been dead all these years? He had blessed us, embraced Mejda and kissed his head. I was choked with awe, unable to speak. I simply looked at Mejda. There was no doubt that Mejda and I had seen and talked with the great Lahiri Mahasaya! the saint whose counsel was sought by householders and sages alike throughout all India; the preceptor to whom people had come in endless streams to receive blessings and spiritual instruction. With Mejda, I had seen the Yogavatar with my own eyes and talked with him. I am thrilled to this day whenever I recall that wondrous experience. It is forever etched in my memory. I am blessed: His endless mercy, his crowning grace, is upon me. My gratitude knows no bounds.

A Bully Is Subdued

At the beginning of the school term, a robust rogue of a boy was admitted to Mejda's class. He bullied the smaller and younger boys whenever he had the opportunity. He forced them to run errands and do menial tasks for him; if they refused, he beat them.

One day a small classmate of Mejda's was assaulted by the intimidating bully. Mejda could not stand to see the unfair contest between two so disparate in size and strength. He challenged the bigger boy, "If you have such a great desire to fight, then fight with me! Let's see who is stronger."

The other boys standing nearby were shocked at Mejda's words; they feared for his life. The ruffian retorted contemptuously, "So, small fry, what are you so riled up about. Do you not know who I am?" Saying this, he jumped on Mejda like a wounded tiger. Instantly they were both on the ground, rolling over and over in the dust. Then suddenly they were on their feet, and the muscular bully picked Mejda up over his head and threw him to the ground. Mejda hit with a cracking thud that sounded as though his back had been broken. Frantically I tried to break through the tight ring of boys surrounding the fighters, but I couldn't budge them. I began to cry. Mejda looked so pale — I felt he was doomed.

The bully bent over to pick Mejda up a second time; but as he did so, Mejda got an arm-lock around his assailant's neck. The bully was startled: he hadn't been prepared for this move. He tried unsuccessfully to unloose Mejda's grip; failing this, he caught hold of Mejda's head and slammed it hard against the ground—again, and then again. Mejda would not let go of his stranglehold, though he was almost knocked unconscious from the blows. The bully was gasping for breath; his face turned red. Mejda, in a voice that seemed to come from far away, said firmly: "Say that you will never pick on anyone again."

Though the bigger boy was suffocating, he swore at Mejda and again grabbed his head and slammed it to the ground. Somehow Mejda kept his senses. He called out: "Unless you admit defeat, I will not release you."

By this time, the bully's eyes were bulging from

their sockets; he knew he could not go on. "All right," he choked, "you have defeated me. Let go!"

Mejda released his hold. Both boys were panting and shaking as they stood up. I ran over to Mejda and saw that the back of his head was bruised and bleeding. But Mejda didn't seem to care. His heart was too full of the victory he had won.

However, the bully could not accept defeat. He suddenly turned and jumped Mejda again. But this time all the boys rushed in to intervene: "You were justly beaten by Mukunda," they shouted. "If you do anything to him now, you will have to fight all of us. And if that happens, we will give you such a beating that you will be bedridden for the rest of your life!" Seeing the boys united against him, the bully retreated step by step; then he turned and fled.

Mejda became known as the protector of the weak. But later, he repented the anger that had driven him into the conflict. As it dawned upon him that his anger had been uncontrolled, the biting pain of his conscience far outweighed his physical pain. He knew that anger has no place in the life of one who has faith in God, for it blots out the very thought of God. He resolved that never again would he give way to anger. Many times after that I saw others hurt him; but he never expressed any anger or lost his temper. When his friends were wrong, he firmly reproved them—repeatedly, if necessary—but it was always with the greatest patience and inner calm.

Paper Boats Calm a Storm

We were at Chittagong for about two months. Then Father was transferred to Calcutta. The circumstances surrounding the move were indeed strange. Father was given only seven days' notice to be in Calcutta. Just at that time a cyclone struck our area, bringing torrential rain. The local inhabitants said the storm would last at least fifteen days; similar reports were given in the newspapers. We feared we would not be able to reach Calcutta in time.

Mejda was impatient to leave and asked Father if we would have to wait out the storm. When Father appeared apprehensive, Mejda told Nalini: "Why is everyone afraid? You will see: I am going to stop this terrible rain." When the household heard of Mejda's ridiculous statement, they laughed.

Resolutely Mejda went to the kitchen and opened the door leading to the courtyard. He sat awhile on the doorstep watching the unrelenting rain pouring from the sky. He told me, "Bring some newspapers." I began to collect the papers; Nalini joined me quietly and helped. Stacking the papers in a pile beside Mejda, we waited to see what he would do next.

Mejda began to make little paper boats. One by one he tossed them into the pool of water that had accumulated in the courtyard. As he launched each boat we could hear that he was saying or praying something, but we could not catch the words.

After about half an hour had passed, we expressed our doubts that Mejda could muster any power against the fierce storm. He looked over at us, but said nothing. He continued making the paper boats and throwing them out upon the water, reinforced with his prayer. He did this for an hour without pause. Then, what wonder of wonders: the rain stopped! The clouds blew away, and a beautiful sunset lit the evening sky. No one in the family had witnessed a miracle like this. Everyone regarded Mejda with an astonishing respect. The next day we began our journey to Calcutta.

As we were crossing the Padma River in a large steamer, Mejda asked me, "What sort of transport do you like best?" I didn't like the boat. It was horrible! I told him I would much rather ride the train.

Mejda replied, "I love traveling by steamer. Oh, see how it rolls from side to side. Yet so many passengers turn upside down and faint! You will see: one day I will go to a very far country on a big ship."

We arrived in Calcutta from Chittagong on July 2, 1906.

CHAPTER 8

Early Years in Calcutta

Mejda as Athlete and Wrestler

When we first arrived in Calcutta we stayed with Father's sister on Sitaram Ghosh Street, and then rented a house at Champatala for a year. Then a distant relative told Father about another house at 4 Garpar Road, which was for rent for forty rupees a month. As this house was more convenient for us, we moved. Years later, the owner decided to sell the house for 17,000 rupees; so Father purchased it, on July 25, 1919. It was then a two-storied building; in later years I added a third floor. Garpar Road was at that time a very narrow lane; it was almost impossible for two cars to pass. The Calcutta Deaf and Dumb School, surrounded by a high wall, was located across the street.

Mejda and I were admitted into the Hindu School from our Champatala residence; Mejda in class eight, I in class three. We both completed our high school education in this school. Here we met Sri Satyendra Nath Basu, who later gained fame as a renowned scientist and a National Professor.* Satyendrada often came to our Garpar house and became one of our close friends.

* An honor bestowed on eminent retired professors by the Government of India through the University Grants Commission. They received the coveted title and a stipend for their outstanding contribution to learning. This practice has prevailed since India's independence. During British rule, famous professors were knighted. The title of National Professor connotes a similar honor.

Mejda and he would sit on the veranda and spend the evening talking.

Mejda loved sports. He joined the College Street Branch of the YMCA. Boys of all ages could join; monthly dues were only four annas (one-quarter rupee). We also often watched games played on the field of the deaf-mute school from our second-floor veranda. Then the school added another story to its building, and our view was blocked. Shortly thereafter, Mejda met Manomohan Mazumdar, son of one of the founders of the Calcutta Deaf and Dumb School. (In later years Manomohanda was initiated in *sannyas* by Mejda and became the respected Swami Satyananda.) After we met Manomohanda, he invited Mejda and me to the playing field of the school, and made its sporting facilities available to us. We exercised frequently with the boys of the school, and had many opportunities to compete in the school games. Often we won prizes.

Greer Park was also located near our home. Adjacent to the park was the Greer Club, which was quartered in the home of the manufacturer of Lakshmibilas Oil. After members of the club had finished using the park for their games, Mejda had me and many of the boys do running exercises, sprints, and longer races around the field. Then after racing, we all ran ten or fifteen laps to develop our breathing. Mejda always led the field.

Mejda also competed in YMCA races in Marcus Square, and won many awards. I vividly recall one particular event. I sat on the sidelines of the field, holding Mejda's jacket and shoes. Other athletes competing in the races were sprinting a few laps to warm up. They wore running shoes and shorts; Mejda was barefooted and in his knit undershirt and *dhoti,* which he had tucked tightly up above his knees.

Mejda had entered two events: the 440-yard race and the half-mile. He astonished everyone by winning the 440. The half-mile was scheduled later in the afternoon. At the beginning of that race, Mejda trailed three or four of the more experienced runners. But he gradually overtook one after the other. And on the final lap he pulled ahead to win the race.

The spectators cheered and clapped. Everyone wondered: "Who is this new runner?" Mejda looked over at me and smiled happily. The organizers of the races were surprised, but the winners of previous years' races were dejected and dumbfounded! "How could this totally unknown runner beat them?" Mejda received as first prize an air gun for the 440-yard run, and a beautiful pair of cut-glass inkwells for the half-mile race. (Later, while he was using the air gun for target shooting, a sparrow was accidently killed. Mejda was so heartsick, he broke the gun. Bishnu and I had pleaded with him to give the gun to us, but Mejda wanted to be sure no further harm would come from its use.)

Mejda became widely known as a fast runner. Many were jealous. Former champions arranged a race in Greer Park, planning to defeat the new hero. Though I was very young, their scheme appeared ludicrous even to me. Mejda soundly defeated every one of them, running even faster than in the previous races. The sad thing was, his challengers wanted to be sportsmen without having the corresponding sportsman's spirit.

Mejda's success encouraged Bishnu and me to train strenuously. Owing to our diligent efforts, we won many prizes in the annual competitions at the Hindu School—

so many prizes, in fact, that a servant had to help us carry them home.

Mejda himself organized a sports competition in Greer Park. He worked to create an atmosphere of impartiality that fostered fairness and the spirit of true sportsmanship. His planning and coordination of the program was professional. He set up three divisions: one for small boys, one for intermediate boys, and a division for older boys. All those who participated—and the spectators as well—were highly pleased.

Many persons asked Mejda to organize similar competitions every year, and he had thought a great deal about creating annual exemplary competitions. But he met with much resistance from some already established sectors of sporting competitions. It hurt him that those responsible for fostering sportsmanship were neither supportive of his efforts nor always impartial in their dealings. He didn't want to enter into any clash with these groups, so he withdrew his efforts.

Mejda's interest turned to wrestling. The gatekeeper of the nearby Atheneum Institution—a giant of a man—had a wrestling gymnasium on Garpar Road near our home. Many young men trained there. Mejda took some of us to the gym with him every morning. Fascinated, we stood at ringside and watched. Sometimes, when one of the wrestlers was in a difficult position, Mejda would prompt him what to do. Following this sideline advice, the wrestler would gain the advantage and defeat his opponent. Afterwards, Mejda would be treated with *jalebi* (a crisp, juicy sweet) and hot *chola dal* (sprouted garbanzo beans). As friendship grew, Mejda ventured one day to ask if they would teach him to wrestle.

The men were surprised to hear this request from

such a refined boy. "You're joking, aren't you?" they laughed. Mejda assured them he was serious. Then one of the young men said, in a mixture of Hindi and Bengali, "Respected lad, you are a puzzle to us. You obviously are the son of a gentleman and do not seem suited to this type of sport, yet you know many of the holds. You even coach us. You don't look like a wrestler, yet you appear familiar with the sport. Please explain yourself."

It took a lot of talking on Mejda's part to convince the young men he knew nothing of wrestling, that the coaching he was doing came spontaneously to his mind. Finally, the men agreed to teach him. And after a time, Mejda allowed me to take instruction, too.

About a fortnight after Mejda began training, a friend of his, Shishir, approached him for help. He had been attacked with gout, and had undergone extensive treatments, but nothing had relieved his condition. He couldn't even walk. The night before he came to Mejda, he had dreamt of Mejda and heard a voice telling him: "Go to Mukunda tomorrow. He can cure you." Mejda first taught Shishir Lahiri Mahasaya's *Kriya Yoga* technique, which he had learned from Father, and had him practice it regularly. His condition began to improve. Mejda then brought him to the gymnasium for exercising. He taught Shishir a special set of muscular exercises to increase the blood circulation. In a few months Shishir was completely well.

Shortly after the healing, Shishir confided to Mejda, "Mukunda, if I had not seen you in a dream that night and heard those words telling me to seek your help, I believe I would have committed suicide; it would have been unbearable to be an invalid and a burden to others the rest of my life."

A New Spiritual Friend for Mejda

One November afternoon, the boys that Mejda had organized into an athletic club, including myself, were preparing for a soccer match with another team. The soccer ball was deflated, and our only pump suddenly went out of order before we had finished filling the ball. We were in real trouble, as it was almost time for the game to begin. Mejda asked me if I knew anyone who had a pump, there being no bicycle shop nearby. I knew some boys, but they refused to help us because they were not on our team. Mejda only accepted boys of good character, and these had been considered unfit. Kalinath Sarkar, a friend of ours who lived on Parsi Bagan Lane near the Science College, and who also was a member of our team, suggested we try at the Calcutta Deaf and Dumb School. "I am a friend of Manomohan Mazumdar, eldest son of one of the founders, Mohini Mohan Mazumdar."

We all went as a group to the school. Manomohan was standing at the gate. Kalinathda said, "Mano, we're so happy to find you here."

Manomohan inquired, "What are all of you doing in this scorching heat? Are you really going to play?"

"Yes," replied Kalinathda, and, pointing out Mejda, he added, "This is Mukunda Lal Ghosh, our captain. The boys on Sukia Street have challenged us to a game, boasting that they will soundly defeat us. Mukunda has told them, 'I promise by my name that we will beat the shirts off you.'"

Mejda and Manomohan looked soul-stirringly at each other. Though Manomohan was about three or four years younger than Mejda, they were attracted instantly in a friendship that transcended their difference in age; they felt the magnetic drawing of the heart's pure love.

Watching the two, Kalinath spoke up: "Our football pump is broken. May we borrow the school's? Our prestige is at stake."

Looking intently at Mejda, Manomohan replied, "Can his wish be unfulfilled? No, never. Come with me." Saying this, he led us into the school building and provided us with the vital pump.

From that day, Mejda and Manomohanda were fast friends. One evening, coming home from the playing field, most of our teammates had gone on ahead of us. Manomohan, his second brother, Mukul, and Mejda and I were walking together. The footpath took us alongside the railroad track on the east side of Upper Circular Road. The last rays of the setting sun had beautifully colored the western sky. Clouds had shaped themselves into hills, animals, and waves along a vermilion seashore. But Mejda's mind was not there—it was in the Himalayas. He said to Manomohan, "Just imagine how right now the saints in the Himalayas are meditating in their caves. Throughout all ages they have lifted the souls of men out of the darkness of *maya.* I see the spiritual heights of the Himalayas ascending into Infinity and merging with *Aum.** I feel the entrancing beauty of the holy mountains drawing me."

After a moment's pause, Mejda continued, "Come! Let us follow the footsteps of the ascetics. I will teach you that *sadhana.* But the way is not easy; it is fraught with ridicule and the misunderstandings of those who

* The sound of the cosmic creative vibration; "Amen" and "the Word" of the Christian Scripture.

do not believe in the path of renunciation. There are many obstacles. You must learn to keep your mind fixed on the Divine Goal alone, even to the exclusion of home."

The following day Mejda taught Manomohan the technique of meditation for hearing the holy sound of *Aum,* and seeing the Divine Light. Inwardly Manomohanda accepted Mejda as his guru. They were frequently to be found meditating together—in the drawing room of our Garpar Road home, at Kali Temple and Belur Math in Dakshineswar, and on the cremation grounds during nights of the new moon. Their devotions were focused on Divine Mother as Kali.

The three of us made an image of Mother Kali. The founder-principal of the Deaf and Dumb School, Sri Kamini Mohan Banerjee, arranged for *puja* on the school grounds. After the service, he distributed *prasad* to all who participated.

Encouraged and inspired by Mejda, Manomohan and I dug a cave for meditation in the embankment of a pond inside the school compound. It took us a long time, for we had to conceal our efforts: we could work only after the schoolboys had finished their play in the afternoon. We made the cave to look like those used by Himalayan yogis. Unseen by anyone, we began to meditate in our secret grotto. But before long we were discovered by the school authorities, who abruptly evicted us from our "Himalayan" sanctuary.

Flight to the Himalayas

We didn't dream that Mejda was thinking so seriously of running away to the Himalayas to be with the saints and to search for his guru. He planned every detail of his trip in complete secrecy. On the chosen day of his flight, he stayed home from school on the pretext that he was not well. He spent all morning in his prayer room. It wasn't until three in the afternoon that we discovered he had fled.

Ananta went to Mejda's school to ask his friends if they knew his whereabouts, and learned that Mejda's friend, Amar, also had not attended classes that day. The next morning Ananta made inquiries at Amar's home. Amar had left behind a marked railroad timetable showing the transfer stations en route to Hardwar, ancient and holy site of pilgrimage in the Himalayan foothills. As Ananta was leaving, he overheard Amar's father talking with the coachman who usually took him to work, dropping Amar off at school at the same time. When the driver asked where Amar was, his father replied sadly that Amar had run away. The carriage driver then revealed that another coachman had told him he had taken Amar and two other boys—all dressed in European clothing—to Howrah Railway Station.

When Ananta heard this he knew that Mejda, Amar, and another friend had disguised themselves as Europeans and left Calcutta by train. Consulting the marked timetable, Ananta sent telegrams to the police and stationmasters at the stopovers marked in the timetable. The telegram requested aid in apprehending three Bengali boys, dressed as Europeans, proceeding to Hardwar via Moghal Sarai. "I will generously reward your assistance," the telegram promised. Ananta also sent a cable to our friend Dwarka Prasad, in Bareilly, another stop underlined on the timetable.

Shortly thereafter we learned from our relatives that Jatinda, a cousin, had been missing from home the previous night but had just returned — dressed as a European. Quick to seize the opportunity to learn from Jatinda what had happened, Ananta invited him to lunch at our house.

Jatinda arrived at noon. Ananta himself had supervised the planning and preparation of the food so that it was a veritable feast! Happily consuming course after course of the delectable meal, Jatinda was completely unaware that Ananta had a scheme in mind. The royal treatment he received blinded Jatinda's reason; he remained oblivious to the fact that Ananta's patronizing behavior was quite uncharacteristic.

After the sumptuous meal, Ananta suggested, "Jatin, let's go for a walk." Unsuspectingly Jatinda agreed, not realizing Ananta had planned the route so as to pass by the police station. Ananta led him right into the station where imposing, fierce-looking officers on duty had been specially chosen by Ananta for their roles in his plot. They fixed the hapless Jatinda with accusing stares. Shocked by the sudden turn of events, and threatened by the grim officers, Jatinda broke down and confessed everything.

"All we wanted to do was go to the Himalayas to find a guru," he cried. "Amar brought a hackney carriage to Mukunda's house." (When Mukunda heard the carriage he tossed his little travel bundle from his rooftop prayer room to Amar in the alley below. The bundle contained a copy of the Bhagavad Gita, a picture of Lahiri Mahasaya, a string of prayer beads, two loincloths, and a blanket. He then ran out the front door and into the waiting carriage.) "Amar and Mukunda picked me up on the way to the railroad station. First they went to Chandni Chauk to purchase our travel clothes: We had to buy canvas shoes, for we discarded all items made of leather. We also put on European suits as a disguise. At Howrah we entrained for Hardwar by way of Burdwan.

"While we were riding along in the train, Mukunda said, 'Imagine what joy we will have when we receive initiation from a guru. We will become so magnetized by spiritual power that we will be able to control the wild animals in the Himalayas. Even tigers that come around us will behave like pussycats!'

"Though Amar was filled with enthusiasm at Mukunda's words, I was terrified. I knew that if ever I came face-to-face with a tiger, I would end up in its stomach. I stuck my head out of the train window, hoping the fresh air would revive my spirit. But fear so constricted my throat that I could not speak during the rest of the trip to Burdwan. I decided then to give up my spiritual journey.

"I suggested we divide our travel funds into three parts so that each of us could purchase our own tickets in Burdwan. In this way we would not arouse the suspicion of the authorities. Mukunda and Amar agreed. When we alighted at the station and separated to buy our tickets, I hid in the station and then bought a ticket to Calcutta. That is how I arrived back home."

Mejda related to us later: "After we had waited for Jatinda for some time, I felt he had abandoned us. We searched for him in the station and on the platform, but I knew he had returned home. I told Amar that this was an ill omen; our trip was doomed to failure. Discouraged, I suggested that we, too, return to Calcutta. But Amar would not admit defeat so easily. His confidence and encouraging words convinced me that this was a divine test.

"The bell was announcing the departure of our train. As we were about to board, Amar urged me not to answer if anyone questioned us. Just at that moment an English conductor came running down the platform waving a telegram. He looked suspiciously at us for a few moments, then asked us if we were fleeing from home. The phrasing of his question enabled us to give a negative reply. He asked us repeatedly where the third boy was. Then he asked our names. Amar spoke so convincingly of our half-European heritage that the conductor was completely persuaded we were not the fugitives described in the telegram. He said, 'Come with me. You shouldn't get into this compartment with natives. I will put you in the first-class coach with other Europeans. If anyone gives you any trouble, tell them who I am and that I have placed you in this compartment. I will return shortly.'

"The funny thing was, he didn't tell us his name, nor did he ever return. Since we were alone in the compartment, we resumed talking in Bengali. I scolded Amar, 'Why did you leave that marked timetable in your house? Ananta has surely found it.'

"When we reached Bareilly, Dwarka Prasad was waiting on the station platform. I realized that Ananta had wired him, too, asking him to stop us. I invited Dwarka to join us in our holy quest. I don't know what he thought, but at least he didn't hand us over to the police. He simply said to me, 'Go home, Mukunda. Your entire family is worried about you.' I didn't reply, and returned to the train.

"The next leg of our journey took us to Hardwar. Anticipating that another of Ananta's telegrams was one step ahead of us, we planned how we could escape the officials there. We decided to press on immediately to Rishikesh. But in Hardwar we were caught by a policeman. He detained us there in his home for three days, until Ananta and Amar's brother arrived."

Ananta did not conceal his consternation. He said to Mejda, "If you really want to associate with saints, then seek one who knows God. I understand your aspirations, but fleeing home again and again worries all of us. In our anxiety we neither eat nor sleep well. You make us feel as though we offend you.

"You are searching blindly for a preceptor, but I know of an illumined master in Banaras who can forever quench your thirst for the Divine. On our return journey we will stop there to meet him. When you see him you will behold God in his form; from him you will learn how the Divine may be attained."*

When they reached Banaras, Ananta took Mejda to the saint. A large group of devotees was gathered around the holy man. They appeared overly eager to please their guru, whom they believed to be God incarnate. The room was fragrant with costly incense, and a brass pot in each corner contained scented water. A similar container had been placed in front of the saint. His disciples would take water from this jug and drink it and sprinkle it on their heads, feeling it to be blessed because it had touched the feet of the saint.

* In *Autobiography of a Yogi,* Paramahansa Yogananda wrote about a cleverly hatched plot that Ananta had prearranged with a pundit in Banaras who had agreed to try to dissuade Mukunda from the path of renunciation. That was an incident separate from the one here related by Sananda Lal Ghosh. Ananta was trying all means available to prevent his ardent younger brother from leaving home. As noted in the Introduction to "*Mejda,*" Paramahansaji purposely omitted from his autobiography some stories about himself. *(Publisher's Note)*

Dressed in expensive clothing, and supported by a large pillow that was elaborately covered with ochre silk and bordered with silver lace and tinsel, the saint lay back in a half-reclining position. His eyes were closed, as if he were withdrawn into another sphere. From time to time he opened his heavy eyelids to reproach his disciples for worshipping too boisterously: they were disturbing his inner serenity.

After a time he spoke condescendingly, "If you want to worship me, do so; but don't make such a fuss about it! I exist *within* you. In time you will receive my compassion and blessings."

Ananta's intrusion was not welcome. The saint's disciples refused to let him near their reclining Godhead. "What do you want? Can't you see he's resting. He gets *very* angry if he is disturbed."

Ananta hesitated, for he had not had much experience with saints. Having come this far, however, he determined to carry out his plan. He gripped Mejda's hand and forced his way through the cluster of devotees. Those who saw the reverence in Mejda's face gave way readily. Soon Ananta and Mejda were seated near the august presence.

Ananta addressed the sadhu respectfully: "Your Holiness, kindly grace us with your glance. I have brought my brother to receive your blessing." Mejda bowed humbly. The saint opened his eyes and gazed at Mejda's quiet, serene countenance.

The saint's disciples marveled that Mejda had attracted their guru's attention, when all their service and devotion had been seemingly ignored. What had he offered? How had his simple bow commanded this response? But the saint's shrill voice dispelled the moment of awe: "Young man! Are you seeking the Divine? Your search is at an end: *I* am God!"

Mejda's face registered shock.

"I see you don't recognize me," the saint fumed. "You are still blinded by delusion and attraction to family life."

Mejda was calm as he spoke with deep conviction, "Respected Soul, never say that *you* are God."

Indignation clouded the saint's face; it became dark, as though ink had been poured over his body. He resented the impudence of this young boy. His chest heaved and swelled; his face became distorted with anger. Mejda took a small mirror from his shoulder bag and held it up before the sadhu.

"Look at yourself! Is this the face of God? Can the God of love and beauty Whom I have sought day and night, month after month, year after year, have such a face? No! God is not greedy. He does not deceive His devotees in order to procure a following and the gifts they bring. He shows His devotees the path of enlightenment. Neither God nor truth can be obtained through deception. Unless one forgoes ego-consciousness, he cannot attain deliverance.

"You are leading your disciples into greater ignorance by flattering your ego and theirs. Show them instead the path of liberating truth. Give them the knowledge by which they can taste the joy of deliverance from delusion. Help them to understand the transitoriness of life on earth as compared to the everlastingness of life in God. We are only playing make-believe for a time in these garbs of flesh. We come into this world naked and without possessions; and when we again merge in His greatness, we will leave everything behind. There is nothing we can claim as our own. Everything and everyone belongs to God; He *is* all. Help your disciples realize this truth. Or if you cannot rightly guide them, then let them seek their own paths to God. All they are quarreling and fighting for is useless. It vanishes in time. Open their eyes to the true knowledge that deliverance can come only when we have freed our souls from the encumberment of sense-born passions and desires.

"Enlighten your devotees! Make them realize that this universe—the planets, the sun, the moon, the earth, the sky, the clay and water, the day and night, life and death, His blessedness and delusion — is moving through time and space by His will alone.

"The first necessity of life is to avoid causing pain and misery to others and to seek harmony in oneness of mind and soul as we surrender everything worldly to Him. He is Truth; we have to abandon everything in search of this Knowledge. Nothing on earth can be exchanged for its value. To receive this Knowledge our life must follow His will. Only He who can impart divine wisdom to others and show them the path to God is a real guru."

Saying this, Mejda stood up and started to leave the room. Ananta followed.

The saint was thunderstruck. A violent earthquake could not have shaken him more than Mejda's words shook his egocentric attitude. Slowly his face lighted with amazement.

Before Mejda reached the door, the humbled saint came running after him crying, "Stop! Stop!" He stood in front of Mejda. "Young sir," he uttered, "you have freed me today from a great delusion. I did not realize my ignorance until you spoke. Though you are much younger than I, I bow to you in gratitude, for you have given me enlightenment."

"Oh Sadhuji!" Mejda replied, "you truly have a great heart, for otherwise you could not have admitted your weakness in front of your disciples. No man can ever say, 'I am God.' The wave on the ocean cannot say, 'I am the ocean.' It can only say, 'The ocean has become the wave.' God is the ocean of light out of which have come the waves of human forms. Can a man contain the Infinite Ocean in the finite wave of his bodily form? With our human limitations, we cannot even comprehend — let alone encompass — His magnitude, which pervades every atom in the universe. It is only when we have attained realization of Truth that we may speak with divine authority."

Mejda later recounted that the sadhu indeed awoke from his egoistic delusions and became a truly great saint.

Swami Kebalananda, Mejda's Sanskrit Tutor

Mejda's roving nature, fed by his insatiable desire to find his guru, and to spend his time in holy places and in the company of saints, resulted in serious neglect of his studies. Father worried about this, and talked with Ananta. They decided to hire a tutor, one of spiritual inclination who, they hoped, would not only coach Mejda in academic subjects, but would also help to quench his spiritual thirst and perhaps thus divert the child from his quest for Himalayan saints. Father engaged Sri Ashutosh Chatterji, a devout and highly regarded Sanskrit scholar. He was respectfully known by the title of Shastri Mahasaya.* The private tutor proved

*The title *Shastri* denotes respect for one schooled in India's *shastras,* or scriptures; *Mahasaya,* a religious title, means "large-minded."

to be no ordinary teacher. Unknown to Father, he was an advanced disciple of Lahiri Mahasaya. Some time later, when Father came to know this, and that Lahiri Mahasaya often referred to him as a *rishi,* illumined sage, Father was embarrassed and asked the saint's pardon if in any way he had not shown him due respect.

Intuitively feeling their spiritual kinship, Shastri Mahasaya and Mejda were instantly and deeply attracted to one another. They "compared notes" on their meditative practices and experiences. Mejda told Shastriji of his meditations on *Aum* (the holy Word) as Sound and as Light. They discussed aspects of the *Vedas* and *Puranas,* ancient Indian scriptures. The revered tutor shared with Mejda his knowledge about the lives of India's great saints, and inspired him to learn all he could about their exalted examples. Secreted in Mejda's attic room, teacher and student devoted most study periods to *Kriya Yoga* meditation. He assisted Mejda in his practice of Lahiri Mahasaya's *Kriya Yoga* (including *Maha Mudra* and *Jyoti Mudra*), which Mejda had already learned from Father. The saintly Sanskrit tutor enhanced his student's understanding of *pranayama,* life energy control, and how the life and consciousness in deep yoga meditation are withdrawn from senses, nerves, and spine into the *sushumna,* or astral spine, with its spiritual centers of divine awakening.

Kriya Yoga works on the principle that breath and life are intimately related. *Kriya* masters the breath and transforms it into pure *prana,* the subtle energy that sustains life in the human body. Were this "life energy" to cease its activity, instant death would result. In the ordinary man the life current is restless, tied to the breath and to endless perceptions of the senses. Through *Kriya* practice, one learns control of the life force and mind by natural means, producing in time the spiritually exalted state of breathlessness. This process is called "yoga," and its end result is, as the very word implies, "union" of the soul with God. The restless consciousness becomes anchored in the vibrationless, nondual realm of Spirit.

The resulting mental poise yields perception of the purest joy—a joy that cannot be known by a mind made restless with material pleasures. A technique such as *Kriya Yoga* is needed to make of the body and mind a receptacle for the bliss of Cosmic Consciousness: oneness with God as ever-existing, ever-conscious, ever-new Bliss. The guru shows the way to attain this Bliss.

God's bliss awakens universal love; it removes the fear of death; it permeates one's life with peace and joy and vitality. Thus, through action of *Kriya* upon man's life currents, the devotee acquires health and well-being, and a mental poise and supreme happiness that free him from restlessness and sorrow—the seemingly inescapable state of the ordinary man.

Through the instruction and exalted company of Shastri Mahasaya, Mejda advanced remarkably in spiritual knowledge and realization. Some years later, the beloved Shastriji took *sannyas,* initiation into the Swami Order of renunciants, and became known as Swami Kebalananda.

A Story of Lahiri Mahasaya

A great yogi must at all times keep his powers "insulated," lest their potency cause an overreaction in this world of grosser energies. Shastri Mahasaya related to me the following incident in the life of Lahiri Mahasaya:

Swami Sri Yukteswar, Shastri Mahasaya, and Lahiri

Mejda at 16

4 Garpar Road, our family home in Calcutta. “X” marks window of Mejda’s attic room, where he spent long hours in meditation. Interior is shown at right. In later years I made a permanent shrine of this holy place.

Mahasaya's two sons, Tincouri and Ducouri, were eating lunch one day with the great master. The household cat was sitting on the right of Lahiri Mahasaya, about a meter away. It was obviously intent on getting some of the food from his plate. Unthinkingly, Lahiri Mahasaya gently waved his hand in the air and told the cat to keep away. Though Lahiri Mahasaya's hand was far from contact with the cat, the animal gave a jerk and fell over senseless on the floor.

Shocked at what had happened, Lahiri Mahasaya poured some milk onto his plate and mixed a little rice with it. He then went over and picked up the unconscious animal and stroked its fur gently. The cat regained consciousness immediately, and Lahiri Mahasaya fed it the food on his plate. When the cat had eaten its fill, it contentedly resumed its former place by Lahiri Mahasaya's side.

Another plate of food was brought for Lahiri Mahasaya, and with bowed head he continued his meal in silence; he felt, humbly, that he had committed an offense.

Mejda's Love for Music

Mejda had a natural ability to pick up a tune. If he heard a song once, he could reproduce it. He loved to sing. His voice was sweet and musical. So his friends often asked him to sing for them. With unrestrained fervor, Mejda would chant "Kali-Kirtan" and "Shyama-Sangeet" (songs of devotion to Divine Mother) or the *bhajans* of Tagore.

Sometimes Mejda's friends would chide him for his single-minded dedication to the love of God, even in his songs. "Life is so short," they would remark. "If from this early age we give all our time to loving God, when shall we be able to enjoy this world?"

Mejda would laugh when he heard them speak like this, but their ignorance deeply pained him. "Just as a man who has been in a dark room cannot see when at first he emerges into the bright daylight, so your eyes are blinded by your preoccupation with the perishable objects on this earth."

"Mukunda!" his friends would protest in unison, "don't give us another sermon!"

"All right, my brothers," Mejda would reply. "But remember, things that appear beautiful from a distance do not always look so beautiful when you come up close to them. No earthly object is lasting, nor does it have real value, for of itself it cannot produce happiness. Test your pleasures to see if they can give you lasting joy."

Mejda's friends urged him to seek out a good music teacher and take lessons, not only to develop his natural ability, but also to give them greater pleasure in listening to his songs. Mejda pondered their suggestion and realized he knew only a few devotional songs, and didn't know how to play any musical instruments. So he purchased an *esraj* (a stringed instrument), a harmonium (a hand-pumped reed instrument), and *tablas* (drums). He engaged the services of a competent teacher.

One of Mejda's favorite songs was "Mandire Mamo Ke" ("Who Is in My Temple?") by Rabindranath Tagore. Mejda later translated this song into English for his Western students. I was privileged to teach Mejda this song, which I had learned from a schoolmate, Kishen Chand Baral, the eldest son of the late famous musician Lal Chand Baral.

To sing Indian *bhajans* properly, one must be able to blend intuitive feeling with the modulations of the tune. Mejda was so adept at this that those who heard his devotional songs became enraptured.

When Mejda practiced, I often sat beside him, mentally humming the tune. He always kept his harmonium locked up for he thought I was too young to play it properly and might break it. But one day he forgot to put the lock on it. I tried to calculate the length of time he would be away, and decided I had enough time to play his harmonium. With eyes closed like a professional musician, I swayed back and forth as I played enthusiastically some of the songs Mejda was learning. I didn't hear Mejda come up behind me. He listened for a time, then gave a low cough to attract my attention. I jumped, like a thief caught in the act. "Where did you learn to play the harmonium?" he asked in a low, stern voice.

"I watched you when you practiced. And then I drew a sketch of the keys on a piece of paper and practiced the fingering that way."

The sincerity of my effort pleased him greatly, and so he said, "You have a beautiful voice. From tomorrow we shall practice together." The inspiration of singing with him, and the encouragement he gave, enabled me to become accomplished in singing devotional songs, which I have enjoyed doing throughout my life.

One day the brother of Mejda's music teacher came to our house and said, "Mukunda is attending a music function. He has been requested to sing some songs in praise of the Divine Mother, so he asked me to come for his *esraj*."

I believed the boy, and gave him the instrument. Foolishly, I didn't consult anyone else in the house.

When Mejda returned home he was astounded to hear of the incident, for not a word the boy said was true.

Mejda went directly to the music teacher's house, but the wayward brother was not at home. When Mejda received no sympathy or help from the teacher, the cordial relationship between teacher and pupil ended. Mejda returned home discouraged. His gloomy countenance focused on me for a moment, and then he went straight to his meditation room.

Ananta rebuked me, but the damage was done and I could not undo it. Even today I feel penitent for my foolish act, but I learned a good lesson that day.

About ten years later, I was on an errand for the family: I went to the Bose Pharmacy to purchase some medicine. At that time, it was the only allopathic pharmacy in our locality, situated at the crossing of Sukia Street and Cornwallis. While returning home, I heard a man playing an *esraj* on the terrace of a nearby house. Several boys had gathered around him. I joined the group. To my great surprise I saw the man was playing Mejda's *esraj*!

I ran home in a near panic of delight and conveyed the news to Ananta and Mejda. The three of us returned; but it wasn't until after some threatening discussion that the man finally admitted that the brother of Mejda's music teacher had pawned the *esraj* for ten rupees. Mejda ran home and got the money from Father and bought back his *esraj*. He was so happy to have it that he touched the instrument to his forehead, and then gave it a big kiss. He also gave two extra rupees to the man to buy sweetmeats for his friends — in those days, two rupees bought a lot of sweets!

Undaunted Determination and Courage

We spent one of our summer vacations at our ancestral home at Ichapur. Everything had changed; the village seemed new to us. Many of the boys liked Mejda. They were attracted by his calm, dignified behavior. But several others, resenting his popularity, felt he had intruded into their domain. Mejda didn't want to be drawn into another fight such as had happened at Chittagong; so one day he told the group of boys that followed him not to ignore their old friends altogether: "They might become angry and even think that I have asked you not to associate with them anymore."

Some of the boys replied: "Don't worry about them. They were never really our friends. They are bent on making mischief. Do you know why they don't like you? It's only because they are losing many of their gang, while our group is increasing. They aren't worth giving another thought to. Come, let's sit under a tree and you tell us more stories!" They loved the way that Mejda could narrate a story; and so they listened with great enthusiasm. Afterwards, the boys would ply him with all kinds of questions. Mejda, bubbling with mirth, always had a humorous answer. The boys laughed until the tears ran from their eyes.

Three weeks before our arrival, a fierce southwest storm had passed through Ichapur. Now, in the intense heat of the summer sun, ponds, ditches, and tanks had almost dried up, leaving the soil baked and cracked. All life seemed to wither in the blast of Nature's furnace.

We stayed in the house during the heat of the day, especially at midday, for the relentless heat would have roasted us. But it didn't deter Mejda. "I will test my mind to see if I can meditate outside—to see if God is more important to me than the interference of the scorching sun." So he went outside at noon to meditate. Everyone in the house warned him that he would collapse. But he simply smiled and said: "Though I have to go about with sorrow and suffering as my only conveyance, I will not forsake my determination."

Mejda seated himself in meditation posture in an open paddy field. The sun blazed overhead. The stifling hours of the afternoon finally faded helplessly into evening, their wrath spent before Mejda's undaunted will. Night followed on the heels of the fleeing sun. At last Mejda arose from his meditation to feel the cool touch of the evening breeze on his skin, and to see the soft, silvery light of the moon. In the silence he felt his meditation-expanded mind stretch across the starlit sky. Slowly he began to walk back toward the house.

From a distance he saw a pack of boys coming toward him. There must have been thirty or more in the group. As they neared, he recognized the dissidents who had expressed their ill will toward him. When they reached him, he saw their eyes glinting with the hunter instinct: they had found their prey. One of the boys said, "At last we have you! Where are your friends now? Can any of them help you?"

Another joined in: "Now that he's alone, see how defeated he looks. Perhaps he knew we wanted to settle the score today, so he fled to this field to hide like a coward."

Someone else taunted: "That was pretty intelligent, wasn't it?"

Mejda, unmoved, said firmly, "Why do you call me a coward? You are so many; I am only one."

The leader said scathingly, "So what! We could bury you here in this field and no one would ever find a trace of you." With this he tried to push Mejda backward.

Mejda stood like a rock; he didn't budge an inch. His eyes shone with the fire of his inner strength. Aroused now, he roared like a lion, "Which of you has the nerve to fight me? Come! Now! I am ready for you!" Not one of the boys ventured forward to accept the challenge.

The leader, having prudently backed off, said, "Hey! Are you angry? We aren't serious. We were just joking. Actually, we want to be your friends. Let us be friends from today."

Mejda instantly reciprocated the offer of friendship. "Then come to my house with me. We will feast on sweetmeats until we can hold no more."

Mejda never wavered before an injustice. His belief in principle, his divine inner strength, permeated his teachings, which have inspired a struggling mankind worldwide. He taught: "Even a man who practices *ahimsa,* nonviolence, has a right to 'hiss.' Stand up for what is right, all the while recognizing that love is the greatest power in creation."

Mejda's Compassion

Mejda was always looking for quiet, secluded places to meditate. One day he took me to the temple of the Nababidhan Brahma Samaj. There we met the late Jnananjan Neogi, who later became an intimate friend of the family. On other occasions we also visited the Parasnath Temple in Gauri Beria, and the Pagoda at Eden Gardens. Manomohanda joined us many times for meditation. After one of their meditations, Mejda and Manomohan decided to collect funds to help the poor. They planned to distribute the proceeds to the needy at the Kalighat Temple during the next auspicious festival, *Ardhodaya Yoga.*

On the day of the festival, I accompanied them to the Kalighat Temple to distribute the money. Our spirits uplifted by the selfless act, we were returning to the streetcar to ride home when we came across some pitiful lepers asking for a few paise. Though we had only the tram fare in our pockets, Mejda gave it all to them. We walked home, a distance of about ten kilometers. I was still a very young boy in that year of 1908, but I did not feel the least bit tired. I stoutly walked the entire distance, thinking of myself as a brave soldier marching for a noble cause.

One December night, about eight o'clock, I was talking with Father on the veranda in front of his room when we heard footsteps in the corridor below. Father said, "That must be Mukun." I turned and saw him ascending the stairs dressed only in his *dhoti* and shoes; his entire upper body was bare. He had on neither shirt nor coat to protect against the chill winter air.

Father asked him, "Where are your clothes? Why are you out in the night air bare-chested this way?"

Like a child, Mejda replied, "I saw an old man lying on the street. He was shivering, and had nothing on except a torn rag. I thought to myself, 'We have enough money to protect ourselves from the cold, but this poor man has nothing. He is helpless and has nowhere to go.' So I gave him my garments. And I have also had the chance to know how others feel who have not the means to keep themselves warm!"

Father wanted to scold Mejda, but he restrained himself to a practical suggestion: "All right. You could have given the man your shirt and coat only, you know. You didn't need to give him your *ganji** also. If you catch cold now, what then?"

Smiling, Mejda reassured Father, "Nothing will happen to me. All will be well, with your blessing."

Father realized that no matter what counsel he might give, Mejda would have a logical argument in reply, so he wisely said, "You did very well. But there is no sense in your standing here in the cold now. Go put on some warm clothing."

"Rama Ho!"—Taking the Lord's Name in Vain

Some villagers from out-of-state who were employed at the Calcutta Deaf and Dumb School, across the street from our house, took it upon themselves to celebrate the holidays between Shyama Puja and Holi Festival by chanting the name of Lord Rama every evening. Though they had no musical training, they did their best to surpass the professionals. In Bengali *kirtan*† style, the leader would sing a refrain, and then the others in the group would repeat it after him, accompanied by drums, cymbals, and tambourines. Their bodies swayed to and fro with the rhythm of their chanting. Singers attempted to outdo the instrumentalists and the latter applied all their strength to drown out the singers.

Their "*kirtan*" often lasted until midnight. Unmindful of the disturbance they were causing to the neighborhood, their enthusiasm became more zealous with every bottle of homemade liquor they consumed: their

* An undershirt.

† Group chanting of devotional songs.

"devotional" chanting metamorphosed into cacophonous ranting. Being simple in nature, they couldn't understand why anyone would object to the chanting of the Lord's name. They dismissed all complaints with the reply: "You mind your business; we are minding ours." No one in the school hostel complained: this was one time when it was a blessing to be deaf!

Holi festival was drawing near. Impelled by the festive mood, the "devotionally intoxicated" singers extended their outrageous chanting to all-night sessions. No one for blocks around could sleep. In desperation an elderly neighbor took Mejda with him to confront the singers. "Your singing the whole night to Lord Rama is causing all of us grievous trouble," he said. "You used to stop at midnight. Now, what urgent demand of the Lord Rama is causing you to go on for the whole night?"

One of the singers replied: "In this huge city people are dying every minute. Since they have not found salvation, their spirits haunt us at night. We save ourselves from them by chanting the Lord's name."

Another neighbor, passing at the moment, commented dryly, "You are right, my friend. Your singing does indeed wake the dead!" As the village songsters excused themselves and hastened away, Mejda exclaimed: "I have it! I have it!"

The neighbor who had just arrived asked, "What are you talking about? What is it that you have?"

"They are superstitious. They're afraid of ghosts. Please ask Anup (the passerby's son) to come to my house at once."

Mejda held a secret meeting with all the neighborhood boys. At the conclusion of the closed-door conference, sweets were passed and the boys dispersed happily, promising to gather at our house that night at nine-thirty.

By midnight the "Rama Ho!" chant was throbbing with clamorous cadence as drums, cymbals, and tambourines kept resounding pace with the vociferous singers. The neighborhood boys easily scaled the low wall of the school and stealthily approached the *kirtan*. All of us carried tin pans and enameled spoons; Mejda had a box of large firecrackers. When we were about five yards from the men, we began to beat our tin pans and made weird vocal noises of laughing, crying, groaning, howling, and meowing. Our outlandish cries startled the chanters; they abruptly ceased their singing. We, too, became absolutely quiet. Nothing stirred in the darkness except the pale lights of darting fireflies; no sound except the crickets. With a trembling voice one of the men called: "Who…who…who's there?"

Only the dark silence pressed in around the tense group. The men began whispering among themselves. Finally the leader said in a shaky voice, "One of you go see what that was." Paralyzed with fear, not a man could move.

Mejda was waiting for this moment. With perfect timing and aim he threw a huge firecracker into the small clearing around which the men were seated. Its explosion shattered the night in a brilliant flash. We beat our tin plates and wailed in our high-pitched voices. Instantly the men fled in all directions, each calling loudly upon Lord Rama to save him from certain doom.

News of Mejda's prank reached the singers the next day. They complained hotly to the school principal. "We were disturbing no one and we always ceased chanting by ten p.m.," the singers maintained. The principal sent for Mejda. When Mejda confronted the singers in the principal's office, he said only, "You have not told the truth!" He looked at them so sternly, they faltered.

"Well, sir, though we did not always stop at ten o'clock, we *never* went beyond midnight," said the leader defensively.

But by now the principal understood what had happened. He led the singers on by saying, "But why did you stop at midnight? Such devotional singing should have continued until dawn."

The leader responded: "Oh, yes, we felt the same way; often we did chant throughout the night. If more respected persons like yourself appreciated what we are doing, perhaps more and more devotees would join us."

"Listen very carefully, each one of you," the principal said firmly. "If ever again a complaint reaches me that you have disturbed this neighborhood with your singing, I will dismiss you immediately. Now go!"

The deflated "musicians" left the principal's office with an air of discouragement. How could their pious endeavor have come to such an untimely end?

Chapter 9

Mejda Explores the Realms of Mind and Spirit

SAMADHI AT DAKSHINESWAR

Mejda, Manomohan, Jitendra Nath Mazumdar, whom Mejda called Jitenda, and I often visited the sacred Kali Temple in Dakshineswar to spend the day in meditation. We usually went by horse-drawn carriage. On one occasion we traveled by boat up the Ganges from Ahiritolla Ghat, but that day we returned home very late because the boat could not be rowed against the current, so we had to wait for the ebb tide. Father scolded Mejda severely for keeping me out so late.

Whenever we went to Dakshineswar, we first received the *darshan** of the beautiful statue of Mother Kali. Then we meditated in the portico in front of the temple. Next we would meditate in the room of Sri Ramakrishna Paramahansa, and then Mejda would spend several hours meditating outside under the sheltering branches of the large banyan tree in the *Panchavati,*† where Sri Ramakrishna received illumination. Sometimes Mejda would also sit under the *bel* tree to the east of the temple, another of Ramakrishna's favorite meditation spots. Immersed in the thought of God, sitting beside the silently flowing Ganges on these

* The blessing received from the sight of a holy image, place, or person.

† A grouping of five trees held sacred: *amalaki, ashvattha, bel, ashoka,* and *vata* (banyan).

sanctified grounds—it is difficult to describe the peace and joy of our pilgrimages. At sunset, *arati* was performed in the temple before the image of Kali. After joining in the ceremony, we would take *prasad* and return home.

One evening we went to call Mejda from his meditation under the *Panchavati* tree, as it was time for *arati.* The quiet eventide had wrapped Mejda's meditation nook in deep shadows. As we approached, we saw a halo of soft light encircling Mejda's body. A snake had coiled itself around his neck! another lay in his lap. The scene immobilized us for a moment; then I called out, "Mejda! Mejda!" When at first he didn't respond, Manomohan and Jitenda also called him.

In a few moments Mejda stirred slightly. Then he gently clapped his hands and the snakes slipped away quietly into the dense underbrush surrounding the tree. When we mentioned the incident to Mejda later, he spoke lightly about it, saying it was nothing.

Today the dense undergrowth around the *Panchavati* is no longer there. The area has been cleared and protectively fenced to prevent zealous devotees from stripping the sacred banyan of its leaves and branches.

Saints Pseudo and True

Whenever Mejda heard that a saint was in the area, he sought him out. Often he took me and others with him. One day he heard that a sadhu had come to Kalighat and was camping under a tree near the Adi-Ganga, the old course of the Ganges River. The sage was 105 years old, the informant had told Mejda, and he had healed many people. Manomohan, Jitenda, and I set out with Mejda.

When we reached Kalighat, we found that a large crowd had gathered around the hoary-headed savant. Somehow we managed to work our way up to a place immediately in front of his campfire. His hair, in the tradition of some sadhus, was matted and hung in long strands. He had a strikingly attractive face. Mejda sat down near the saint, and we sat behind Mejda. After a brief conversation with the august personage, Mejda arose to leave, and motioned us to follow. We had not been able to hear the conversation, and wondered what had happened. Mejda was silent as we threaded our way back through the crowd, and he made no comment about the saint as we rode the tram home.

It wasn't till we reached the house that he finally said, "I have just seen a beautiful whitewashed tomb!"

"What do you mean?" His statement seemed strangely inappropriate.

"A grave looks so nice from the outside: It is either whitewashed or covered with marble, and decorated with flowers. But what does it contain? Nothing but rotting flesh and bones. The sadhu, too, looked lovely from the outside, but from our conversation I found him spiritually dead and decayed inside."

I am grateful that by keeping Mejda's company I did meet several real saints. Not far from our house, on Circular Road, lived the venerable Sri Nagendranath Bhaduri, "the levitating saint" about whom Mejda has written in *Autobiography of a Yogi.* Mejda often visited Sri Bhaduri. He occupied a three-story house, and was cared for by several of his disciples.

One evening Mejda took me with him to visit the sage. The house was dark and quiet: it looked as though no one was home. Sri Bhaduri had invited Mejda to come any time, so we entered and went upstairs to Bhaduri Mahasaya's room. Quietly we opened the door. A faint glow from the gas light on the street came in through the shutters and barely illuminated the room. At first I saw and heard nothing. But as my eyes became accustomed to the darkness, I was astonished to see the saint sitting high up in the air above his bed. I thought there must be some raised pedestal or platform supporting him, but I could see none. A cough I tried vainly to suppress startled Bhaduri Mahasaya. His weightless body oscillated slightly and slowly settled on the bed.

Then Bhaduri Mahasaya spoke, his voice quietly resonant: "Welcome, Mukunda. How long have you been here? Light the lamp."

We talked with Nagendranath Bhaduri for some time. Then he gave us sweets, for he never allowed any visitor to leave without extending this hospitality.

Never in my life will I forget what I had the rare good fortune to witness that day.

Mejda Discovers the Powers of the Mind

The power of mind over matter is unlimited. Early in Mejda's *sadhana,* in the course of his meditations, he discovered miraculous powers of the mind and explored their uses. He found he could transcend time and space to gather knowledge of specific events and places. He could also accurately prophesy a person's future. One method of doing this is through a "medium," so he required the services of a second party—me!—to aid in some of the demonstrations of his mental force.

I well remember the first time he asked my help. Our youngest uncle had lived for some time in our house and had been afflicted with a chronic illness. One day Mejda called me to his prayer room and asked me to sit in a cross-legged posture facing him. Slowly he passed his hand over my head and body. I felt a soothing, relaxing sensation spread through every cell. We talked for a few minutes about trivial matters, then Mejda asked me about our uncle's health. "Uncle's condition is most serious," I replied. Then I made a remark out of context: "Someone will call you in a moment."

Almost immediately a knock on the door interrupted us. Mejda was told that someone was at the front door downstairs and wanted to see him.

Not long after this session, a Bengali boy, Sunil, whom Mejda had met in Banaras, came to stay with us for a few days. He had no relatives in Calcutta, he told us. The "few days" extended into weeks, but Sunil showed no inclination to leave. Mejda was worried, for he had learned in Banaras that Sunil was of dubious character, and now he had often observed Sunil avariciously eyeing the high-necked silken coat Father had given him. Still, Mejda could not bring himself to ask Sunil to leave.

The coat meant a great deal to Mejda because it had been given to Father by our mother. Father had always dressed only in the most ordinary clothing, even when visiting our relatives. Mother received so many complaints that he didn't dress in a manner fitting his station in life that she purchased the coat, even against Father's wishes. Father wore the coat only twice or thrice. After Mother's passing, and when Mejda had reached a size proportionate to the coat, Father gave the lovely garment to Mejda.

Mejda shared his concern about Sunil with Jitenda,

who agreed to help him keep an eye on the delinquent house guest.

One night we returned late from visiting some of our relatives. Instead of taking the coat to its usual storage place upstairs, Mejda left it in a downstairs room. The next day, Father asked Mejda to take me to a shoe store on College Street to purchase some sandals for me. It was evening when Mejda, Jitenda, Sunil, and I left on the errand. As Mejda's coat was conveniently at hand, Sunil took it from its hanger and put it on. Mejda made a half-hearted objection, but then decided it sounded selfish; so he let the matter go.

On the way to College Street, Mejda stopped briefly to see our third sister, Nalini, who was by then married. Before entering her house, he called Jitenda aside and asked him to keep a close watch on Sunil. In a few minutes Mejda was back, and we continued our walk to College Street. As we arrived at the crossing of Cornwallis Street and Keshab Sen Street, Sunil suddenly jumped aboard a rolling tram. Jitenda was alert and grabbed the door of the second car and swung aboard. Sunil knew that Jitenda would catch him so he jumped off at the next busy intersection and vanished in the evening crowds.

We searched the area for a long time, but without result. Utterly dejected, we purchased the sandals and returned home. Mejda changed his clothes, and then took me to his prayer room and had me sit in front of him. As he used again the same technique he had employed to find out about Uncle's illness, I soon felt a soothing relaxation come over me. Mejda queried me as to Sunil's whereabouts. I described the house he had gone to and gave Mejda the address. But because it was then so late in the evening, we decided to wait until the next morning before going there.

Shortly after sunup, Mejda, Jitenda, and I went to the address Mejda had written down. The door was answered by a kindly-looking gentleman. Mejda asked him if he knew Sunil, and gave him a description of his appearance. The gentleman, a distant relative of the boy, said that Sunil had spent the night there, but had gone before sunrise. He asked why we were looking for him. Mejda then told him about meeting Sunil in Banaras, his doubts about his behavior, and the stealing of the coat.

The gentleman said, "You should have come last night. We would have caught him red-handed. I know this boy is a thief: this morning he stole money from my wife before he left. I will write to his relatives in Banaras to make certain your coat is returned."

"He'll probably sell it," Jitenda interrupted gloomily.

The gentleman then invited us inside and offered to reimburse Mejda for the coat. "I sheltered that thief in my home, so I feel I bear some of the responsibility for your stolen coat."

"Oh no," Mejda objected. "Why should you pay for the wrong actions of someone else?"

Mejda told the whole story to Father, who was glad we had acted as we did. We never heard anything further about the coat, and dropped the matter entirely.

Mejda was then experimenting with spiritualism; he used me as a medium to contact departed souls. On one occasion a soul took possession of my passive mind and body, and was unwilling to give up its newly acquired residence. He said that he had been murdered near

Talla Bridge and desperately wanted another physical form. He was determined to keep mine!

Mejda tried without success to drive the unwelcome spirit out of my body. Finally, he took the holy photograph of Lahiri Mahasaya, given to our parents by the great master, and threatened the tramp soul: "Leave now. Go away at once or I will touch you with this sacred relic." Mejda repeated this two or three times. The unholy spirit left reluctantly.

Mejda was also able to talk with our mother in the astral world using me as a medium. When our relatives heard of Mejda's uncanny powers, they came as a group to see a demonstration. Mejda began by telling them, through me, what they were thinking. When it was the turn of Ranga-Boudi, the wife of cousin Lalit Mohan Mitra, the other relations remarked: "If you can read *her* mind, then we will believe in your power."

Mejda hesitated, saying, "Why are you trying to embarrass her?"

"We won't believe you until you tell us what she is thinking. Even God has difficulty knowing what is in her mind!"

Addressing Ranga-Boudi, Mejda said apologetically, "Please excuse me for reading your thoughts. Not only do our relatives doubt me, they doubt my God as well."

He gazed at her piercingly. She returned a frowning look. Mejda seemed a little disturbed, but said to me in a moment, "What is it that Ranga-Boudi craves at this moment?"

"A glass of ice-cold water," I replied.

The other relatives laughed merrily. Ranga-Boudi

flushed and denied it. "How silly! This is nonsense," she said.

But Mejda insisted, "Tell me if I'm right or not." Finally Ranga-Boudi assented by nodding her head ever so slightly.

One day Mejda and I went to the house of our friend Upendranath Mitra, who lived on Garpar Road not far from us. With his family, we went into their drawing room. Mejda asked Upen to select a book at random from the bookshelf behind me. Upen took down a book and held it behind my back so that I couldn't see it. I spoke aloud the name of the book, its author and publisher, the printer, and the price. Mejda then asked Upen to open to any page. I gave the page number and repeated the entire contents of the page verbatim. Understandably, Upendranath's family was astounded.

A week later, some of the officials of the Calcutta Deaf and Dumb School asked Mejda to demonstrate his mental power for them. Because they had been such good friends to us, Mejda couldn't refuse. Standing me in front of them, Mejda handed me a clod of soil and asked me to eat it. "Isn't it sweet? Is not its taste most relishable?" he said.

I began to devour the clod with the greatest pleasure and said, "It is delicious!"

Then Mejda countermanded forcefully: "How dirty and distasteful it is."

Immediately I vomited everything I had just eaten.

Not long afterwards, Mejda and I had just come out of our house when a stone lodged inside my shoe. I leaned against the neighbor's house with my hand so as to balance on one leg and remove the stone with the other hand. Mejda said, "Oh my, your hand is stuck to the wall."

How right he was! Try as I might, I could not pull my hand away from the wall. The more I struggled, the more firmly my hand adhered to the neighbor's house!

Mejda said, "Just a moment. I'll be right back." He went inside our house, but returned shortly. "Okay," he said, "let's go." My hand was instantly free, and we continued on our errand.

When Father learned that Mejda was using me as a medium to demonstrate his mental powers, he told him, "You must never use Gora for such things. Eventually both his body and mind will weaken." From that day Mejda never again asked me to become his mental instrument.

One Sunday, Panchudi,* who used to help look after us motherless children, came to Mejda. "Mukun, someone has taken twenty-five rupees from my cash box. I suspect Kanu Thakur did it, for no one else goes into that room where it is kept."

Mejda questioned Kanu closely, but he denied any knowledge of the theft. Mejda then asked him to sit on the floor of the drawing room. He passed his hands lightly over Kanu's face and body. Kanu lay back on the floor with his eyes closed, completely relaxed in a hypnotic state. Panchudi, Ranga Mama (our maternal uncle), Binu (the youngest son of our second sister) and I stood in a group around Kanu. Mejda asked him:

"Did you take the money?"

* Panchudi was the daughter of Father's maternal uncle. When she was widowed at a young age, she was taken into our household. She had a very spiritual nature; and though she was quite a bit older than Mejda, she became his disciple.

"Yes, I took it."

"Where did you hide it?"

"Under a brick below the northern staircase."

After the money had been recovered, Mejda attempted to bring Kanu back to consciousness, but without success. Mejda had always been able to arouse me in a moment, but for some reason he could not awaken Kanu. We even tried sprinkling water on his face, but to no avail.

In the meantime Binu had gone to get Father. When Father came into the drawing room he said, "Mukun, what have you done? Have I not forbidden you to do such things?"

Father then sat down beside the still form of Kanu. He pressed his finger between Kanu's eyebrows and performed a *pranayama* technique. Then he passed his hands lightly over Kanu's head and body. Kanu's eyes fluttered, then opened fully. He sat up and gazed at us wonderingly.

Heeding Father's stern request, Mejda gave up his practice of hypnotism.

The Nonchalant "Naga Sadhu"

Every morning Mejda awakened before dawn, washed, and then sat for meditation. After meditating, he would sometimes walk to the Ganges to bathe, singing songs of devotion as he wended his way through the quiet streets in the early morning light. Sometimes I would beg to accompany him, and he would allow me to come along.

I remember one such occasion; Mejda was in class ten at the time. When we set out for the Ganges, the morning star was still shining brightly in the western sky. Golden-colored clouds above the eastern horizon softly heralded the coming of the sun. God's beauty gently called to sleeping earth to awaken from its rest of the night.

Calcutta was not quite so congested in those days. There were large open areas, covered with dense foliage of green trees and shrubs. These surrendered their deep shadows to the dawning light in the east. Among the branches, gaily colored birds called musically to sleepy households to arise for prayer, rejoice in God's beauty, and share His love with all in this new day. Then, unfolding their wings, they flew into the measureless blue of the sky, with a trill of assurance in their sweet songs that they would return again in the evening.

Mejda loved birds, and spoke often of how they serve us: Their songs remind us of the joy of God. They awaken us in the early morning that we might enjoy the beauty of God's creation from the first moment of the dawn. When they fly into the sky, they tell us that this world is transitory; we must free ourselves from earthly bondage to fly on wings of freedom in omnipresence. We have spent our days in earthly delusion, oblivious of God, the only Reality, who has hidden Himself in the many guises of nature. Realize His immanence and sing His glory! Time is passing so quickly. Begin your journey now; and take others with you as you fly to the Divine Abode!

Thus enthralled, Mejda reached the banks of the Ganges. Taking the name of the Divine Mother, he immersed himself in the river. And then he stood in the quietly flowing waters, transfixed in his songs and prayers to God. As I watched him—only his head above the wavelets — he seemed the embodiment of Spirit come to dwell for a time amongst deluded humanity.

The bright hours of the morning flew by. Still immersed in the river, his songs of love for God were mixed with fervent prayers for the salvation of humankind.

The sun had passed its zenith when he came out of the water. Intoxicated with the joy of God-communion, he was oblivious to his surroundings as he started up the lane from the river bank. On this day he was totally unmindful of dress—or the lack of it! I didn't have the courage to disturb him. But passers-by seemed to take no notice: they were enraptured by the singing of this young "*naga sadhu.*"*

He hadn't gone far, however, when he was accosted by one of our aunts. Seeing Mejda naked she frowned, "How shameful, Mukunda! I didn't know that in the name of God you indulged in such indecency. Can't you see that many mothers and sisters are walking along this road? Have you lost your senses?"

Mejda didn't recognize who was speaking. In a faraway voice he asked, "What do you mean?"

Infuriated, our aunt cuffed him sharply on the ear. "You don't understand what I am saying? Look at yourself! Where are your clothes? What an evil boy you are to walk on the street like this. You are a disgrace to your family!"

Mejda was jolted from his joyous state of God-consciousness. With a shudder he returned to the world of duality, which is very much bound by the proscrip-

* A sect of ascetics who wear no clothing in honor of the Lord who owns nothing — and everything. Certain Shiva sects who wear no clothing are called *digambara,* sky-clad, as is the Lord Himself.

tions of society. He realized then that he had left his clothing on the bank of the river. But with a calm, beatific smile he said to our aunt, "The 'evil' is in *your* mind."

Auntie was enraged by Mejda's nonchalance. It is a wonder he wasn't burned alive by her fierce gaze.

But Mejda was not affected in the slightest by the castigation nor by the sudden realization of the bare facts of his condition; he calmly turned back toward the river to fetch his clothing.

A Vision of Lord Krishna

One day Mejda was talking to a classmate. He was always trying to rouse in others the enthusiasm he himself felt for God. His friend was obviously interested, but skeptical. Mejda was assuring him that God would come to anyone who was sincere and persistent enough. The friend wanted to share Mejda's faith, and so met him halfway: "Well, perhaps in the distant future—or in the next incarnation—I might be able to realize the truth of what you say."

"Why speak of the future? Why not find Him now," Mejda insisted. "If a devotee prays wholeheartedly, 'Lord, You *must* come to me,' He *will* appear. When the devotee's prayer spreads the sincere longing of his heart into the very atoms of the universe, where then can God hide? He will have to reveal Himself."

Mejda's faith was contagious. He saw its sparks igniting a flame in his friend's mind also, so he continued, "If this very night we were to try sincerely to see God as Lord Krishna, He would appear in that form."

To Mejda's classmate, the prospect of seeing Krishna that very night seemed suddenly not only possible, but excitingly probable. The two agreed to meet that evening at Mejda's house. They would meditate until Krishna came to them.

The shadows of the approaching night covered the earth when the two determined friends entered Mejda's meditation room. They bolted the door from inside, sat cross-legged on *kusha*-grass *asanas* (meditation mats), and with divine enthusiasm began to sing and pray and meditate.

To the devout Hindu, Bhagavan Krishna represents the loftiest incarnation of God, to whom His worshippers have given 108 names. As a great king of ancient India, Krishna is the supreme example of wisdom, justice, and love that should characterize a leader of men. When his disciple Arjuna was loath to fight for righteousness in the battle of Kurukshetra, Krishna exhorted him, symbol of all mankind, to fulfill his divinely ordained duty, and satisfy his spiritual destiny. The Bhagavad Gita contains the sublime teachings that Krishna gave to Arjuna during the battle of Kurukshetra. Materially and spiritually it is a scripture of unsurpassed beauty and wisdom.

Down through the ages, Krishna has become "all things to all men," and has been approached confidently by his devotees as the greatest Divine Friend and Lover of Creation; as the Protector of the Innocent; as the Destroyer of Evil; as the Lord of Creation, Preservation, and Destruction. To many, he is the Divine Cowherd, the youthful Gopal, whose flute of celestial love calls errant souls back to Spirit. He has responded in every form to his worshipping devotees.

A transcendent peace enveloped the meditating boys. Mejda's face radiated a perceptible glow as he chanted songs and prayers to Lord Krishna. In moments of quietness, the ardent devotees practiced *pranayama* meditation. Their bodies and minds became stilled as they patiently and persistently offered inner prayers to Bhagavan. The darkened room became divinely illumined with their fervor; joy pervaded their expectancy. As the rest of the city slept, the young boys maintained their wakefulness of devotional longing. Throughout the night, two yearning hearts melted as one in songs and inner prayers of love to the Lord. But toward morning, weariness and doubt began to creep over Mejda's companion.

"Mukunda, perhaps we were mistaken. God doesn't come so easily."

"We mustn't give up. Concentrate more deeply. He *will* answer the call of our souls."

After another period of renewed effort, Mejda's friend sighed dejectedly, "There is no hope, Mukunda. It's almost dawn. Let's go and get some sleep."

"You go if you want to; I won't give up," Mejda said firmly. "Even if I die sitting here, I won't move until God comes."

Suddenly Mejda sucked in his breath. His body became rigid in the ecstasy of the vision. His face glowed with a smile of enchanting sweetness. He cried out: "I see him! I see Krishna!"

Mejda's friend was lacking in spiritual sight as well as determination: "Where is he, Mukunda? I can't see him." Mejda reached out his hand and placed it over the heart of his doubting friend. Mejda's magnetic touch transferred the beatific vision.

"Oh! I see Krishna. I see him, Mukunda!"

Tears flowed from their eyes. Humbly, both boys bowed to Bhagavan.

"Beloved Krishna," Mejda prayed, "suffering humanity no longer hears the sweet melody of your flute, played on the banks of the Yamuna River. Your enchanting melody of divine love enraptured all: the birds, the beasts, and mankind. Please play your celestial music in the hearts of humankind once again, that they may see the light of your salvation. Bless my *sadhana*! Accept my devotion! I bow to thee!"

Bhagavan Krishna smiled, and raised his hands in blessing, then melted into the rays of the dawning sun.

The Transference of Spiritual Vision

Nothing is impossible to one who unites his will power with the unlimited will of God. Mejda had full faith in this. He could easily demonstrate the power of the mind, and had the ability to transfer his own spiritual perceptions to others by mere touch or suggestion.

One day Mejda, Manomohan, Atulya (a distant relative), and I spent the afternoon and evening in a park near Fort William. We were sitting quietly as the stars began to appear like specks of light piercing the evening sky. Suddenly, pointing to a star, Mejda exclaimed: "Look, Lord Krishna with his diadem!"

We started in wonder, the tranquility of our silence broken. Manomohan looked intently but couldn't see the beauteous form. Atulya cried, "There he is! Can't you see him?" Manomohan looked again, but in vain. He was very discouraged. He had for a long time been a constant companion to Mejda, and had shared his spiritual aspirations; and yet it was not he but Atulya, who seldom prayed and never meditated, who had been blessed with the vision. I too felt sad that I couldn't see Lord Krishna.

Manomohan turned to Mejda and said, "My brother, I am not fit to be your spiritual companion nor to receive your guidance. It is better that you give your time to Atulya. Your efforts with me are wasted."

Not long afterward, Mejda, Manomohan, and I were together on the grounds of the Calcutta Deaf and Dumb School. Mejda had asked me to bring along a betel leaf rubbed with oil. He handed the leaf to Manomohan and said, "Look intently at this betel leaf. Throw everything else out of your mind and think deeply of someone who is in the other world. You will see his face on this leaf."

Manomohan concentrated on the oily surface for some time, then exclaimed, "I see a beautiful bluish figure—Krishna?"

Mejda said, "Ask him what your spiritual advancement is."

I do not know the answer Manomohan received, nor what he told Mejda; but the experience seemed to fully satisfy the previously disappointed Manomohan.

Not long after this incident we three went together to the solitary graveyard at Narikeldanga. We had just entered when Mejda said, "Let us all bow down, for perhaps some virtuous soul is here." We immediately prostrated ourselves, following Mejda's example. We neither questioned nor wondered. Nor can I say whether or not I felt any fear. But I do know that in Mejda's company I was becoming more and more interested in those matters beyond the ordinary. From him I learned to believe in the metaphysical world; and what is more important, to understand that the greatest awakening in man is the realization of his own potential. Any achievement is possible when one properly unites will, intelligence, conscience, and right action.

The Manifestation of Mother's Astral Form

I followed Mejda like a shadow. He loved me, and wherever he went he often allowed me to accompany him. One day we visited a schoolhouse at 50 Amherst Street, site of our mother's passing. As I looked with apprehension upon the place that had been the scene of this tragedy, I said to Mejda, "Our mother died in this house."

"A great sage lives here now," Mejda consoled me. "His name is Sri Mahendra Gupta. He is headmaster of this school and author of *The Gospel of Sri Ramakrishna.* Unknown to many, he is an exalted devotee of Divine Mother." Mejda had been here before and wanted me to meet the saint.

We had arrived in the evening. Master Mahasaya, as we later came to address him, was meditating in his prayer room. When we bowed before him, he embraced us affectionately. His sweet love made us feel we had known him always. He kindly asked us to sit down. He enquired who I was, and what classes I was attending. I felt much blessed to be in his holy presence.

A large photograph of Mother Kali, garlanded with China rose flowers, graced the altar of his meditation room. When we arrived during his meditations on subsequent visits, we would remain quietly behind him or at his side in the room, absorbed in the aura of devotion that saturated the atmosphere.

One day I asked him if he thought this house was haunted. We told him of Mother's premonition when she first entered the house, and how on the eve of our brother's wedding our mother and cousin had died here of cholera. We had learned later that in this same house a similar incident had happened. The dwelling had been engaged for a marriage celebration; the day following the marriage, the groom and his father died of cholera. And in another startling instance, the groom died on his wedding day, under the canopy where the rites were to be performed. After these tragedies, no one would rent the house; it was believed to be haunted.

Master Mahasaya told us, "Since the house was vacant, I took it for my school. I am a devotee of the Divine Mother; what evil can befall me? I have no fear of inimical ghosts. It is true that the grieving spirit of a man who had committed suicide haunted this house; thus the tragedies that were destined to happen anyway were attracted to this place for fulfillment. The spirit tried to frighten me as well. But as I am a blessed son of the Mother, he could do me no harm. Instead, he entreated me for deliverance from his plight. I prayed to the Mother for release of his earthbound spirit, and performed many oblations for him. He was freed, and since then the house has had only peaceful vibrations."

One day as we sat quietly behind Master Mahasaya during his meditation, the eyes of the picture of Mother Kali in front of him moved. Seeing this miracle, Mejda and I silently looked at each other in utter amazement. Simultaneously, though his back was turned to us, Master Mahasaya said, "What are you seeing?" He knew that we had been blessed to behold the living eyes of the Mother.

On another occasion we asked him if he would call our mother from the astral world to appear before us.

Mejda as a high-school youth; from a painting by the author

Shastri Mahasaya (Swami Kebalananda)
Mejda's Sanskrit tutor

At first he refused; but we were persistent. Finally he acquiesced. "Come on a Tuesday evening. But you must promise to sit very still and not detain her for long." We readily agreed.

The appointed evening found Master Mahasaya deep in meditation. We sat behind him without moving. For almost two hours the great saint meditated. Then, without turning around, he softly said, "Look behind you and see who is standing in the doorway." We turned and saw our beloved mother smiling at us, her hands resting on either side of the doorway.

We cried out, "Mother! Mother!" We wanted to rush up to her, but Master Mahasaya told us not to move.

"You may speak to her if you wish," he said.

"Mother, do you remember us?" we asked.

She replied sweetly and clearly: "I keep constant watch over all of you. The Divine Mother is protecting you." Saying this, she vanished.

We kept this marvelous event secret from everyone except Father. He mildly rebuked us, "It is troublesome to a soul to make such demands upon it." From that time, I often saw our mother in dreams, but never again did I behold the vision of her form as we did that day in the house on 50 Amherst Street.

Symbology of Kali—the Divine Mother

From his childhood, Mejda had worshipped God as the Divine Mother; in his youth he worshipped Her in the form of Goddess Kali. Though Christians usually call God "Father," Hindus have developed also the concept of "Divine Mother."* In our human life we usually

* God's greatest manifestations to His children, said Paramahansa Yogananda, are as Father, Mother, Friend, Beloved. *(Publisher's Note)*

feel a special closeness to the mother, for she is quick to forgive, and loves us unconditionally. She responds instantly to her child's needs regardless of whether or not the child is "deserving."

I will explain here the symbology of Goddess Kali. In this I gratefully acknowledge the help of a respected acquaintance, Sri Mahanam Brata Brahmachari.

Kali represents the *shakti,* the creative power or energy, of Unmanifested Spirit. She is the symbol of all that has existed, that exists now, and that will exist in the future. Creation, preservation, and destruction are Her manifest powers. The destructive quality is not negative. Just as the seed "dies" to produce the plant, and the youth "dies" to mature into an adult, the annihilative quality of God's creative power renews indestructible Spirit's outward manifestations for continued expression and evolution. In this renewal is to be seen the wisdom, beauty, and compassion of Spirit's creative power. Above all things, Spirit is good and merciful. We must always remember that the Creative Power destroys old and useless forms only to create anew and preserve the form of the universe. Thus in the dual-sided aspect of Kali we have an accurate representation of Nature. Her cosmic form is revealed in meditation.*

Kali has four arms. Her two right arms represent Her power to create universes and to bestow blessings and salvation on Her devotees. Her two left arms hold a scimitar and a severed head, respectively. These represent Her power to preserve the cosmos and to cause its

* In *Whispers from Eternity,* in the selection, "I beheld Thee in Thy dances of creation, preservation, and destruction," Paramahansa Yogananda describes his vision of the Divine Mother Kali in Her dance of cosmic creation. *(Publisher's Note)*

dissolution in Spirit when Her dance of creation is ended. In this imagery we have a beautiful synthesis of the opposing forces of Nature. No other symbol better represents both the unconditional love of God and the inexorable laws of creation.

Kali is garlanded by a wreath of fifty human heads; the heads represent generally the power of knowledge, and specifically, the fifty sounds that comprise the Sanskrit language. India's rishis rooted the ancient language in the primal sound of creation, *Aum,* the cosmic "Word" or creative vibration. From this science of sound vibrations, they perfected *mantras* (correctly intoned Sanskrit words) to bring about desired, lawful changes in creation. Thus, the wreath of human heads represents the knowledge and power inherent in creation.

The flowing hair of the Goddess resembles a curtain, the "screen of *maya*" (illusion, duality) behind which is hidden the unifying Intelligence, the essence of Spirit.

Black is the color of Kali. Creation originated in the realm of "lightless light and darkless dark." As Kali represents the primordial creative force, Her natural color is black. In the beginning, creation had no form. Black represents formlessness. Black is also the absence of color, therefore the absence of variety. The various-hued facets of truth, all knowledge, all religions, are thereby totally absorbed and unified in the all-knowing, all-pervading Mother who is black.

Her unclothed form suggests infinity.

Her waist is girdled by human hands, symbolizing man's endless rounds of desire-produced reincarnation that result from actions performed under the influence of delusion. Man's desires for sensory fulfillment pursue him even beyond the portals of death to bring him back again and again into material existence. Thus the Infinite Mother is circumscribed by mankind's ignorant delusive activity.

Kali has three eyes, representing the sun, moon and fire, each a source of darkness-destroying light Omnipresent in creation, the Mother beholds through her three eyes the past, present, and future; and in the ignorance-destroying light of those eyes, She reflects for man to see, beauty, truth, and bliss.

The Mother's breast feeds creation with the swee milk of sustaining cosmic energy; and to Her God seeking children, She gives a taste of Her blissful Presence.

With flashing white teeth the Goddess bites her red tongue. Red is the color of *rajas,* the activating quality of Nature; white represents *sattva,* Her discriminating purifying, and elevating quality. The activating impulse is to be controlled by discriminative wisdom.

In Her whirling dance of creation, one foot of the Cosmic Mother strikes the breast of sleeping Shiva (Spirit) who is lying at Her feet. During creation, relatively speaking, Spirit makes Itself subservient to the laws of Nature; Kali reigns supreme. But the moment Nature touches Spirit, She is subdued.*

The Mother is often worshipped in cremation grounds. She resides there to receive those who come to take rest in Her. Death is looked upon as Her transfigur

* Paramahansa Yogananda writes in *Whispers From Eternity:* "Shiva or the Infinite is transcendent (inactive in the phenomenal worlds). He has relegated to His 'consort' Kali all powers of creation, preservation, and destruction. In ancient Hindu texts, the universe is said to vanish when 'Kali's flying feet touch the breast of Shiva.' That is, when the finite meets the Infinite, the world of appearances dissolves in Reality." *(Publisher's Note)*

ing touch that removes pain, sorrow, anxiety, and gives freedom and peace.

Although Kali's form is terrible to look upon—because Her power will not compromise with evil—Her smile reveals a heart that is the essence of mercy. As Spirit's creative energy, She is Mother of the universe, of all human beings. Her strength is unsurpassable. And yet Her love, soft as a flower, bestows benevolent motherliness on all.

Worshipping the Supreme Being as Mother, the Hindu thinks of Her not only in cosmic form but in universal human motherhood. When we see Her in all mothers as the one Mother of all, every human being becomes our brother. The devotee sacrifices petty selfishness at Her feet and lives the ideal of brotherhood. When passion for self-gratification is transformed into divine love through love for the Mother, unity among human beings is the result. And this is our greatest need today.

Mejda's Last Kali Puja

As his meditations deepened, Mejda soon spiritually outgrew reverence for images of Divine Mother as a part of worship. He sought the Supreme Being beyond form and ritual. I remember helping him at our Garpar home when he made his last statue for the annual celebration of Kali Puja. As our mother had done, he used straw and wood to form the basic framework. This he carefully covered with clay, molding it into a figure of the divine Kali. When cracks appeared in the drying clay a few days later, he covered the statue with a wet cloth to moisten the clay and fill the cracks. Hair for the statue was prepared from jute. Obtaining the fiber was a matter of some doing: Jute bales were hauled along Upper Circular Road by bullock cart. Mejda had me stand at the entrance to Sukia Street while he himself went to the crossing of Manicktala. When the bullock-cart drivers were distracted by traffic, we could catch a few of the tufts of jute that dangled from the bales in the back of their carts. We then dyed the jute black. It looked just like hair.

By helping Mejda I thus learned the art of clay modeling. For about five years after Mejda had stopped performing *puja,* Nalini and I continued to make statues of Kali, and worshipped the Divine Mother in that form.

Nalini was by this time married to a renowned doctor, Sri Panchanon Bose. She and Mejda loved each other affectionately. She clandestinely helped Mejda finance many of the religious functions he organized at our house. I didn't know how she got the money to him until one day he sent me to her house with a note: "Please, may I borrow your beautiful harmonium." Curious to see the instrument, I opened the box and discovered the money from Sejdi inside.

Mejda used this means often, and Nalini was more than happy to help with all his spiritual projects. Her husband's practice brought sufficient income. Besides this, Dr. Bose was a charitable person. He often refused fees from the poor, and instead gave them money to purchase medicines and food. Our relatives were welcome to his help without any charge.

Mukunda Investigates Tantra Worship

Mejda left no stone unturned in his spiritual investigations. He went often to the Nimtala cremation grounds. It was there that our mother's body had been cremated. In the stark atmosphere of death, he contemplated the uselessness of attachment to the impermanent body and its ceaseless demands. At first I accompanied him. Mejda easily became absorbed in his meditations there, but the surroundings only frightened me. I stopped going with him. A short time later I noticed that a matted-haired ascetic, dressed in a dark red cloth, often came home with Mejda. They would go directly to his attic room. I was scared of the sadhu, for his eyes were always red; on his forehead was a long mark of deep vermilion.

One day, when the two of them had left the house, I secretly stole up to the meditation room. I gasped when I saw a human skull and two human bones placed crosswise, resting on a wooden stand. The skull had a vermilion mark like the sadhu's. As fast as my legs could carry me I ran back downstairs. When Father returned from the office that night I told him about Mejda's visits to Nimtala, and also about the sadhu and the human bones. Father spoke quietly to Mejda; he explained the harm that could come from *Tantric* practices.* Mejda took Father's words to heart, and soon thereafter the sadhu came to take away the human skull and bones. Mejda never again performed the rites prescribed in the *Tantras,* and he also counseled others to stay away from them.

Putrid Grain or Rice Pudding?

Some sadhus in India follow a practice of mixing

* *Tantra* deals primarily with ritualistic worship and the use of *mantras.* The purpose is to gain knowledge of and mastery over the forces of *maya,* and thus to reunite the individual soul with Spirit. The pure *Tantra* of the Hindu scriptures, however, is understood by only an enlightened few. More commonly to be found are its many degenerate offshoots, whose followers seek after phenomenal powers and experiences. *(Publisher's Note)*

together various foods that would not ordinarily be palatable in combination. To this mixture they add contradictory flavorings of spice, sugar, and salt. The purpose is to make individual flavors indistinguishable, and thus help the ascetic to overcome gustatory likes and dislikes.

Mejda enthusiastically tested any theory he thought might advance his spiritual progress. He prepared his own mixture, heavily flavored with both salt and sugar, so that it was virtually impossible to recognize what was being eaten. It was terrible! For five or six days he ate nothing but this hodgepodge.

One day Mejda, Surenda, and I were walking along Upper Circular Road towards Sealdah. Suddenly a repulsive smell of rotting rice wafted in our direction. Nausea overwhelmed us. We held handkerchiefs to our faces, but there was no escape from the putrescent odor. A cow walking ahead of us caught a whiff and abruptly changed course to the opposite side of the street. Several persons walking nearby exclaimed in disgust and diverted their footsteps posthaste. Traffic came to a halt as astonished drivers inquired about the stench.

But Mejda was unaffected. With a nonchalant air he walked along as though nothing were amiss. "Don't you smell that overripe garbage?" we asked him. He smiled, and kept walking unconcernedly. We had no alternative but to go along with him. There was a distant look in his eyes; his mind was withdrawn.

"Mukunda, let's go to the other side of the street! This maggoty rice is covered with crawling flies; they're getting all over us. Even an ignorant cow had the sense to avoid it."

"An ignorant animal cannot comprehend that God

exists in everything, even something as offensive as this pile of decaying rice," Mejda answered. "But *I* realize that God is in everything; therefore I know I could eat some of that rice and not come to any harm."

"If you can eat some of that rotting stuff so can I!" Surenda jeered, confident that Mejda would never do anything so drastic. Shock registered on Surenda's face as Mejda bent over and scooped up a handful of the noxious mess. He ate it as though it were a delicacy carefully prepared with sweetening and milk.

As if he had seen a ghost, Surenda ran for the other side of the street. Mejda scooped another handful of the rice and sped after the fleeing victim. Catching him, he stuffed it into his mouth. I cried out in protest, but it was too late. Overcome with revulsion, Surenda promptly vomited, and seemed about to faint with suffocation as he fell to the ground. In my boyish imagination loomed a fear that he wouldn't recover, and that we would be apprehended by the police. I started to weep. Mejda was rubbing Surenda's chest, smiling all the while. Pretty soon Surenda stood up, fully recovered, and said to Mejda, "I admit defeat! I will think a hundred times before I challenge you again!"

What amazed me was that Mejda experienced no ill effects. At the time, I could not but wonder whether that Light which relieves pain and suffering in God's devotees and *sadhakas** had likewise removed the foul smell and taste of the putrid rice before it reached Mejda's mouth. I know now that Mejda was engrossed in God, aware only of His presence. Beyond physical sense perceptions, he was tasting only the sweetness of the Lord who is hidden within all forms in creation. Mejda's

* Those who follow a spiritual discipline for realizing God.

amazing feat on that day demonstrated that without doubt he had realized God in everything.

Founding Sadhana Mandir and Saraswat Library

It was probably around 1908 that Mejda founded his first ashram. He and his faithful band of spiritually inclined friends often had difficulty trying to meditate together and practice *sadhana* in our Garpar Road home. So, for some time, he had been looking for a more suitable place for our meetings. Pulin* found a small, one-room hut with a thatched fan-palm roof near his own house at Bagmari, in the Kankurgachi area of Calcutta. Mejda rented it for Rs. 1.25 a month and named it "Sadhana Mandir" (Temple of Spiritual Discipline). Mejda felt very proud to have an ashram, and we spent much time there with him. We would gather regularly, and Mejda would read *slokas* from the scriptures and lead us all in *kirtan* and meditation.

Late every night, after the family had retired, Thamu would quietly let Mejda out the middle door of the drawing room on the ground floor, and open the door to let him in again before morning. He would spend his nights at the Sadhana Mandir. No one in the family knew he had been gone except Thamu.

It was at this time that Mejda became acquainted with the famous athlete, Purna Chandra. He occasionally came to the meetings. An ashram run by such young spiritually minded boys attracted quite a lot of attention and visitors. Near the Sadhana Mandir was a beautiful garden called *Panchavati.* Mejda sometimes sat in this garden with the devotees for meditation.

The Sadhana Mandir was in this location for about

* Pulin Bihari Das, who later became an ascetic, Swami Sivananda.

a year. But it was very small for our purposes, and quite some distance from all of us. During this period we met Tulsi Narayan Bose, son of Sri Harinarayan Bose, the headmaster of the Art School.

Tulsi offered Mejda a tile-roofed adobe building owned by his family on a lot adjacent to their house. The building had several small rooms. We moved Sadhana Mandir from Kankurgachi to this location: 17/1 Pitambar Bhattacharya Lane, Calcutta. A little alleyway to the property opened onto Garpar Road. We established a small library here, which Mejda named "Saraswat Library."* He stocked it with many books, magazines, and papers; and furnished it with a table and some chairs from our home. A new boy named Prokas Chandra Das, a close friend of Tulsi's, was attracted by our activities and joined us.

The opinions of Tulsi and Prokas differed from that of Mejda as to how the library should be developed and operated. When they paid no attention to his ideas, and an agreement could not be reached, Mejda decided to re-establish Saraswat Library elsewhere. Fortunately, Mejda became acquainted with Upen Mitra, a neighbor of ours, at that time. After hearing Mejda's story, he said, "Never mind. I'll see to it that you can use the sitting room in the house of Sri Hari Nag for your library."

When the room was ready, Tulsi and Prokas would not let Mejda take any of the books or papers from the ashram. But this did not discourage Mejda. "Gora," he said, "we shall start a new library!" With the help of a couple of other boys, he enthusiastically collected many books by going from door to door throughout the local-

* Saraswati, Goddess of Learning.

ity, and founded a new Saraswat Library.* That library still exists today. It functioned for many years in the Nag home. After the death of Sri Hari Nag, the books were stored in a warehouse for a time. On May 9, 1978, the Saraswat Library was reopened in a new building at 69 Garpar Road across the street from Sri Nag's house.

From 1910 to 1915 Mejda was in college and at Serampore with his guru, Swami Sri Yukteswar Giri. In 1916 Mejda again started to build up the ashram at Tulsi's house. By then, Mejda had become Swami Yogananda. The old Sadhana Mandir was refurbished. It included a meeting hall, and a kitchen and room for Shastri Mahasaya. The grounds were landscaped with many plants.

Meetings were held regularly, with scripture readings, devotional songs and *kirtans,* spiritual discourses, and *Kriya Yoga* meditation. At the end of the meetings, fruits and sweets were distributed to all.

One day Sri Netaji Subhash Chandra Bose† visited our Mandir during one of our meetings. After meditation, he walked through the rest of the ashram and the garden. "The work I have yet to do in the temporal world is my meditation," he told us. "For now, meditation with closed eyes is not for me."

Two young boys were resident in the ashram, and several others came in daily for spiritual training. In 1917, Mejda moved his ashram and boys' school to Dihika; and then in 1918 to Ranchi. But he always kept a warm remembrance of his ashram days at Tulsi's. Many

* The founding date recorded in the Saraswat Library annals is January 10, 1910.

† An early disciple of Mahatma Gandhi; and later considered a great patriot of India during World War II.

years later, he sent money from America to buy that same property, and had constructed there a new Yogoda Satsanga center with a meeting hall and altar, and living quarters. It is known today as the Yogoda Satsanga Garpar Center.

CHAPTER 10

Mejda's Guru and College Years

Mejda Meets His Gurudeva, Swami Sri Yukteswar

Mejda passed the entrance examination* of Hindu School in June 1909. He had promised Father he would complete his high school studies; that promise had been kept. Within a few months, when he announced his intention to renounce the world and seek God alone, his freedom to do so could no longer be denied. Jitendra Nath Mazumdar (Jitenda), had taken initiation from Shastri Mahasaya and had gone to the Bharat Dharma Mahamandal hermitage in Banaras. Mejda planned to join him. With Father's reluctant permission, he set out for the ancient holy city.

In the Mahamandal hermitage, Mejda continued his meditative practices. The other ashram residents, not sharing his ardor for meditation, ridiculed Mejda for the hours he spent in seclusion. Unfairly, they as-

* In 1909, there were two examinations to be passed before one could go on to college. The first was the entrance examination, given by the Education Department of Bengal. This was given at the end of the tenth year as a final examination for all class ten students, to indicate that they had successfully completed their schooling. Those who successfully passed the entrance examination and wished to enter the University or an affiliated college then had to take a matriculation examination, which was given by Calcutta University. The last year in which the entrance examination was given was 1909. From 1910 onward, only the matriculation examination was given to college aspirants. Students in class ten were then said to be in the Matriculation Standard in school. *(Publisher's Note)*

signed him more than his share of the hermitage duties. Mejda tolerated all this silently.

Father regularly sent Mejda a small allowance for his personal needs. When the head of the monastery, Swami Dayananda, learned of it, he asked Mejda to return the money. Mejda told Father to discontinue the stipend. Adding to Mejda's difficulties was the unusual schedule for dining: the first meal of the day was not served until noon. At home, Mejda had always enjoyed an early morning repast.

On one occasion, Swami Dayananda was absent from the hermitage for fifteen days. Mejda fasted the day before his return, quieting his hunger pains with assurances that his austerity would be amply rewarded by a sumptuous feast at noon the next day when Dayanandaji was expected to arrive. Mejda eagerly awaited the promised hour, but the Swami's train was delayed. Out of respect for their leader, the entire ashram waited to serve the banquet until Dayanandaji at last reached the ashram and had bathed and meditated. Mejda was sure he would not survive the delay. How well he recalled the loving care he had received in "the good old days" at home! Finally, at nine p.m., the summons for dinner was given.

The Swami proved a real renunciant, utterly detached from the needs of his body. "It is God's power alone that sustains life," he told Mejda. "He knows our needs and supplies them all. Food and money are merely instruments; they are not the Divine Life. Until man breaks his dependence on the instruments, he cannot perceive the Great Cause of life."

Mejda's heart was stirred, for above all things he desired to find God. He decided to discard all excess material possessions. While going through his box to sort out his belongings, he saw that the silver amulet had disappeared, and he remembered the prophecy the saint had given Mother: "When the amulet has served its purpose, it shall vanish."

Grieved that he seemed to be making no progress toward realizing God, he was meditating one morning soon after and heard a voice speaking to him from the ether: "Thy Master cometh today."

Mejda was then called to accompany one of the young ashram priests to the market to make some purchases. Their errand took them past a small lane, at whose far end stood a noble-looking sage dressed in ochre. The saint had a stalwart, erect body. Long curly hair and pointed beard softly framed his strong face. When Mejda glanced at him, he felt as though he had seen him before, and wanted to stop and talk to him. But because he and his companion were hurrying to get back to the hermitage, Mejda turned away and walked on. After some time, however, his legs became heavy; they seemed rooted to the ground. Realizing that the saint was magnetically drawing him, Mejda dumped the parcels into the arms of his astonished comrade and ran back to the saint.

Humbly he knelt and touched the sadhu's feet: "Gurudeva!" This was the saint whose face had appeared in many of his dreams and meditations, holding a promise he had not fully understood until this moment. "I have been searching for you for years. I know that you, only you, can take me to God."

Sri Yukteswar joyously greeted Mejda, "O my own, you have come to me! How many years I have waited for you!" He took Mejda's hand and led him to a house on the Ganges, in the Rana Mahal district of Banaras. It was the home of the sage's mother, whom he was visiting. As they sat on the balcony overlooking the river, he said to Mejda, "I will give you my ashrams and all I possess."

But Mejda replied, "I desire only God; no other wealth has meaning for me."

Sri Yukteswarji then promised him, "I give you my unconditional love."

When they had gone inside to take food, the saint said, "The amulet has vanished because its purpose was fulfilled. You need no longer stay at the hermitage in Banaras. I would like you to return to your home in Calcutta. Why exclude your relatives from your love for mankind? Wisdom is better sought from a true guru than from Himalayan forests."

Mejda could not help remembering Ananta's last remark before he left for Banaras: "Let the young bird fly in the skies of spiritual aspiration. The weighty air will tire his wings. Then he will return to the nest. The way of the world is thus: a bird accustomed to resting on a perch always returns to that perch." Mejda was not about to give Ananta the satisfaction of saying "I told you so"; he thus refused to follow his newly found guru's wish that he return to Calcutta. Instead, he asked for the saint's name and the address of his ashram.

"My name is Swami Sri Yukteswar Giri. My main hermitage is in Serampore, on Rai Ghat Lane."

Though Mejda said he would not return home, Sri Yukteswar insisted that he would do so in thirty days. Mejda was obstinate. Sri Yukteswar told him: "There must be complete surrender by obedience to my strict training."

Mejda wondered afterward at the cosmic play: he had been willing to go to the ends of the earth to find his guru, and all along Sri Yukteswarji was in nearby Serampore, right on the outskirts of Calcutta!

The following weeks in the Mahamandal hermitage became increasingly painful. Swami Dayananda was away in Bombay for a time. Mejda was accused of enjoying ashram hospitality but not paying for his share of the expenses; it was implied that though he was well-off, he never gave a paisa to the hermitage. Mejda wished that he had not returned Father's money as advised by Swami Dayananda. Deeply hurt, he told Jitenda, "I am going to leave. Please convey my *pranams* and apologies to Dayanandaji. I have met a great saint who lives in Serampore. I am going to his hermitage there."

"I will go with you, Mukunda," Jitenda said. "I also do not have the opportunity here to meditate as much as I would like."

Resistance to a College Education

Reaching Swami Sri Yukteswar's ashram in Serampore, Mejda knelt at his guru's feet, his soul at rest in the joyous contemplation of spending the rest of his days in the holy presence of the *Jnanavatar.** Instead, he was told by his guru that he should return to Calcutta to continue his education. "Someday you will go to the West. Its people will be more receptive to India's ancient wisdom if the strange Hindu teacher has a university degree."

Perhaps Mejda wasn't very happy about returning home, but we were overjoyed to have him back!

Mejda had a keen intuitive intelligence and a re-

* Incarnation of wisdom.

markable memory; he could have been a great scholar except for the fact that he rarely studied his books. Only to keep his promise to Father had he persisted just barely enough to graduate from Hindu School. The family had then kept pressure on him to continue his education in some specific field, so that he could have a means of earning his own livelihood. Mainly, they were trying to curb what they felt to be his over-zealous interest in spiritual matters. Halfheartedly, Mejda had enrolled at Sabour Agricultural College in north Bihar. But agriculture was not part of God's plan for Mejda's future. After only a short time, he left. He had not been happy in that environment, having found no companions there who had spiritual interests akin to his own. He returned home with a large cabbage—his only harvest from his agricultural "education."

Back in Calcutta, Mejda had entertained an even briefer interest in becoming a doctor. He enrolled in the Intermediate Science Class of the Metropolitan Institute (now Vidyasagar College). He filled an almirah in our house with stacks of books and reference materials—and then discarded them all, along with his interest in medicine. I don't think he attended even one class. He had then left Calcutta to join the Mahamandal hermitage in Banaras. He was free at last, and forever, from the unrelenting pursuit of school books—he thought. But his new-found guru had now told him that a university degree was important for his future mission in life. It was with loving obedience, but woeful reluctance, that Mejda entered Scottish Church College in Calcutta about August or September 1910.

Still, Mejda spent more time with his *sadhana* and with his guru in Serampore than with his books. He was a college student in name only. Toward the end of his second year, when he was to take the I.A. examinations, Mejda became very ill and could not appear. He had to wait for several months until they were held again in the following year, 1913. He passed those exams and got his Intermediate Arts diploma.* Now, he felt, he had had enough of college. He went to his guru in Serampore with his diploma and his decision to quit school. "To tell you the truth, sir, I want to discontinue my studies altogether. My real wish is to be near you all the time," Mejda told his guru.

Sri Yukteswar frowned disapprovingly. "You must remember, Mukunda, that someday when you go to the West you will find a university degree helpful to you."

"You are evading my request to be near you *all* the time," Mejda argued.

Sri Yukteswar thought for a time and then said, "Seek admission in Serampore College."

Mejda looked at his guru in puzzlement. Didn't he know that Serampore was only an Intermediate Degree college? However, it was but a short time later that Serampore became a fully accredited college, affiliated with Calcutta University. Mejda could indeed continue his studies for an A.B. degree and yet be near Sri Yukteswar's hermitage. It is well known that it was only through Sri Yukteswar's blessings that Mejda passed his exams and got his degree. When he was assailed with doubts as to whether he would pass, his guru comforted him:

* In India, the completion of two successful years of college brings an Intermediate Arts diploma. Another two years are required to obtain a bachelor's degree. Because Mejda's illness delayed his schooling, he did not enter Serampore College until the fall of 1913 to begin the last two years of his formal education. Thus, he obtained his A.B. degree in 1915.

"Mukunda, it is more likely that the sun and moon will change their positions in space than that you will fail to get your degree!"

On the day of his graduation Mejda knelt at his guru's feet in gratitude. "Get up, Mukunda," Sri Yukteswar told him. "The Lord simply found it more convenient to make you a graduate than to rearrange the sun and moon!"

Mejda's First Public Speech

Mejda was a first-year student at Scottish Church College in Calcutta when he received an invitation to deliver a lecture at one of the local school festivals. The request was made by an acquaintance, Sri Atul Nandi, founder and headmaster of the Atheneum Institution. Mejda hesitated, but then agreed. Later he told us, "I had never spoken in public before, so naturally I was taken aback. When I thought it over more calmly, an inner voice said: 'You have nothing to worry about; pray to God and everything will be all right.'"

The afternoon of Mejda's speech, several of his friends, including Manomohan and Jitenda, and myself, accompanied him to the school. We were sympathetic, knowing he must be nervous. As we walked along, Mejda's countenance, usually smiling, was grave. Although I don't recall the subject of his lecture, I remember well some of the thoughts he expressed—they made a deep impression on my mind:

"Every man seeks happiness: Some seek it in drink; others seek it in sex and sense pleasures; others seek it in marriage and family life with their children. And there are those who seek happiness by renouncing the world and all possessions; clothed only in a little loincloth, they meditate in Himalayan caves to realize the Source of all happiness.

"Gratification of the senses does not produce happiness. The pleasure of sense indulgence is temporary and results in misery. The sensualist is like a moth that destroys itself in the burning flame of a candle.

"*Maya* or ignorance is what attracts man to worldly life. From this attraction come desire and wrong actions. These produce the alternates of temporary pleasure and subsequent sorrow."

Mejda's speech was listened to attentively by all. Afterwards, he was highly praised by the headmaster and other respected persons of the locality who attended the function. I noticed that the smile had returned to Mejda's face.

In the "Valley of the Shadow of Death"

For years it had been Mejda's practice to frequently slip away from the house without telling anyone where he was going; nor would he even ask Father for a railway pass, lest he have to disclose his plans. But invariably he invited some of his friends to accompany him. His journeys were undertaken to seek out saints and temples and secluded places to meditate. At first, Mejda's preoccupation with spiritual matters brought strong criticism and resistance from members of the household. They urged Father to do something about it. But after a while, Mejda's independence was accepted as part of the normal family routine. It was not uncommon, either, for Mejda to seclude himself in his room, locked away from the family and all household affairs, for long periods of meditation. After he met his guru, Swami Sri Yukteswar, the length of those periods increased, up to thirty or forty-eight hours at a time.

One day, during our summer vacation, we all sat down to lunch together. Mejda had just come from one of his prolonged meditations; we hadn't seen him for two days. He was withdrawn and silent. As he absentmindedly ate some of the rice on his plate, it was as though he was oblivious of everyone and everything except the presence of God he felt within. Panchudi was silently scrutinizing Mejda's behavior. After a while, I caught a twinkle in Mejda's eye and thought: "He is planning some fun."

Suddenly Mejda fell backwards, unconscious. Panchudi shouted: "What happened? Are you not well?" We could see that he was not breathing. Panchudi felt for his pulse. His heart had stopped!

One of the relatives groaned, "It's due to this yoga he's practicing. I always knew it wasn't good for his health. Surely his head is reeling."

A doctor was called. He had us place Mejda on a bed; then he examined him carefully. At length, finding no signs of life, he shook his head sadly and left the room.

A pall of deep mourning fell over the household. We youngsters cried and called to Mejda, "Get up! Get up!" The elders, too, wept despairingly. They shook Mejda: "Moko, Moko, talk to us!"

Jhima, our maid-mother, who was Mejda's most ardent protagonist, came running into the room. On hearing what had happened, she took the lifeless form of Mejda in her arms. In tears she rocked back and forth, crying: "Where are you, Mukun? O dear God, please don't take him away. I swear I will never scold him or say anything harsh to him ever again. He is such a good boy. Please bring him back."

We had never seen Jhima weeping like this. She was always after Mejda for one reason or another: he spent too much time with his friends; he was wasting his life and would amount to nothing, and squander his father's hard-earned money. She never liked his bringing his friends to eat at the house—which he did all the time—and they constantly fought about this.

As suddenly as he had fallen unconscious, Mejda sat straight up, shaking with laughter. "So, Jhima, you will never scold me again?"

Because of old age, Jhima had to use a cane to get about. Infuriated, she raised it as if to strike Mejda. "Naughty boy! I knew you were only playing; I knew it! Do you think you could fool me? I will show you. One day I, too, will sit and consciously leave this body."*

The tussle between Jhima and Mejda brought an immediate feeling of normalcy back to the household. Peals of laughter replaced sorrowful sobs. The ache was gone from our hearts.

Later, Mejda told me that meditation and yoga *pranayama* enable one to completely control all the natural functions of the body, even for hours at a time. Our doctor was astounded. He could hardly believe what had happened, nor accept the limitation of his learning when faced with such a situation.

Mejda received a proper scolding from the elders, but it was obvious that they had enjoyed the charade.

Mejda Demonstrates the State of Samadhi

I often listened to Mejda and Manomohan discuss *samadhi* (ecstatic union with Spirit). One day when I was alone with Mejda I asked him what *samadhi* was, and if I

* This prophecy was fulfilled.

could see him in that state. At first he hesitated, saying, "You are too young. You wouldn't understand." Then he paused and said, "All right, come to my room tonight after midnight." I had the lamentable childhood habit of wetting the bed at night, so Father used to wake me up about that time and send me to the latrine. Mejda told me to be sure that Father had gone back to sleep before I came to his room.

Excited, I had no difficulty in remaining awake that night. (Bishnu, Thamu, and I slept on the floor of our father's room; he slept on a wooden cot. Nalini was married and living with her husband in her father-in-law's house. Mejda slept in the middle bedroom.) Father had sent me to the latrine and was sleeping soundly again when the clock struck twelve. I quietly got up and made my way to Mejda's room. He was sitting on his bed, meditating. A mat had been spread on the floor in front of his bed in readiness. He asked me to sit on it, then told me:

"*Samadhi* is withdrawing the mind from the body and merging it in God through a method of concentration. Salvation from this world of *maya* is achieved through *samadhi*. When the mind of the devotee becomes wholly absorbed in the sound that arises from the *anahata chakra,* the twelve-petaled lotus of the heart center, the center of feeling,* then *buddhi,* or the intellect, at the *ajna chakra,*† becomes pure and fixed upon God. All motion in the body ceases. This state of mind-

* The fourth of seven successively higher cerebrospinal yoga centers of spiritual consciousness. The *anahata* is in the spine opposite the heart. Each center emits a characteristic sound, an expression of the cosmic creative vibration of *Aum* as it operates in that center to enliven man's body and mind.

† The sixth yogic center, at the point between the eyebrows. The

interiorization and body stillness, and resultant inner awareness of God, is called *yoga* (union). The devotee realizes that he is not the mortal body; he is the immortal Spirit that became the body. This perception frees him from all sorrow. He realizes that, like Spirit, he is ever-existing, ever-conscious, ever-new Joy."

After saying this, Mejda began to sing in Bengali:

Nahi surya, nahi jyoti, nahi shashanka sundara
Bhase byome chhayasama chhabi viswa charachara
Asfuta man-akashe, jagat-sangsar bhase,
Othe bhase dobe punoh ahang-srote nirantara.
Dhire dhire chayadal, mahalaye probeshiio
Bahe matro "a me" "a me"—ei dhara anukshan
Se dharao baddhwa halo, shunye shunyo milaiio
"Abangmanasogocharam," bojhe—pran bojhe jara.

Translated, the words mean:

Lo! The sun is not, nor the comely moon,
All light extinct; in the great void of space
Floats shadow-like the image universe.

In the void of mind involute, there floats
The fleeting universe, rises and floats,
Sinks again ceaseless, in the current "I."

Slowly, slowly, the shadow multitude
Entered the primal womb, and flowed ceaseless,
The only current, the "I am," "I am."

Lo! 'Tis stopped, ev'n that current flows no more,
Void merged into void—beyond speech and mind!
Whose heart understands, he verily does.*

---

advanced yogi's consciousness remains at all times between the *anahata* and *ajna chakras,* thus intellect and feeling in their pure, spiritualized state guide all his actions, perceptions, and understanding.

* I had never heard the song before and was sorry I didn't write it

When Mejda finished singing, he sat completely motionless. The clock struck one a.m. When, by two-thirty, he had not moved, I was becoming alarmed. I touched his body lightly and called his name. But he remained inert. I held my hand near his nostrils, but there was no sign of breath. I felt his chest, but there was no movement. Then I shook his shoulders firmly, and called louder to him; still no response. By now I was distraught. Fortunately, Father awoke, as was his custom, at three o'clock. Seeing that I wasn't in bed, he came to Mejda's room. In tears I told him what had happened.

Father sat beside Mejda and practiced *pranayama*. Then, touching Mejda's chest with one hand, he chanted "*Aum*" softly in his ear. He continued this for more than half an hour. Finally Mejda's body moved slightly, and after some time he opened his eyes. But his consciousness remained withdrawn. Father gently massaged Mejda's body for a long time. It was almost dawn before Mejda returned fully to waking consciousness. Father told me to open the windows. Seeing Father beside him, Mejda felt very shy. Nothing was said. Father silently returned to his own room, and I followed. Soon I was fast asleep.

A Classmate Becomes Mejda's Disciple

Mejda was always surrounded by spiritual friends. As bees are attracted to honey, so high-minded boys sought out Mejda as their leader.

In his first year of college, Mejda met a talented,

---

down at that time. After diligently searching for the words, I found them written in our eldest sister's diary. ["The Hymn of Samadhi" by Swami Vivekananda. The English translation given here is also by him, as published in *The Complete Works of Vivekananda, Volume IV.*]

intelligent, and religious-minded youth, Basukumar Bagchi. As their friendship deepened, Basu confided to Mejda, "Mukunda, I have difficulty meditating at home. It is impossible to find a place where I can have the privacy I need."

A short time later Mejda invited Basu to come to our house to live. "When both of us travel the same path with heart and soul," Mejda told him, "we can find a way to work things out."

In the beginning, Mejda kept Basuda's residence with us a secret from Father. Basuda lived in Mejda's attic meditation-room and shared all of Mejda's food. He came downstairs only when Father was at the office. But of course, in time, his presence became known, and Basuda was accepted as one of the family members. Instead of disapproving, as Mejda had feared, Father commended Mejda for his generosity and openheartedness.

Basuda was a close associate of Mejda in those days, and a fervent follower in all spiritual matters. In later years he was known as Swami Dhirananda.

One day, in college, Mejda acquired an unexpected follower. As the students were reading in the first period of the day, Mejda heard a Voice as though whispering in his ear: "Mukunda, accept the youth sitting beside you as your disciple. Illuminate for him the way to salvation."

The Voice startled Mejda. "Who spoke?" he wondered. He looked over at his classmate, but the lad only smiled. Doubting that he had heard anything, Mejda turned his attention to the teacher, standing in the front of the room. The teacher was asking questions of each of the boys in turn, but for some reason he skipped Mejda. Again Mejda heard the beautiful Voice repeat the same command. He leaned over and spoke to the boy, but his classmate frowned. "Be quiet, I am listening to the professor."

Mejda replied, "I am your guru. You should listen to me."

The boy was outraged at Mejda's presumptuous words. "You scoundrel of a boy!" he retorted, his voice just controlled enough that the professor couldn't hear. "If ever you say such a thing again, I'll box your ears!" Mejda smiled a knowing smile.

The next day, the boy went very early to school and waited at the entrance, so as to be sure to meet Mejda when he arrived. As usual, Mejda was early, too. He saw from a distance that the lad was waiting by the gate. Mejda hid behind a post so that he couldn't be seen. When some of the other students came along, they asked Mejda why he was hiding.

"Don't ask me now," Mejda said in a hushed voice. "Do me a favor. All of you surround me so that when we go into the classroom my friend standing by the gate will not see me. I am going to have a little fun."

Mejda's classmates were always eager for a prank; but they were curious, too.

"What are you trying to do?" one of them asked.

"Wait until we are inside, then I'll tell you."

Mejda somehow knew that the boy had been shown in a dream that the portentous message was indeed true. The lad's heart was filled with joy; he was also repentant for rebuking Mejda the previous day, and had come to school early to see his new-found guru before classes. Now it was Mejda's turn to be "hard to get." He was playing hide-and-seek with the young disciple, even as God Himself plays hide-and-seek with His devotees.

Mejda the Photographer and Artist

During his first year at college, Mejda purchased a box camera. In those days it was a remarkable instrument, and cost only eight rupees. It could take six pictures in succession through manipulation of six quarter-inch plates inside the camera. We darkened the drawing room downstairs to load the camera, and used the same room as a laboratory to develop and dry the negatives—a wooden box served as the drying rack.

Mejda also set up a "studio" in the drawing room. Father posed, sitting on a chair Mejda himself had rebuilt from some broken, discarded parts. Next came our other relatives and friends. Mejda enjoyed his hobby for some time. Then, seeing how enthusiastic I was about photography, he gave me the box camera.

To encourage my interest and talent, a few years later Mejda sent to me from America a stereoscopic camera. A friend, Nagendra Nath Das, taught me how to use the camera and develop the film: the right negative was printed as the left-hand picture; the left negative became the right-hand picture. In a special box fitted with ground glass we could view the two prints as one photograph. We were fascinated with the three-dimensional effect of the pictures. Years later I became a professional photographer; I am grateful to Mejda for his gift of that camera, and to Nagen Das for the early lessons he gave me.

I have previously mentioned my predisposition toward art, inherited from Mother. Mejda also had natural artistic talent. Seeing a picture I had painted of Krishna, he decided to paint one. It was completely original, not like so many stereotyped presentations. He then painted some of the other deities, expressing the same creative originality. Those who saw his paintings were truly astonished, for he had not received any formal instruction. His talent was the natural ability of a great soul to draw creativity from within. I deeply regret that through carelessness his paintings were eventually lost and cannot be displayed today.

A Motorcycle for Mejda

In 1911, while enrolled at Scottish Church College, Mejda traveled daily by train from Calcutta to Serampore to see Sri Yukteswarji. The trip took valuable time that could have been better spent in the company of his guru. When Mejda complained of this, Sri Yukteswar suggested he get a motorcycle so that he could come to Serampore "flying like a bird."

When Mejda talked to Father about it, Father gave his characteristic reply: "The conditions of my early life are not unknown to you. I have told you often how poor our family was. Through unending patience and ceaseless perseverance I have established some financial security for our family."

Mejda replied, "But your sons do not have a poor father!" Father capitulated and gave Mejda the money to purchase a motorcycle. Mejda bought a Triumph with a sidecar. The sole agent selling motorcycles in Calcutta at that time was M/s.T. Thomson. Mejda engaged one of their staff to teach him to drive the vehicle. Afterwards, he hired a mechanic named Suren to keep the cycle in perfect running order. Often, when Mejda drove to Serampore, Suren rode with him in the sidecar.

A month after Mejda had purchased the motorcycle, he went to Darjeeling for a few days. The motorcycle sat unused at home, except for occasional runs by Suren as instructed by Mejda. Nagen Das, who was a close friend of Mejda's, was living at Pitambar Bhattacharya Lane, not far from our house. At that time he was taking the Intermediate Science examinations. Mejda had asked Suren to drive Nagen to his examinations each day on the motorcycle, and bring him home again after the examinations were over.

Taking advantage of Mejda's absence, Bishnu and I asked Suren to give us rides, too. Unfortunately, Suren had an accident: with Bishnu in the sidecar, he overturned the motorcycle on Manicktala Bridge. Bishnu's head was injured, but not seriously. To escape a scathing reprimand from Father, Suren returned the motorcycle quietly to our house and then fled.

The next day Nagen came for his ride. He waited for Suren until there was no more time left even to catch a bus or tram. Having no other alternative, he asked me, "Do you know how to drive the motorcycle?"

"Yes," I replied, but not without trepidation. I had never actually driven the motorcycle before; I had only carefully watched Mejda and Suren whenever I was riding in the sidecar. I felt I could duplicate their expertise. I mustered what confidence I could and asked Nagen to sit in the sidecar. Then nervously I started the cycle. I don't know how I did it, but I drove him safely all the way to the college. Oh! what pleasure of success was mine! I purchased a gallon of gas and invited a neighbor boy of my age to go for a ride. We drove to Dakshineswar and back. In the afternoon I met Nagen and brought him home; and I continued my chauffering service until Mejda returned from Darjeeling two or three days later.

Nagen told him everything. Although Mejda seemed outwardly angry at me, he was actually pleased

Swami Sri Yukteswar Giri (1855–1936)
Mejda's guru

Serampore College, where Mejda received his A.B. degree

Entrance to Serampore College

Room in Uncle Sarada's home in Serampore where Mejda occasionally stayed during his college years. Uncle Sarada's son, Prabhas Chandra Ghosh, later made the room into a meditation shrine, which he named *Anandalok* ("place of bliss").

Swami Sri Yukteswar
Mejda named this picture "The Lion of Bengal."

Rai Ghat on the Ganges, Serampore, where Sri Yukteswar often bathed, and where he met Mahavatar Babaji (as described in Mejda's *Autobiography of a Yogi*)

Mejda's passport photo for trip to Japan, 1916—the only time, after childhood, that his hair was ever cut short

Father seated in a chair made by Mejda, who also took this photograph

that I had been clever enough to drive the motorcycle. "Come," he told me, "I will sit in the sidecar and give you lessons."

I made the most of this unexpected opportunity. Thereafter I sometimes drove Mejda to Sri Yukteswar's ashram; and at other times Mejda and I would ride on the motorcycle, with Sri Yukteswar in the sidecar. Everyone on both sides of the street turned his head to look at us! On occasion we brought Sri Yukteswar to our house. When I became more experienced, I was sometimes given the privilege of driving. Once Sri Yukteswar told Mejda, "Your younger brother drives better than you do." I was so proud!

Our friend, Nagendra Nath Das, went on to obtain a doctorate degree in medical science, and became widely respected. He lectured at many seminars in Europe and America. He spoke before eminent scientists in universities, presenting new theories. Part of his education had been under the renowned Sri Jagadish Chandra Bose at Basu Vijnana Mandir (The Bose Institute). For several years, until he passed away, he served as a member of the board of directors of Mejda's Yogoda Satsanga Society. He received the Ghosh Travelling Fellowship for advanced study abroad in neurophysiology and electroencephalography. He had been a year at the University of Michigan when in the fall of 1950 he was blessed to visit Mejda at Self-Realization Fellowship in California. Upon his return to India, Dr. Das became head of the Department of Practical Psychology in the Science College in Calcutta.

My First Darshan of Swami Sri Yukteswar

While in high school in Calcutta, I concentrated more on athletics than on my studies. When Mejda transferred to Serampore to complete his last two years of college, he arranged—with Father's permission—to have me admitted into class ten at the Serampore Union School. I lived with Uncle Sarada Prasad, and occupied the room formerly used by Mejda when he first went to Serampore.* Because our uncle constantly scolded Mejda for returning so late at night from Sri Yukteswar's ashram, Mejda had moved to the Panthi, a student boardinghouse fronting the Ganges near Rai Ghat Lane. Uncle's house, the Panthi hostel, and Sri Yukteswar's ashram were all just a short distance from one another. Mejda would come to get me and take me with him to Sri Yukteswar's ashram.

I remember the first time Mejda took me to his guru, while we were still living in Calcutta. It was about nine o'clock on a Sunday morning. We entered a large old house, the ancestral home of Sri Yukteswar's family. An inner courtyard and a hall set apart for worship graced the premises; behind the house, a large garden had been cultivated. The mansion was hung with decorative chandeliers, shields, and swords. We spent the entire day in Sri Yukteswar's company; we could do this on all Sundays and holidays. Hearing me called "Gora," Sri Yukteswar inquired its meaning. Mejda explained that it was a short form of "Gorakhnath," and that the choice of the name of that saint was related to my having been born in Gorakhpur.

Visits to Sri Yukteswar's ashram always included a long period of meditation in a secluded room. Then we would sit at the Guru's feet to listen to his sublime dis-

* Years later, when Paramahansaji's beloved cousin Prabhas Chandra Ghosh lived in Uncle Sarada's home, he made a shrine of that room in memory of the Yogiraj and called it Anandaloka (Place of Divine Bliss).

courses, which filled our souls with nectar. Often he interpreted passages from the Bhagavad Gita. When I returned to my room in Uncle's home, I would make notes of what I remembered.

On one of my visits, Sri Yukteswar initiated me in *Kriya Yoga.* I had received initiation earlier from Shastri Mahasaya* at our Garpar Road home; but because I was very young then, and more interested in sports than meditation, I had not applied myself to spiritual practices. Under Sri Yukteswar's influence, I improved considerably.

I graduated from the Union School and was admitted to Serampore College. But during my second year I was severely stricken with dysentery. Father had me transferred to City College in Calcutta so that I could stay at home where he could take care of me.

While I had been living with Uncle in Serampore, I came to know from him some of Sri Yukteswar's past. His family had been wealthy landlords, which explained some of the furnishings in his home. From the many tenants on their large estates the family received a sizable income. Sri Yukteswar inherited those estates. Though it is said he enjoyed his material comforts, he was known for his philanthropy and generosity. He exercised equanimity in the management of his affairs, and came to be respected throughout a large area. He was kind, thoughtful, and fair to all in his employ.

I learned from Uncle that Sri Yukteswar had met our maternal grandfather, Govinda Chandra Bose, who was a Deputy Magistrate for a time in Serampore. Sri Yukteswar was also acquainted with our second maternal

* Swami Kebalananda. See "Swami Kebalananda, Mejda's Sanskrit Tutor," Chapter 8.

uncle, Shiva Chandra Bose, the Inspector of Police in Serampore; they often rode on horseback together along pathways by the Ganges.

After the passing of his wife, and his meeting with Lahiri Mahasaya, Sri Yukteswar took up the life of an ascetic. He sold his estates to his tenants for a nominal price and invested the proceeds in government bonds, so as to provide a modest income for his later years. He founded an ashram in Puri, and used to spend the summer months there.

Notes from Swami Sri Yukteswar's Discourses

Following are some of the summary notes I made of Swami Sri Yukteswar's discourses on Yoga references in the scriptures.

Jnanam yogatmakam viddhi yogaschashtanga samyutah
Samyogo yoga utyukto jivatma paramatmanoh
Yoga Yajnavalkya 1:44

"True knowledge, which comes from yoga, or union of the individual soul with Spirit, is attained by (practicing) the eight steps of Yoga."

Jnana Yoga (the path to wisdom) itself is *jnana* (wisdom). There are eight *yogangas* (steps or parts of yoga); *Yama* (forbearance); *Niyama* (observance of rules); *Asana* (posture for pacification of the body); *Pranayama* (pacification of the breath); *Pratyahara* (pacification of the mind); *Dharana* (fixation); *Dhyana* (contemplation); *Samadhi* (union, final pacification).

Obstacles to the practice of yoga arise from *kama,* lust; *krodha,* anger; *lobha,* greed; *moha,* desire; *mada,* pride; *matsarya,* envy. When these impediments are destroyed by faithful practice of the eight *yogangas,* knowledge is attained. Yoga is union of the *jivatma* (soul) with *Paramatma* (Spirit). Without the practice of yoga it is impossible to win control of the restless mind, or to achieve true knowledge. But through mastery of yoga, there is nothing that cannot be attained.

Nahi jnanena sadrisham
Pavitram iha vidyate
Tat svayam yogasamsiddhah
Kalena 'tmani vindati

Bhagavad Gita IV:38

"There is nothing on earth more purifying than wisdom. He who becomes perfected in Yoga will realize this in himself, in the course of time."

Realizing the Self (through yoga) is the highest *sadhana.* One may banish the fire of sin by *Karma Upasana* (worship through noble works); but good works alone do not necessarily destroy ignorance, the *cause* of evil actions. So the chance remains that one may sin again. Many advanced and well-intentioned devotees have so fallen because of the overpowering influence of ignorance. Without *jnana,* the true knowledge that destroys ignorance, one cannot know God.

But *jnana* is not independent of *karma* (action), any more than work can be independent of *jnana.* Success in *Karma Yoga* is also necessary to gain knowledge of the Self. *Karma Yoga* is action performed without worldly attachment and with the consciousness centered in the *Kutastha* (the seat of wisdom and divine consciousness at the point between the eyebrows), so that *jnana* comes automatically (and guides one's actions).

When true knowledge is revealed to the *sadhaka,* he enjoys *Brahma-sthiti* (the blissful state of God-awareness).

Yam labdhva cha param labham
Manyate na dhikam tatah
Yasmin sthito na duhkhena
Guruna pi vichalyate
Tam vidyad duhkhasamyoga
Viyogam yogasamjnitam
Sa nishchayena yoktavyo
Yogo 'nirvinnachetasa

Bhagavad Gita VI:22, 23

"That, on gaining which the yogi considers there is no other gain greater, the state in which he is not shaken even by the deepest sorrow—

"That (state) is Yoga—disconnection from identification with pain. The practice of Yoga is therefore to be followed with determination and a heart undismayed."

Sarvadharman parityajya
mam ekam sharanam vraja
Aham tva sarvapapebhyo
Mokshayishyami ma shuchah

Bhagavad Gita XVIII:66

"Abandoning all other duties, seek refuge in Me alone. Be not grieved, for I shall release thee from all sins."

Giriji Maharaj* said that this stanza has been interpreted in different ways by many people. Sri Krishna did not mean that we should only worship Him and

* *Giri,* meaning "mountain," is the branch of the Swami Order to which Sri Yukteswar belonged; his full name and title was thus Swami Sri Yukteswar Giri. The addition of *ji* at the end of a name or title connotes respect. *Maharaj,* literally, "great king," is also a title of respect that may be used in place of or after the name of a holy man. *(Publisher's Note)*

relinquish all dutiful responsibilities. The deeper meaning is that within the spinal *chakras* are manifested the primary elements of all created matter: *kshiti,* earth; *ap,* water; *tejas,* fire; *marut,* air; and *vyoma,* ether.* The body is composed of these elements. After death the body returns to these elements. The five senses of the body (smell, taste, sight, touch, and hearing) are made manifest by these elements and draw the mind outward into the body. The result is that the mind becomes utterly forgetful of the Self within. Thus "sin" is that which keeps the mind attached to sense perceptions and objects of the senses. Such attachment produces restlessness, which clouds perception of the soul.

The soul is ever pure, stainless, true, and eternal. It is ever untouched by any earthly experience. It may be likened to a mirror covered with dust. Wipe away the dust, and the mirror shines bright and clear. So the soul is covered by restlessness of the mind; and because of that, one does not know or perceive the soul.

He who remains under the influence of the attributes of the primary elements is subject to the alternating waves of pain and pleasure. So God tells us to find eternal shelter in Him through practice of *Kriya Yoga,* by which the consciousness is raised above the disturbing effects of the elements in the lower *chakras* and becomes established in the *ajna chakra* (the *Kutastha*). In this state, the devotee remembers God constantly with devotion; that is, becomes anchored in Him.

This, then, is the meaning of the message of God that He will release the yogi from all sin. Becoming established in God, he becomes a *jivanmukta,* one who is liberated while living. But even though such assurance

* Other terms used are *prithivi* (earth), *vayu* (air), and *akasha* (ether).

has been given by God, mankind for the most part remains bound to the senses and hence lives in ignorance.

Mosquitoes and Meatless Menus in the Serampore Ashram

For as long as I stayed in Serampore, I visited Swami Sri Yukteswar's ashram with Mejda almost every evening. On my first visit, Giriji Maharaj told us to go upstairs to meditate. The twilight-darkened room was occupied: by huge mosquitoes! It was impossible to sit quietly, for warding off their fierce attacks became a major undertaking. Sri Yukteswar appeared at the height of the "battle."

"How will you be able to meditate if you move about so much? You are concentrating on the mosquitoes, not God. Practice *titiksha* (endurance with even mind) and self-control. Pay no attention to the mosquitoes and you won't feel their stinging." To our great surprise, from that moment the mosquitoes did not come near us; and thenceforth whenever we meditated there in the evening we were not bothered by the ubiquitous insects.

Many devotees came to Swami Sri Yukteswar to discuss spiritual matters and to listen to his discourses. One day a gentlemen happened to mention that he intensely disliked cooked green bananas. A few days later he was a dinner guest at the ashram. After several courses had been served, all prepared by Sri Yukteswar, the guest praised the meal lavishly.

"Do you know what you have just eaten?" Giriji asked.

"No. But I do know it was delicious!"

"Every dish was prepared with green bananas."

The gentleman left the ashram happily satisfied by Sri Yukteswar's cooking—and the wiser for his wisdom.

Sri Yukteswar himself often cooked the meals for ashram guests. He also supervised the preparation of food served at the religious festivals he held throughout the year. Everyone enjoyed his cooking; and it was from Sri Yukteswar that Mejda acquired his culinary talent.

When religious festivals were observed — such as Lahiri Mahasaya's birthday or the autumnal equinox — Sri Yukteswar's ashram was decorated days before with flowers and leaf garlands. On the day of the festival, at dawn, a *kirtan* group marched in procession through the streets. A public meeting was held at Rammohan Library Hall in Calcutta, and was attended by many well-known dignitaries and scholars. The activities were concluded with a feast, ofttimes served on the roof of No. 3 Garpar Road, the house adjacent to ours.

Once Mejda had learned the preliminaries of cooking from Sri Yukteswar, he developed many delicious recipes of his own. On special occasions, he often cooked these dishes for us at home, and showed us how to prepare them. Of course, all these dishes were from vegetables only. Some that I remember particularly were *luchi,* a delicately puffed unleavened bread; potato curry (a favorite of Mejda's); *pulau,* flavored rice; vegetable "meat"; vegetable-egg curry; vegetable "fish head"; and some other meatlike dishes. After meals, sweetmeats (confections made primarily from milk and sugar) were always served.

Some of Mejda's recipes were prepared as follows:

Vegetable egg: First, *channa* (a soft cheese made from the curd of milk) was cut and molded into large, round "eggs." Then a small portion of *channa* was colored yellow with saffron and put inside the "white" of the "egg." They were then fried and added to a curry.

*Vegetable fish head:** A large cabbage was cut into four pieces. Each piece was tied with a string and cooked in a delicious, seasoned sauce.

Vegetable cutlets: Potato and spices were cooked with banana cone (flower pod). The mixture, when soft, was mashed and shaped into cutlets. The cutlets were soaked in liquid arrowroot, and then covered with cracker crumbs and fried.

Vegetable meat: 1) Flour was mixed with water to form a soft dough. The dough was then kneaded and washed in water until only gluten, the essence of the wheat, was left. Potatoes were cut lengthwise, and the gluten was molded around the potato slices. The preparation, when flavored and fried, tastes very much like meat.†

2) Jackfruit, when cut and properly prepared, renders a textured, meat-flavored dish.

3) *Guchi* (a special variety of large black mushrooms), prepared with *gram* (a pulse resembling garbanzo beans) also tastes meatlike.

Mejda Helps Me to Overcome a Bad Habit

While I was a student in Serampore College, I succumbed to the influence of some of my friends and developed a strong liking for cigarettes. In India it is considered a discourtesy to smoke in the presence of one's elders or superiors, so our relatives did not know that I

* Fish heads are considered a delicacy in many nonvegetarian Bengali households.

† Gluten meat substitutes are very popular today with vegetarians in the West. Several companies manufacture a variety of these products. But Paramahansaji was the first to make gluten "steaks" in America. *(Publisher's Note)*

had acquired this noisome habit. I soon realized that I was a slave to smoking, so I tried several times to quit. But the habit had such a pernicious hold, I couldn't give it up.

I am sure Mejda knew of my inner struggle. One day while we were waiting for Sri Yukteswar in the main hall of the ashram, Mejda suddenly said: "You should realize, Gora, that anyone who accomplishes something great in his life does so only through the power of his will. The potential strength of the mind is unlimited; it can do anything. Those who are addicted to harmful habits, such as smoking, chewing betel leaf with tobacco, taking snuff, or drinking, do not use sufficient will power to stop. If one's mental strength is exercised to control little habits, he will have increased power to do greater things."

His words struck a deep chord in my mind. I realized he was trying to help me break my hidden habit of smoking. "If I can't even control the desire to smoke," I thought, "how will I accomplish anything worthwhile in life?" That day I promised myself I would never smoke again, even if it killed me. It was difficult; the withdrawal symptoms were painful. For several days I experienced digestive problems. A little soda water and some digestive medicines helped. And after some days, I knew the habit had been broken. When I next saw Mejda, I bowed at his feet. He just smiled, and said nothing. We understood each other.

At the time I was also accustomed to eating meat* and fish. It seemed unthinkable to me that vegetarians could exist—except Mejda, who was an exception to

* Usually goat, lamb, or fowl. Traditionally, Hindus do not eat beef or pork.

everything! I had given up smoking; I decided to see if I could do without meat. Again I experienced a few initial difficulties, the worst of which was to eat only vegetables when I returned home to Calcutta, while my younger brother and my sisters enjoyed their meat and fish. But I was determined to strengthen my will. Even when I took my friends out for meals, and purchased meat dishes for them, I strictly adhered to a vegetarian diet. I continued for an entire year, until I had proven to myself that I could live without meat and without the desire for it. Once I had accomplished that objective, I occasionally took meat again when with others.

Mejda's invaluable instruction on the importance of using will power to get rid of petty habits has been a great blessing to me.

CHAPTER 11

Sannyas and a Worldwide Mission

Mejda Refuses a Job and a Bride

In June 1915 Mejda passed the Calcutta University examinations and received his A.B. degree. Father hoped Mejda would then accept a position with the Bengal-Nagpur Railway offered by the general manager, Mr. Godfrey. The manager had told Father: "Bhagabati, because of your service to the company I am offering your son the highly coveted position of Assistant Traffic Superintendent. Under ordinary circumstances, this post may be filled only by an Englishman. Even if the Lieutenant Governor were to recommend an Indian, that recommendation would not likely be accepted. Your son should not let this opportunity slip by."

Our cousin Prabhas Chandra Ghosh was to pass his A.B. examination in the coming year. Mejda urged Father to ask Mr. Godfrey to give the post to Prabhas, but Father wanted Mejda to take it. Mejda didn't want the job! He continued to press Father. Every day he walked with Father part of the way to his office, and met him again on his way home, to argue the point. Finally, Father gave in and took Prabhas to meet Mr. Godfrey; Prabhas got the appointment.

Our relatives were hard at work in an attempt to keep Mejda in the family. On many occasions I had accompanied our elder sisters to seek a suitable bride for

Mejda. Finally, one had been found, and his marriage was arranged. Actually, the family had tried unsuccessfully on two previous occasions; this was their final attempt. "If he is betrothed he will give up the idea of becoming a monk," they counseled Father. Father listened quietly, but I never knew his personal thoughts on the matter.

When Mejda learned of the arrangement, he went straight to Father: "What is the purpose of my marriage? To make *you* happy? If you think that *I* will be happy, you are mistaken. I will *never* be happy in marriage. No one knows this better than you."

Father gazed into Mejda's intense eyes for some time. Then he said, "All right. I can be happy only in your happiness." Mejda's marriage plans were canceled.* He was free to become a *sannyasi,* which had long been his resolve.

Mejda's illness in 1912, which made him postpone his sitting for the Intermediate Arts examinations, was a very serious one. He had dysentery and other debilitating symptoms. The illness was short, but the severity of it left him very weak. Though his health was still unstable, he determined to begin the practice of religious austerity to prepare himself for the life of a monk. He gave up everything he considered a luxury so as to become totally self-reliant. A week before *Janmashtami* (the birthday of Lord Krishna) he began walking barefooted. On *Janmashtami* he fasted the whole day. That night he took Basu, Sishir, Manomohan, Pulin, and me to the "Yoga-Uddyan" gardens at Kankurgachi. It was late at night when we sought out a quiet, lonely place to medi-

* The bride-to-be was given instead to our cousin Prabhas, the beneficiary of the Bengal-Nagpur Railway post also intended for Mejda.

tate, near what is now known as the new canal. In his newly adopted role as a neophyte monk it was fitting he have a monastic name. He called himself "Yogeshwara," in accord with his aspiration to find God (Ishwara) through Yoga. That name was known to only a few of us.

My own fate had been sealed when I was sixteen, in class nine of the Hindu School. Because I was Mejda's constant companion, our family feared I would want to follow in his footsteps. They decided to tie me securely to the family tree. Our relatives arranged for my betrothal. I had neither Mejda's strength nor purpose to resist the tide of family opinion, and so on the 14th of May, 1914, I was married to a niece of our sister-in-law.*

Our beloved mother had always looked forward to making the marriages of her sons occasions of pomp and splendor. Because she had passed away before any of her sons married, Mejda sought to fulfill that wish for her by making my marriage an elaborate one. A large celebration was arranged: colorful lights were placed everywhere; a band was hired; delicious foods were prepared. I was carried on a palanquin in a long procession of relatives and friends. Joyously blowing a conch shell, Mejda himself led the procession along its five-mile route to the house of the bride. He enjoyed the gala festivities of Indian weddings — so long as they were someone else's!

Ananta's Death

After Mejda graduated from college with his A.B. degree, there was thought of his going to America to study for a Ph.D. degree. But owing to the involvement

* As was the custom in India in those days, betrothals were sometimes made at a young age, but the bride and groom lived apart until they reached maturity.

of both England and America in World War I, these governments were not issuing passports or visas from India to the United States. Mejda reasoned that if he could go to Japan, perhaps there he would be able to obtain a visa to the West.

Father was against the trip. He had reluctantly agreed to Mejda's adopting the life of a monk; but he could not tolerate the thought of Mejda's living in a foreign country, even for a short time. He asked Mejda to accompany him to visit Ananta in Gorakhpur, secretly hoping that Ananta might be able to persuade Mejda not to undertake the journey. But Mejda could not be deterred, even by the fact that Ananta was not well. Father had to admit defeat again. Mejda sailed for Japan from Calcutta in late August 1916.

He returned early in November, much sooner than expected. It was his first experience outside India. He said the environment was too restless and too much directed toward outer material accomplishments. Also, the Japanese government would not grant him a visa to go to America.

Before Mejda arrived back in Calcutta, we received from him a huge parcel of gifts. Included was a bamboo chest for Ananta. Strangely, on the inside were inscribed the words: "For my beloved Ananta, now gone." We were amazed, for we had not told Mejda of Ananta's passing. The day Mejda returned from Japan, I met him at the gate of our house. Weeping, he said, "Our elder brother has died. Though Bishnu told me at the dock, I knew of his passing on my way home from Japan."

"But how could you?" I asked in wonder.

"You remember our visit to Ananta in Gorakhpur? On the second day there, the realization came to me that

Ananta would not live long. My feeling was confirmed by a vision I had of our sister-in-law that same morning: she was preparing the midday meal, when suddenly I saw her dressed as a widow.

"I was so saddened I could not bear to remain there any longer. I couldn't say a word to Ananta or Father; and in the face of their arguments that I should not go to Japan, my determination must have appeared ludicrous. Barda's approaching death was the real reason I insisted on leaving when I did. I could not endure seeing him taken from us.

"On the way home from Japan, in Shanghai, I was selecting presents for all of you; I had picked an artistically carved bamboo chest for Ananta. It slipped from my hand and fell to the floor and cracked. As I bent over to pick it up, I saw Ananta's face within it. I knew then that he had died. Stricken with grief, I handed the chest to the shopkeeper. He thought my distress was because I had broken it; he kindly said he would give me a new one. But I told him it was because I had bought this for my brother who had just passed away in Calcutta."

Mejda's account left me speechless. When I recovered, I related to him the details of Ananta's passing.

"Our elder brother fell seriously ill just after you left for Japan. The doctors in Gorakhpur diagnosed his condition as malaria because he had all the symptoms. His condition deteriorated rapidly. One of the physicians in attendance, Dr. Binay Roy*—the brother-in-law of Netaji Subhash Chandra Bose—suggested to Father and Ananta's father-in-law that the best course would be

* It should be mentioned also that Dr. Roy was the son of Rai Bahadur Yagneswar Roy, Civil Surgeon and husband of our cousin.

to bring Ananta to Calcutta for treatment by specialists. So, with Dr. Roy's assistance, they brought him here to Garpar. We put him in the central room on the second floor.

"Father asked Lt. Col. Dr. J. T. Calvert, principal of the Calcutta Medical College, to come and see Ananta. Dr. Calvert was furious with the Gorakhpur doctors; Ananta's illness had been wrongly diagnosed and treated. Ananta actually had typhoid fever; there was little that could be done as the disease had progressed so far.

"Ananta remained in critical condition for seven days. Manomohan was staying here at the time; he lovingly helped in every way to make Ananta comfortable. He held the ice bag on Brother's head, so as to reduce the fever, while I held the oxygen tube to help Ananta breathe.

"Toward the end of the week Ananta told me: 'Call your sister-in-law. Ask her to come at once.'

"When Boudi came into the room, Ananta said, 'My time has come. I am sorry that I must make of you a widow.'

"Ananta could say nothing more. His delirium increased throughout the day and evening, until midnight. About two a.m. I left his room to get more ice chips for the bag. When I returned I saw that he was lying perfectly still; he had entered the eternal sleep. Manomohan sat beside him, his head bowed."

Founding Yogoda Satsanga Brahmacharya Vidyalaya

Shortly after Mejda graduated from college, he took *sannyas* from Swami Sri Yukteswar Giri and became

Swami Yogananda. Giriji Maharaj encouraged him to begin organizational work. In 1916, as mentioned earlier, he started an ashram in a small building on the grounds of Tulsi Bose's residence. Two young boys lived there to receive training, and others came regularly to visit. The boys had to go outside the ashram for academic schooling, so Mejda wanted to start a residential school.

Mejda had long felt the lack of moral and spiritual values in modern-day education. He wished to start a school that would balance academic studies with spiritual training. He discussed his ideas with many people, but none came forward with practical support. At last he met Maharaja Manindra Chandra Nundy, who was overjoyed with Mejda's ideas. "You have come to me as a messenger of God," he exclaimed. "Only yesterday I was thinking how sad it is that our educational system lacks such training."

A program was soon outlined and plans laid for the establishment of the school. In March 1917, Mejda started with seven boys in a small house belonging to the Maharaja, in Dihika, West Bengal.

After a year the fast-growing school required larger accommodations. The Maharaja provided the use of some of his property a few miles from his Kasimbazar Palace in Bengal. The area was infested with malaria, however, and after only a few days most of the teachers and students were sick. The school was moved temporarily to a guest house on the spacious Palace grounds, but the malaria outbreaks continued. The Maharaja then offered his summer palace at Ranchi in Bihar. The school moved to that location in 1918. The Maharaja not only gave Mejda the use of the land and buildings, but also a monthly grant of two thousand rupees toward the expenses of the school.

The twenty-five-acre estate provided the perfect location for Mejda's Brahmacharya Vidyalaya. The grounds were resplendent with luscious fruit orchards, which, in combination with spacious fields and a healthful climate, gave the school a serene, forest-like atmosphere, ideally suited for the development of young minds and bodies. The Vidyalaya was patterned after the ancient Indian hermitages where children were once instructed out-of-doors in a natural setting. They were taught subjects that contributed to their all-round development of body, mind, and soul — not academics only. Such educational institutions are rarely to be seen.

At first a residential school with accommodations for one hundred students was started. The high academic and spiritual standards of the school created such favorable publicity that soon the number of applicants exceeded accommodations ten times over. Every available nook and cranny of the school was made serviceable. Maharaja Nundy was overjoyed at the success of the school and gave Mejda another plot of fifteen acres with a large house—called "Madhukam House"—on the outskirts of Ranchi. Here Mejda started a school for *Adivasi* (aborigine) students. The primary school, begun with five students and one teacher, expanded in two years into a grammar school of one hundred students and five teachers. A boys' school was started also in the Puri ashram of Sri Yukteswar. In all of the schools the academic curriculum and spiritual routine were balanced with recreation, sports, and picnics and hikes to nearby scenic spots.

All who had the opportunity to come into contact with Mejda knew that his spiritual ideals and precepts of justice could not be compromised. But his manner was so charming, and his heart so loving, that no one felt rejected or uncomfortable. His sweet smile was always present; and in the warmth of that glow, all hearts and minds were caught. On the other hand, when Mejda decided to get to the bottom of a matter or to make it a point of issue, there was no avoiding the sharpness of his perception. His testing was severe indeed.

The rules and regulations of the Ranchi ashram-school were strict. Rising at five in the morning, the boys lined up outside for group chanting of prayers. After bathing and cleaning their rooms, at six o'clock they again met together for exercises and meditation. Mejda himself taught advanced methods of meditation to boys over twelve years old.

It seemed as though the school's perennial condition was one of barely meeting its financial obligations. The monthly grant from the Maharaja and the nominal room and board fees paid by the students were just enough to make ends meet. But all basic necessities were provided. The students wore the simple, coarsely woven cloth of villagers. Clothing was kept spotlessly clean, as were dormitory quarters and the ashram grounds.

Under Mejda's watchful eye the ashram-school flourished in an orderly manner. No undisciplined behavior escaped his attention; but he approached every infraction with love and understanding. He would draw the offender aside and explain to him clearly the consequences of his wrong action. He was so compassionate and understanding in his discipline that students were prompted to be good from the force of his love rather than fear of punishment.

Mejda was like a father and a friend to the boys. No one ever felt any hesitation to approach him with a personal problem or difficulty, knowing he would always be sympathetic and helpful. He participated with the boys in all their activities, even games. His presence in the school was a constant source of inspiration, hope, and reliance.

To all the students and teachers Mejda's word was like the word of God. He constantly spoke of the need for seeking God, for uniting heart, mind, and soul with Him. And he inspired everyone to make that sincere spiritual effort. All those who came in contact with Mejda felt his power to open their hearts with a mere touch or look. They used to say that, like Jesus Christ, he could infuse his own spirituality into the hearts of his disciples—to the degree that they themselves were receptive.

Mejda taught that the very basis of spiritual development was right behavior: *yama* and *niyama,* the moral code based upon religious statutes from time immemorial. And along with right behavior, he urged the harmonious development of body and mind. He said that a sick body aggravates the mind; a lazy mind destroys both health and spiritual development. To attain a significant degree of realization, one needs a sound mind in a healthy body, and a positive mental attitude.

Mejda was acquainted with the priest of the Ranchi Catholic Church. They frequently exchanged their views on religion and found a broad basis for understanding and agreement. The good Father came often to the school, on invitation from Mejda, to explain the Bible to the boys; and, as a consequence, the Bhagavad Gita was taught in comparative religion classes in the Catholic school.

In 1920, Mejda was invited to lecture at the Congress of Religious Liberals in Boston, Massachusetts. His guru told him he must go. The teachers and students of the Ranchi schools felt his absence keenly. They counted the days until his return. How they missed his words of wisdom, his thoughtfulness for their welfare, his loving touch that took away their pains and sorrows!

The passing of Maharaja Manindra Chandra Nundy in 1929, while Mejda was in America, left the Ranchi schools without their major source of income. The kind Maharaja had continued his donations to the school even though he himself was in debt. After his passing, creditors filed suit against his properties, but the Maharaja's son, Sri Shrish Chandra Nundy, had earlier transferred the Ranchi property to the name of his wife to save it from receivership.

This serious situation became more critical when in 1930 the British government stopped its nominal financial aid to the Ranchi school because many of the teachers were supporting India's protest for independence. Mejda had always promoted the idea of a free, independent India. Better an impoverished free India than a subjugated nation financed by a foreign country. Had Mejda not dedicated his life entirely to the spiritual path, India would have found in him one of her foremost leaders for independence. So the Ranchi schools were ultimately deprived of all outside financial aid. Madhukam had to be discontinued. Mejda sought financial assistance from many people in India, but none was forthcoming. It wasn't until 1935, when Mejda returned to India, that the Brahmacharya Vidyalaya was reestablished on a sound financial basis. He had saved income from his lectures in America and collected donations from his followers there. With these funds and a donation from Father, he purchased the land from Sri Shrish Chandra Nundy, and secured the future of the school by incorporating it.

I will never forget Mejda's return to Ranchi in 1935. Many of his former students came to welcome him back. How could those who were not his relatives love and respect him so deeply? They offered their devotion so wholeheartedly that I was moved to tears. I saw the years roll back: again his transfiguring presence lifted their burdens and renewed their inspiration.

Mejda Goes to America

In 1920 Mejda received an invitation to speak at the International Congress of Religious Liberals in Boston, organized by the American Unitarian Association. At the time, he was busily engaged in expanding and making improvements in his Ranchi school. But he had a broader work to do, and Sri Yukteswar Giri told him it was time to fulfill that mission.

Mejda was happy with the thought of traveling to America. He always felt there was some special link between India and America; and that combining the spiritual knowledge of the East with the industrial and scientific technology of the West would give the world a golden, middle path of balanced living. He sometimes cited the fact that Columbus reached America when actually he had sailed for India.

In spite of his enthusiasm, Mejda was apprehensive. He had never lectured in English before. He sought out

Sri Yukteswarji and told him of his grave doubts. "English or no English, your words on Yoga shall be heard in the West," his gurudeva assured him.

Father was shocked when Mejda told him of his plans. He could not believe that his son would be so far removed from him; there was fear in his heart that he would never see Mejda again. Sternly he asked him, "Who is going to finance your trip?"

Mejda replied with a smile, "Maybe God will inspire you to help me."

"No! Never!" Father answered, with an anguished look.

So Mejda was greatly surprised the next day when Father gave him a check for a large amount. "I am giving this money to you, not as your father, but as a disciple of Lahiri Mahasaya. Go to the West: preach there the liberating, universal science of *Kriya Yoga*."

Mejda was deeply moved. "I will do my best. I have never entertained a single thought of anything but serving God. I pray His blessings will be with me."

Still, there was no little trepidation in Mejda's mind about leaving the spiritual atmosphere of India to brave the materialistic environment of the West. One morning he prayed and wept for a sign of God's blessing. There was a knock at the door. Upon opening it, he was astounded to see standing before him a youthful ascetic dressed only in a loincloth. The saint entered the room. For a few moments no word was spoken. Seeing that the holy man resembled Lahiri Mahasaya in his youth, Mejda's heart leaped with the realization that he must be the great Babaji!

"Yes, I am Babaji," the sage answered, though

Mejda had not spoken. "Our Heavenly Father has heard your prayer. He commands me to tell you: Follow the behest of your guru and go to America. Fear not; you shall be protected. You are the one I have chosen to spread the message of *Kriya Yoga* in the West. Long ago I met your guru Yukteswar at a Kumbha Mela; I told him then I would send you to him for training." Mejda was thrilled to receive this personal assurance from the deathless Mahavatar. Babaji gave him instructions and blessings, and then left as unobtrusively as he had come.

On the appointed day of departure in August, with the blessings of his gurudeva and the good wishes of all, Mejda sailed for America on *The City of Sparta,* the first passenger liner to go to America after the First World War. I was to have gone as his companion, and my papers were ready, too. But fate intervened: an unexpected family matter required my presence at home.

Mejda's lecture on "The Science of Religion" was received enthusiastically by the assemblage of great thinkers and devoted representatives of all religions attending the Boston conference. Mejda was flooded with requests for further lectures and speaking engagements, and soon he had a following in Boston. In all his lectures he advocated the time-tested, universal methods of Yoga for harmonious development of body, mind, and soul; and showed the ancient lineage and foundation of Yoga in the Bhagavad Gita.

From Boston, he traveled cross-country, lecturing. The impact of his teachings was gradually felt throughout America. Self-Realization Fellowship centers were established in the principal cities, including New York, Philadelphia, and Denver. In 1925 he founded the international headquarters for his worldwide mission atop

Mt. Washington in Los Angeles. The success of his work was highly acclaimed in major American newspapers; it was something of a phenomenon in religion in America.

From the international headquarters, his message in time spread to many countries in Europe, Latin America, Africa, and Asia. Yoganandaji's lifelong *sadhana* was the irresistible force behind his words, and his spirit took root deep in the hearts of his students worldwide. Hundreds of thousands were inspired by his life and teachings.

Mejda believed in and taught the precept that all people of the world are children of the one Heavenly Father. This indisputable truth, if not forgotten by mankind, is the basis for universal brotherhood and unity.

From 1920 until 1930 Father sent Mejda four hundred rupees every month. It was my task to purchase and mail the drafts. Once someone in America criticized Mejda: "You came to America only to make money."

"You would be surprised," Mejda replied, "to know that during these years I have earned nothing for myself. I came here only to teach a spiritual truth. Much of the support for my work came from my own home."

Father had at one time written to Mejda: "How long should I continue to send money?"

Mejda replied: "Please continue. I will let you know when I do not need your help any longer. This I promise you: Every rupee will come back for the welfare of your family."

CHAPTER 12

Return to India in 1935

Homecoming

In 1935, Mejda returned to his beloved India and his innumerable friends and devotees here, but for only a year. During this period he travelled extensively, spreading the Yogoda message, establishing centers throughout his homeland, and initiating many reforms in the Yogoda work, which had long felt the lack of his guiding presence.

One bright morning in that year, our house was abustle with festive mood. Many of our relatives had come to Calcutta; in every room incense sticks were burning. Beautiful decorations hung in abundance from the stairs to the entrance; artistic paintings of rice-paste decorated the pillars and walls. This was the day of Mejda's homecoming: A *sannyasi* son was returning from America for a heartwarming reunion with his father.

A large crowd of relatives, friends, and disciples gathered at Howrah Railway Station to welcome Mejda. In the crowd was the young Maharaja Shrish Chandra Nundy, son of the Maharaja of Kasimbazar, and his entourage. Slowly the Bombay Mail pulled into the station; Mejda alighted from his coach. We garlanded him profusely, then escorted him to the car. The Maharaja was seated beside him. Other friends and relatives climbed into following cars. Our youngest brother, Bishnu Charan, drove Mejda and the Maharaja with the greatest of enthusiasm. I myself rode on a motorcycle, heading the long procession like a pilot! On arrival at Father's home,* conch shells were blown, flowers and rice were strewn over Mejda's path, devotional melodies filled the house with bright, uplifting music.

Then Mejda stood before Father. They embraced one another as though their reunion were a gift from God. Tears of joy flowed copiously—there was not a dry eye in the crowd. Even our stoic father was occasionally wiping his eyes.

First Visit to Ranchi

After a few days with the devotees in Calcutta, and with his guru, Sri Yukteswarji, in nearby Serampore, Mejda made plans to travel by car to Ranchi. He was eager to see the school. Swami Satyananda† was in charge of the school and ashram. Mejda and he were looking forward to meeting again after such a long separation.

Mr. Richard Wright, who had accompanied Mejda on the journey to India, drove Mejda in the V-8 Ford they had brought with them from America. Our eldest sister Roma, Bishnu, and Tulsida rode with them. Prokas Das (who later became Swami Atmananda), Himangshu (a national gymnast champion), and our sister's son Binu rode with me in my car, an eight-cylinder Buick. The tires on my car were new, but the two spares I carried were worthless. I prayed all the way to Ranchi that I wouldn't need them.

Mejda was proudly confident of the American-made tires on his Ford, purported to be self-sealing against punctures, and proof against blowouts. Alas, the American manufacturers had not been informed about our Indian roads. One tire blew out before we reached

* At that time he was living at 4/2 Ram Mohan Roy Road.

† Formerly Manomohan Mazumdar.

Burdwan; Mr. Wright and I put on the spare. About seven miles past Asansol another tire succumbed—victim of a puncture from an iron shoe lost by some bullock as it pulled its cart along the road. We now were in dire straits indeed, for the Ford did not carry more than one spare.

Mejda and the other members of our party found a shady spot under a roadside tree to partake of the delicious picnic lunch prepared by Roma. Mr. Wright, Bishnu, and I returned to Asansol in my car to seek assistance from an acquaintance of Bishnu's whose name had providentially occurred to us while we were discussing our dilemma. The kind gentleman listened sympathetically to our tale and immediately called a local shopkeeper to arrange delivery of two new tires to his house. He also kindly loaned us money for the purchase, since we did not have sufficient funds—we promised to repay him on our return journey.

Night was falling by the time we returned to the crippled Ford and fitted the new tires. We resumed our journey in gay spirits. It was very late when we reached the hills of Hazaribagh. Having been up since dawn, I began to feel drowsy. We had purchased some potato curry from a roadside stand earlier, but the seasoning was so hot with red chilies we hadn't been able to eat it. I told Binu, "When you see my head nod, feed me a bite of that curry." It was an effective stimulant! Every time I felt sleepy, I ate a little more curry. Thus I successfully negotiated the climbing, winding road to the Ranchi plateau. Dick had driven far ahead of us. Alone in the night in that jungly, unpopulated area, my prayers had become more fervent that our tires would hold. They did. Finally, at three in the morning, we pulled through the gates of the Ranchi school.

After a long vigil, and having given up hope of our arrival that night, Swami Satyananda and the teachers and students had fallen asleep. But the noise of the cars on the drive awakened them. With shouts of joy and greeting, they came pouring out of the building. What a lovely sight was this joyous reunion. Mejda and Satyananda embraced warmly, tears streaming down their cheeks. For how many years they had been separated! The reception lasted until dawn lighted the eastern sky.

A Firm Financial Foundation for the Ranchi School

While in Ranchi, Mejda was confronted with the grave financial situation threatening the school. Satyanandaji told him that after the death of Maharaja Manindra Chandra Nundy, the first patron of the Ranchi school, his estate had been taken over by the Court of Wards. The Maharaja's generous monthly grant had therefore been automatically stopped. The adopted son of the Maharaja, Shrish Chandra Nundy, had fortunately transferred the title of the Ranchi property to his wife's name to save the school land. "In an effort to provide an income for the school," Satyanandaji continued, "the teachers and I formed a registered body so that we could solicit donations. We named the society 'Brahmacharya Sangha,' and the Brahmacharya Vidyalaya has been merged into this society. Despite many sacrifices, we have barely been able to raise sufficient funds to keep the school in operation."

"This means the school is now under the control of the society's officers and that I no longer have any jurisdiction," Mejda replied. "In any case, please dissolve the

Brahmacharya Sangha. I shall again build up the school."

Satyanandaji agreed, but the other teachers balked. They did not want to relinquish their private interests. Were it not for the grim, threatening appearance of Bishnu and Himangshu, both national gymnastic champions, the teachers would not have acquiesced. In the end they agreed to accept a compromise payment of rupees 1,200. Taking this amount, they left the school Mejda had founded and started a school of their own some distance away.

Returning to Calcutta, Mejda talked with the Maharaja Shrish Chandra Nundy. The young ruler told Mejda, "As you know, my father's estate is under the Court of Wards till his debts are satisfied. So, though I am ashamed to say it, I must ask rupees 30,000 for the property." (The property was worth rupees 150,000.) Mejda agreed to the price. The question then was how to raise thirty thousand rupees? Mejda had no choice but to ask Father for assistance. "If you do not help me, I will not be able to buy the school property. My lifelong dream which found fulfillment in this school will be shattered. The climate is ideal, and you and the family can go there from time to time for retreat."

Father had a keen interest in helping educational and health-care institutions, remembering his own hardships as a youth. He sent money anonymously to many such organizations. He was also the chief patron of the competitive-sports programs organized by Mejda in earlier years at Greer Park. His generous donations met all expenses.

Father similarly supported Mejda's Yogoda Satsanga Brahmacharya Vidyalaya in Ranchi in its hour of need.

Sadhana Mandir, Mejda's first ashram

First site of Yogoda Satsanga Brahmacharya Vidyalaya, founded in March 1917, in Dihika, West Bengal

Students and teachers of Brahmacharya Vidyalaya, Kasimbazar Palace, Ranchi, soon after the school was founded. *(Seated, left center)* Shastri Mahasaya, *(center)* Maharaja Manindra Chandra Nundy (patron of school), *(center right)* Mejda, who was then Swami Yogananda

Mejda's return to India, 1935, Howrah Railway Station, Calcutta. *(Left to right)* Maharaja Shrish Chandra Nundy, Mejda, the author, Bishnu, and part of the crowd of devotees who came to welcome Mejda home.

Mejda and party, along with other pilgrims, at the Kumbha Mela in Allahabad, 1936

Mejda and party during 1935 visit to old family home site in Bareilly, where they were received by his childhood friend Dwarka Prasad *(seated, center, next to Mejda),* and his family. *(Standing, center, left to right)* The author, Mr. Richard Wright, and Bishnu Ghosh.

Mejda and party, 1935, on site of family's ancestral home in Ichapur. Of the original estate, only an empty field and one tree remained.

He was proud of Mejda's accomplishments in America and of the spiritual understanding and growth he had given to hundreds of thousands through his tireless work. He gladly gave Mejda ten thousand rupees toward the purchase price of the property for the Ranchi school.

Mejda had also written to his Self-Realization Fellowship organization in America. In those early years, Self-Realization had very limited means. But timely donations arrived. The remaining twenty thousand rupees, and additional funds to help offset the difficult financial situation confronting the school and to place it on a firm foundation, came from Mr. James J. Lynn* and other devotees in America. The Maharaja Shrish Chandra Nundy was truly grieved to take the money as remuneration for the Ranchi estate, but he had no choice; he was heavily indebted to his father's creditors.

I returned to Ranchi with the Maharaja's secretary to register the deed. My wife, our two small sons, and Bishnu accompanied me. Mejda told me not to let Bishnu drive because he was fiercely competitive and had a tendency to drive recklessly. He had never allowed Bishnu to drive the Ford. When our work in Ranchi was finished and we were en route to Calcutta, Bishnu was brooding because I wouldn't permit him to drive. So finally I let him take the wheel. As we turned off Grand Trunk Road to cross the Bally Bridge, another car, driven by a European, came from behind and overtook us with a rush of speed. Bishnu was irate and immediately took up the chase. I regretted that I had not heeded Mejda's orders. In repeated reckless attempts to

* Later, this revered devotee became Rajarsi Janakananda, first spiritual successor to Paramahansa Yogananda.

overtake the car, we barely missed colliding with oncoming cars. The Maharaja's secretary and I pleaded with Bishnu to slow down; but he paid not the slightest attention. All we could do was pray. Finally, at the intersection of Manicktala and Upper Circular Road, not far from our home, Bishnu got his opportunity and passed the car, hurling a look of determined defiance and triumph at the driver. We heaved a sigh of relief: God had saved our lives! When we told Mejda of the incident, he was, of course, justly angry.

Richard Wright

Mr. Richard Wright, mentioned earlier as Mejda's companion on his trip to India, and on his first visit to Ranchi, is the brother of Sri Daya Mata.* He drove Mejda in the V-8 Ford through Europe prior to their arrival in India, and did much of the driving in India—no mean task by anyone's standards, considering the roads in those days! He also took on numerous duties to help Mejda during Mejda's heavy schedule of lecturing, meeting with devotees, and administrative work for the Yogoda Society. After each of Mejda's lectures, for example, Mr. Wright would answer inquiries and take down the names of the persons interested in becoming students of the Yogoda/Self-Realization teachings.

Once when Mejda was lecturing in Madras, Mr. Wright and I were standing at the back of the hall. He was deeply absorbed in Mejda's talk. Then he quietly remarked to me: "He's like a different person when he's

* As spiritual successor to Paramahansa Yogananda, Daya Mataji is the present *Sanghamata* ("Mother of the Society") and president of Self-Realization Fellowship/Yogoda Satsanga Society of India; a disciple of Paramahansaji for almost fifty years, since 1931. See Chapter 13. *(Publisher's Note)*

lecturing." He mentioned this because when Mejda was lecturing, he radiated tremendous power and wisdom; at other times he was simple and joyous like a divine child.

Mr. Wright was extraordinary. I had never met such a hardworking and obedient young man. Even if we returned late at night from a strenuous engagement, or came home weary from an extended tour, he never missed any opportunity to serve Mejda, and never failed to write in his diary. Not only was I impressed with his conscientious performance of every assignment, I was delighted to see that he could eat any of the Indian foods offered to him without the ill effects that Westerners usually experience from the highly seasoned dishes. He was never sick or indisposed.

Mr. Wright had a wonderful, open sense of humor. When he saw that I was sleeping with a large oblong pillow, such as is commonly used in India (excellent for supporting one's arm and leg when sleeping on one's side), he teased me: "I thought you were hiding someone in your bed. I looked inside the pillowcase, but saw it was just a long pillow." Soon Mr. Wright found out how comfortable it was, and thereafter he often playfully tried to snatch my pillow! We developed a fast friendship. I was deeply touched one day when he said, "We like each other very much."

Mr. Wright was of fair complexion, tall and slim, and very alert and intelligent. To tell the truth, I have met very few such good-natured and painstakingly dutiful young men as he.

One day I took Mejda to Serampore; when we came back we couldn't find Mr. Wright. Mejda asked where he was, and was told that he had gone to see a circus. Mejda asked me to find him and bring him back home at once. At the time there were three circuses in Calcutta, and when I told Mejda I didn't know which one he was attending, Mejda gave me some money for admission tickets and told me: "Go to each one until you find Dick."

At the first circus I looked carefully for Mr. Wright in the large crowd, but he wasn't there. At the next one I quickly spotted his light-complexioned face among the spectators in the bleachers. I made my way to his side and told him that Mejda had sent me to bring him home. I was sure he must have been disappointed to be pulled away from the performance, but he obeyed the summons immediately and without question.

When he returned home, Mejda scolded him sternly: "You will spoil the work I am trying to do on this visit to India if you are not here when I need you." He then asked Mr. Wright to take dictation on some urgent matters. I went to my room. When I returned much later I saw that the diligent young man was still busy typing. Ordinarily Mejda expressed the heart of a child, showering all with sweet, loving kindness. But this alone does not perfect a disciple; so when necessary, Mejda also knew how to be a strict disciplinarian.

Kriya Initiation in Calcutta, and a Public Satsanga in Ranchi

Many devotees in Calcutta wished to receive *Kriya Yoga* initiation from Mejda. To create an enclosed hall, a tin roof was placed over a portion of Bishnu's large open-air gymnasium in the north section of the compound of our father's house at 4/2 Ram Mohan Roy Road. On the day of the initiation, Mejda asked the devotees to be seated on a large carpet that had been spread in the improvised hall. He called me and asked me to demonstrate for him how I was practicing the *Kriya* technique. I had often meditated with Father and observed his practice of *Kriya,* and on occasion had asked him to check my *Kriya.* After I had done *Kriya* for Mejda, he told me I was performing the technique correctly. During the ceremony he asked me to demonstrate the technique for the new initiates, while he personally bestowed the sacred *diksha* (initiation). It gave me immense joy that Mejda was pleased with my *Kriya Yoga* practice.

During one of Mejda's visits to Ranchi, it was noted that a large conference of local rajas was to be held there. A huge *pandal** had been erected, and an area cordoned off. Seeing the arrangements—and drawing upon his lecturing experiences in America — Mejda seized the opportunity and expressed the wish to hold public lectures in those facilities, as soon as the conference ended, so as to raise funds for the school. An added attraction was to be a physical culture demonstration by Bishnu and his students.

Tickets and handbills announcing the program were printed. The tickets were sold for rupees 10, 5, and 2; general admission (standing) was four annas. Several large picture-posters, such as had been used for Mejda's lecture tours in the U.S., had been brought by him to India. Mr. Wright and I attached some of the posters to the front and back of the car, and drove slowly through Ranchi distributing the handbills. The notices proclaimed that Swami Yogananda, recently returned from America, would lecture on Hindu religion. And that there would also be an extraordinary gymnastic demon-

* An open-air tent-like structure.

stration by Bishnu Ghosh, nationally known physical culture director, and his students.

Bishnu and his party arrived from Calcutta a day early, and were enjoying their stay in the ashram. By chance Mr. Wright and I drove past the conference grounds the following morning, the day our program was to be held. The conference had concluded, and we were shocked to see that the *pandal* and surrounding enclosure had been almost totally removed. When we inquired why the structure was being dismantled, the contractor said that no one had made arrangements with him for an additional engagement. We were in a terrible predicament. We argued that all the reserved seating had been sold. If the people arrived in the evening to find only an open field, they would accuse us of fraud.

The attention of a gentleman standing nearby was attracted by our animated conversation with the contractor. He came over to us and asked what was the matter. We repeated the details of our dilemma to him. After listening to our sad tale, he introduced himself as the Raja of Ratu, and told us he would do everything he could to help us because he himself would very much like to see Swami Yogananda and hear him speak. The kind Raja wrote a letter and told us to take it to his palace. It authorized us to take from his warehouse whatever materials we needed to prepare a suitable place for our evening program. He also told us he would make immediate arrangements for laborers to help us construct a *pandal* and enclosure—all at his own expense. We expressed our deepest gratitude.

Mr. Wright and I had to make several trips to the palace—a distance of about six miles—to bring to the site all the materials we would need. The Ford Mejda had brought from America proved wonderfully functional for this purpose: The large trunk in the back of the car opened up in such a way that it provided a spacious carrying area.

We had only till five o'clock to complete all necessary arrangements. We worked feverishly. It was about three o'clock when we paused briefly to get some food at a nearby foodstall. But, the noonday meal being over, they had nothing left to offer us but tea and biscuits. The *pandal* was constructed, the enclosure erected, ground covering provided, chairs set up, and the ticket counter in place near the entrance. We finished at four o'clock.

When we tried to start the car to return to the ashram, we saw that inquisitive boys had played with the gears and put them out of order. Fortunately, I knew a little about the mechanism and fixed it on the spot. By the time we reached the ashram it was 4:30. Mejda was anxious and began to scold us for being absent since morning, for we had not had time nor the opportunity to send word to let him know all that had transpired. When he heard our story and saw my grease-stained hands from repairing the gears, he lovingly consoled us for all we had gone through, and humbly apologized for having upbraided us about our tardy return.

Anandamoyee Ma Visits Ranchi

Anandamoyee Ma (born Nirmala Sundari Bhattacharya, the daughter of a Vaishnava Brahmin family in the village of Kheora, Tripura) has attracted a large following in India. She impartially gives to all the pure love of Divine Mother. She regards all religions equally; thus devotees of many faiths, including Islam, count themselves among her disciples. Dignitaries of many nations, heads of universities, teachers, doctors, artists—those of every profession, or none—have found refuge in her divine love.

When Mejda was in India in 1935, he wanted to meet this exalted woman saint, for he had heard much about her. During one of her visits to Calcutta, she was staying in the Bhawanipore section of the city to attend the marriage ceremony of a relative. Mejda and Mr. Wright went to see her.

I did not accompany them, but when they returned late in the evening, Mejda called me and said, "Anandamoyee Ma has expressed a wish to come to Ranchi to see the school. She has already departed for Jamshedpur and will go directly from there to Ranchi if I can provide a conveyance for her. I want you to drive to Jamshedpur tomorrow and offer to take her to Ranchi the following day. I myself will proceed to Ranchi by train to prepare for her visit. My train will make a brief stop in Jamshedpur tomorrow night at two a.m. You can meet me at the station and let me know definitely if Anandamoyee Ma will come to Ranchi as planned.

"You are also to pick up a sadhu* of the Ramakrishna Mission early tomorrow morning and take him with you to Jamshedpur. I have told him our car is going and we would be happy to give him transportation there."

It took me the rest of the night to get gas and service the car for the long journey. Shortly after four a.m. I started out in the V-8 Ford for the Ramakrishna Mission on Lord Sinha Road to pick up my passenger. From there the trip to Jamshedpur took all day. At the sadhu's

* I regret that the Sadhu Maharaja's name has escaped my memory.

request, we stopped en route at Purulia for some time. Some distance beyond, there was a river dividing the road between Purulia and Jamshedpur. In those days there was no bridge to connect the road. We had to ford the river. Considerable time was spent in trying to engage several persons to help us push the car through the fast-flowing current.

When at last we reached Jamshedpur in the evening, we went first to the house of my niece, Amiya, the daughter of our eldest brother, Ananta. I had assumed that the sadhu was a vegetarian and had offered him only vegetarian food during the day's journey. When Sri Sudhir Bose, Amiya's husband, invited us to dinner and asked the sadhu if he would take non-vegetarian food, I was embarrassed at what I thought was a discourtesy. I was surprised when the sadhu accepted Sudhir's invitation. I had not known, until that day, that monks of the Ramakrishna ashram are not necessarily strict vegetarians.

After dinner I told Sudhir the purpose of our visit to Jamshedpur, and asked him if he knew where Anandamoyee Ma was staying. He inquired and learned that her camp was about four miles away, and that a veritable *mela* (religious fair) had sprung up around her camp.

Sudhir and I took the sadhu to his destination and then made our way to Anandamoyee Ma's camp. We found her surrounded by a large crowd, but sitting quietly, absorbed in the Infinite. A devotee by her side, Srimati Bhramar, continuously chanted the name of Divine Mother. I met with the devotees in charge of Ma's program and told them of her conversation with Swami Yogananda, and that he was now on his way to Ranchi to make preparations for her visit. I had come with the car to take her to Ranchi. I explained to them that I was to meet Swamiji at two a.m., when the train passed through Jamshedpur, to confirm her visit to Ranchi the next day.

They consulted with Anandamoyee Ma — and amongst themselves — and finally told me that the Mother would depart with me for Ranchi in the morning, and that ten or twelve of her devotees would accompany her. I told them that the car would hold only seven passengers, including Sudhir and myself. They then asked me to engage a taxi. I diligently sought out many taxi drivers, but none was willing to make the trip. When confronted with this fact, Ma's devotees reluctantly reduced the size of the party to five: Ma, her husband,* an ocher-clad retired magistrate, Srimati Bhramar, and another devotee. By the time all these arrangements had been made, it was almost two a.m. Sudhir and I rushed to the railroad station and arrived just in time to meet Mejda's train. We found him asleep in a second-class compartment. We awoke him and informed him that we would be driving Anandamoyee Ma and her party to Ranchi in the morning.

From the station, Sudhir and I went back to Ma's camp to finalize arrangements. We were then told that in the morning she would be relocating her camp to the home of a gentleman six or seven miles distant. I was to pick her up there, for which I was given directions. By the time Sudhir and I returned to his house, it was dawn. I had spent a second sleepless night! We washed, breakfasted, and prepared for the trip. When we reached the gentleman's home, a large crowd had already gathered around Ma. She was, as always, absorbed in ecstasy, oblivious to her surroundings. Srimati

* He had become a devout celibate disciple of the revered Mother shortly after their marriage, many years earlier.

Bhramar was by her side, keeping up the unbroken chanting of the name of the Divine Mother. We were asked to wait until *satsanga* had ended, so it wasn't until late in the morning that we were able to start for Ranchi.

We crossed Chaibasa and Chakradharpur, then drove through mountainous country: the roads were steep and had many sharp curves. Driving with caution, we made the passage safely. Bhramar-didi continued her sweet chanting of "Ma, Ma," the whole time, which gave a serene joy to our journey. Finally I was able to speed up to 75 and 80 miles per hour on a flat stretch outside Ranchi. Even so, we did not reach the school until three o'clock in the afternoon.

Mejda and all the teachers and students were anxiously waiting to receive Anandamoyee Ma. I let the guests out and parked the car. Exhausted after my sleepless marathon, I fell asleep on the front seat, one hand still holding the steering wheel.

Anandamoyee Ma delighted in her visit, surrounded by the schoolboys. Herself a divine child, she felt at home in the natural setting and spiritual atmosphere of the ashram-school. There is always about her an aura of divine aloofness, but with Mejda she conversed freely. A sumptuous meal had been prepared and was served outside under the trees. Afterward, Mejda came to the car and roused me. The Mother's devotees wanted to return to Jamshedpur. He had been hoping Anandamoyee Ma would spend the night at the ashram, but her traveling companions insisted they must return that day. Ma, always in a state of ecstasy, lets others care for her and make all arrangements. So Mejda was compelled to ask me to drive the Mother back to Jamshedpur.

"But I haven't slept for two nights and have spent the last two days driving continuously," I reminded him, with no little anxiety. "I might have an accident."

"Dear Gora, you have to drive. The Mother's devotees feel they must return today. Courtesy compels us to take them back to Jamshedpur. They came on my assurance of providing transportation at their convenience. With my prayers to God and with Anandamoyee Ma in the car, rest assured you will not have an accident!"

The Car Runs Without Petrol

Somehow I managed to get up. I washed my face, then picked up our guests and settled them in the car. I was anxious to cross the mountains before dark. Not only was the road very difficult to negotiate, but tigers and bears roamed the forests freely in that area. We drove very fast across the plains, but darkness had set in by the time we started up through the mountain pass. Suddenly I remembered that I had forgotten to get petrol. I had intended to stop on our way out of Ranchi to fill the tank, but in my anxiety and haste I completely forgot. I looked at the gauge; it registered empty! I could do nothing now but pray.

Srimati Bhramar was nauseated from the car's motion on the mountain road, so we were forced to make several stops to let her get out of the car. Armed with tire irons, Sudhir and I stood guard against any possible attack by wild animals. At each of these stops I reflected: "How can the car keep going without petrol?" I kept praying!

I knew it was unsafe to turn off the ignition and let the car roll downhill in neutral, for then one does not have complete control of the vehicle. But I felt I had no choice. On every downgrade I put the car in neutral, turned the ignition key, and coasted. Sudhir gripped the handbrake to slow the car should the regular brakes fail. Thus we traversed the mountainous region and reached Chakradharpur, where we stopped at a petrol pump. I inserted a measuring stick in the gas tank: it was totally empty, and dry. I was amazed that we had been able to cover so much distance on an "empty" tank. Certainly this miracle was the grace of the Lord through Mejda's blessings and Anandamoyee Ma's presence.

We started up once more, but shortly the car began swerving and slipping from side to side. I slowed down, but this did not help steady the car. I was terribly worried because deep ditches ran along both sides of the road. I stopped and got out to check the rear tires, and sank ankle-deep in mud! The headlights lit up two boys ahead standing in the mire with a bicycle between them. The bicycle was so caked with mud, it was impossible even to push it. They asked me for a lift, but when they saw how crowded we already were, they realized they were still "stuck."

I was surprised at the condition of the road, for only hours earlier it had been dry and firm. Then I realized that the *moram* used to resurface roads—which is usually ground into a hard surface by traffic—had gotten wet in a light shower and had turned into a slippery clay. I cleaned the sticky *moram* off my shoes, got back into the car, and carefully drove over that treacherous stretch of road. We then covered the rest of the distance to Jamshedpur without incident. The night was spent—and so was I!—by the time we reached Anandamoyee Ma's camp.

After taking leave of the Mother and her devotees,

Sudhir and I went to his house. Dawn was just breaking. I took some tea and snacks, and then started immediately for Calcutta, faithful Sudhir still by my side. Had it not been for his help and support, I doubt that I could have driven those great distances without sleep. Though I had worn gloves, I nevertheless had large blisters on my hands from gripping the steering wheel over such difficult roads for three days in succession. By the time I reached Calcutta, I was so exhausted that even my voice was failing. I collapsed in bed in the blissful refreshment of sleep.

When Mejda returned to Calcutta, he overwhelmed me with his affection and appreciation. I have never forgotten it. He blessed me and promised: "As long as you live, you need never fear any danger."

The Kumbha Mela at Allahabad

A *Kumbha Mela* was held in Allahabad during the time that Mejda was in India. *Purna* (full) *Kumbha Melas* are held every twelve years in Hardwar, Allahabad, Nasik, and Ujjain. *Ardha* (half) *Kumbhas* are held at six-year intervals at these sites. The one in 1936 was an *Ardha Kumbha.* In January, Richard Wright, Bishnu, Prabhasda, and I went with Mejda to Allahabad to see this fascinating and unparalleled religious fair. We stayed at the home of the late Prasad Das Ghosh, Prabhasda's elder brother. From there we would go to the *Kumbha* site early in the mornings, dressed as warmly as we could to ward off the winter chill. Still we shivered.

The *Kumbha Mela* is a unique and wonderful sight. Words cannot fully describe its impact; it is something to be experienced. Tents are pitched for sadhus on a large sandy tract near the confluence of the Ganges and

Yamuna rivers. Temporary stalls are erected to supply food and other necessities to the hundreds of thousands of pilgrims who come to partake of the spiritual atmosphere and to meet holy men who leave their hermitages, mountain caves, and forest dwellings to attend. The highlight of the *mela* is the *Kumbha* baptism. During astrologically determined auspicious times, sadhus and pilgrims take a holy dip in the *sangam* (the confluence of the rivers) and pray for removal of sins and rededication of their lives to God.

Among the thousands of sadhus who come to the *mela* are the *Nagas,* ascetics with long matted hair who have renounced even their clothing. They protect themselves somewhat from the cold or blistering sun by smearing their bodies with ashes. On the auspicious day of bathing, the *Nagas* are the first to enter the sacred waters. When we arrived at the *Kumbha* the first morning, a large procession of *Naga* sadhus was making its way to the river. The road was lined on either side with ascetics of all faiths, many sitting by small ceremonial fires. The *Naga* leader was seated on an elephant; behind him rode other *Nagas* on elephants and horses—some carried scepters—hundreds followed on foot.

Mr. Wright was busily taking photographs when suddenly a stout *Naga* called out in Hindi that he would break his camera. Mr. Wright asked me, "What did he say?"

"He said he will smash your camera," I told him. "It would be better not to take any more photographs. You already have a few, so you'd better put your camera away for a time." The sadhus are shy of the exploitation they are often subjected to by non-understanding foreigners.

Mejda had asked me to be the keeper of the purse

during our travels. He said, "Money stays with Gora, but Bishnu is a spendthrift." I maintained our accounts carefully, making everyone sign a voucher for funds withdrawn. And I always noted every expenditure. Mejda was pleased with my efficiency, and used to call me his secretary. At the *mela,* as we were moving along with the surging throng of pilgrims, Mejda suddenly handed me some folded rupee notes. "Gora, keep this with you. Someone pressed it into my hand." I looked at the folded money: it consisted of five one-hundred rupee notes. When I told Mejda, he said, "God has given us our traveling expenses."

Prabhasda's mother-in-law was a devout woman. We heard she was at the *mela* and wanted to find her. Her late husband had been a wealthy landlord; they had three daughters, all married. One married a renowned lawyer, the second had married Prabhasda, and the third married Prabhasda's younger brother, Dr. Prakash Ghosh. Following the untimely death of her husband, her eldest daughter also died suddenly, leaving a son and four daughters. The bereft mother-in-law of Prabhasda and Prakash Ghosh gave all her property to her two remaining daughters and moved to Brindaban, birthplace of Lord Krishna, to live the rest of her life in religious austerity and devotion to the Lord. She spent her time chanting the name of God and worshipping in the temples of Brindaban. Occasionally her daughters and their husbands visited her. Once while in Brindaban I also met her and deeply admired her extremely simple life, so sharply in contrast to the wealth and comfort she had enjoyed during her husband's lifetime. Any of her sons-in-law would have provided a comfortable, even luxurious, living for her, but she preferred her life of renunciation, and her humble dwelling in a small room of one of the temples.

Our inquiries about her at the *Kumbha Mela* led us to a small hut. She was seated inside, her clothing and hair still wet from her immersion in the river at dawn. In spite of the biting cold wind and the chill inside her hut, she had not dried her body nor wrapped herself in a warm chuddar. She had undertaken, for the few auspicious days of the *mela,* a prescribed religious austerity that prohibited drying oneself after the holy immersion in the river, and that permitted only one simple meal a day: rice cooked in *ghee* (clarified butter), which she herself had to prepare. We were shivering from the cold in spite of our wraps, and were deeply moved by her stoic penance. After visiting for some time, we offered our *pranams* and departed, returning to our residence. We usually went to Prasad Ghosh's home to take midday food; later in the day we would return to the *mela.*

In the kaleidoscope of the giant crowds were sadhus and ascetics representing all manner of spiritual disciplines: some were lying barebodied on beds of nails or thorns; some had locked themselves in postures of penance, their bodies contorted without seeming strain or stress; some were sitting before small, ceremonial fires giving discourses. But all the while we were looking for the few truly exalted saints who grace the *Kumbha Mela* with their presence. Suddenly a man appeared out of the crowd; we didn't know him. "Come with me if you want to see a real saint," he said.

We crossed the Ganges on a pontoon bridge and made our way through the crowds until we had left behind a greater portion of the *mela.* In a small cluster of huts made of straw and mud, we stopped before a nondescript dwelling and stooped to crawl on all fours through the small entrance. Night had fallen, and the lantern we carried illuminated the inside of the tiny hut. Seated in lotus posture on a pile of straw was a radiant figure, clad only in an ochre cotton cloth; his eyes shining with a divine luster. Mejda immediately whispered to me, "Look at him! He is a genuine saint."

We learned that his name was Kara Patri, and during our conversation he told us of his simple life: he touches neither money nor fire (i.e. never cooks his own food, but eats only fruits and plain foods offered by devotees); he wanders alone along the banks of India's holy rivers. Our guide told us that Kara Patri was a great scholar and taught from the Gita and *Bhagavata.* Mejda asked him: "I don't see any books with you. How do you teach?"

"I don't need them," the saint replied. "I speak from memory to those who wish to hear, or who ask questions about the scriptures." We were filled with the joy of his Self-realization. To this day I remember his serenely glowing face.

Our guide then took us to the other side of the Ganges to visit another remarkable sage who, it was said, had healed many persons of incurable diseases. He was seated on a hillock in front of a ceremonial fire, and was surrounded by his devotees. We climbed the mound and seated ourselves near the sadhu. Mejda asked him about his healing power. The saint replied in Hindi: "What is unusual about it? You also are healing others with the same power." Mejda remained silent. After a short time we bowed respectfully and left. Mejda remarked: "He truly has the power of God."

While we were resting at Prasad Ghosh's home one

afternoon, his second daughter, Chaya, about eight or ten years old, was either playing on the high wall surrounding the house or climbing on it in order to pick the fruit from a nearby tree. She slipped and fell, uttering a piercing cry. We rushed outside and found her lying on the ground, unconscious. She was carried into the house. From her posture, and from the swelling in the spinal area near the waistline, it was feared that she might have fractured some vertebrae. They were going to rush her to the hospital.

Mejda came into the room and asked the weeping mother and relatives to step aside: "Let me see her back." Laying the child face downward, he began to offer silently some prayer or chant as he sprinkled cold water on her back. This process lasted about fifteen or twenty minutes. Then he sat down beside the still form, placed his hand over the injury, and meditated for about half an hour. We all stood silently around them. Suddenly Mejda stood up and took hold of the little girl's hand, and with a sharp jerk, lifted her to her feet. "Get up!" he said. "Nothing has happened. You are all right."

Fully conscious now, Chaya saw everyone staring at her; she became shy and ran over to her mother and buried her face in her mother's sari. Mejda quietly left the house and went to the car to return to the *mela* grounds.

A Happy Journey Back to Calcutta

We left Allahabad at four the next morning on our homeward journey to Calcutta. We had planned a circuitous route, through Agra, Brindaban, Delhi, Meerut (where our late eldest brother, Ananta, had once lived and worked), Bareilly and Gorakhpur (our childhood homes), and Banaras.

I was driving the car that morning. The road was deserted and the sky was just beginning to lighten, when suddenly a car pulled out across the road ahead of us and signaled us to stop. As we halted, several young men wearing turbans, their faces covered by the tails of the turbans, surrounded our car. Mr. Wright, Bishnu, and I were sitting in front. Mejda, Amiya, and Bishnu's wife and children were in the back seat. The men looked at us for a moment then, inexplicably, turned and climbed back into their car and sped away.

In unison we heaved a huge sigh of relief and all began talking at once. Obviously they were *dacoits* (highway thieves) who had intended to rob us; they might also have harmed us. Maybe Mejda's saintly presence dissuaded them; or perhaps the presence of a foreigner in the car confused them. In any case, we were more than they had bargained for!

In Brindaban we stayed at the splendid ashram of Swami Keshabananda, an exalted disciple of Lahiri Mahasaya. He was a tall, strong, and imposing sage with long, matted hair. I took a photograph of the venerable saint with Mejda and Mr. Wright, which was subsequently published in Mejda's *Autobiography of a Yogi.*

While in Brindaban, Mejda wanted to take Mr. Wright into some of the ancient temples. Foreigners were prohibited entrance, so Mejda asked me to dress Mr. Wright in one of my *dhotis* (a plain white cloth wrapped around the waist, draped between the legs, and then tucked up in back), and to put some garlands around his neck. He was so tall that the *dhoti,* which normally reaches low on the calves, came only to his knees. Hiding our smiles at his ludicrous appearance, we solemly visited the temples. When Brahmin priests objected, Mejda explained that Mr. Wright could not be considered a "foreigner" as he was a converted Hindu. We encountered many foreign tourists outside the temples, and in every case they were staring in astonishment at Mr. Wright's appearance. Finally he could take no more: blushing and ill-at-ease, he lowered his head and quickly made his way to the car!

We proceeded without further incident to Delhi and then to Meerut, where we visited the house formerly occupied by Ananta. From there we went to Bareilly and visited Mejda's boyhood friend, Dwarka Prasad. After leaving Bareilly we went to Gorakhpur and then on to Banaras.

On the stretch to Banaras I drove all night. It rained so hard I was forced to use a hand-held spotlight to help me see along the slippery, muddy road, and to read the roadsigns. The only support I got from the other members of our party was the sound of contented snoring. We reached Banaras at dawn. We wanted to go to the famous Banaras Hindu University, but I was at a loss to find our way. The streets were still deserted at that early hour. We finally made our way to the house of one of Bishnu's students named Mani Roy, a director of Physical Education at the university. The following day he took us to the residence of Pandit Mahamanya Madan Mohan Malaviya, the university's founder and principal. At his home, we met the famous Rama Murti, known for his physical prowess. He had performed such feats as letting an elephant stand on his chest. Unfortunately, during a demonstration in which a two-ton roller was being pulled across his chest, it slipped onto his leg and crushed it. The limb had to be amputated. Sri Malaviya had kindly taken Rama Murti into his own home.

While we were in Banaras, we visited the home of Lahiri Mahasaya, a hallowed shrine indeed, and the temple of Lord Vishwanath. We then proceeded to Calcutta.

The Mahasamadhi of Swami Sri Yukteswar

As soon as we reached Calcutta after our *Kumbha Mela* tour, Mejda wanted to go to Serampore to see Sri Yukteswar, but was disappointed to learn that his gurudeva had already gone to Puri. Soon after, on March 8, Mejda and I were at Father's house when he got news that one of Sri Yukteswar's disciples in Calcutta, Atul Chowdhury, had received a telegram that day from a brother disciple in Puri. It said: "Come to Puri at once." Mejda was anxious at the implications of the message; but instead of leaving that night on the train to Puri, he said we would get some railway passes from Father and would go the next night. I did not understand why, at the time.* The next day, before our departure for Puri, a telegram signed by Atul Chowdhury was delivered to Mejda at Father's house: "Come quickly. Giriji Maharaj never so ill."

That evening, March 9, Mejda, Richard Wright, and I set out by train from Calcutta; we arrived at the Puri

* Paramahansa Yogananda wrote in *Autobiography of a Yogi:*

"As I was about to leave Father's house for the train [on March 8], a divine voice spoke within.

"'Do not go to Puri tonight. Thy prayer cannot be granted.'

"'Lord,' I said, grief-stricken, 'Thou dost not wish to engage with me in a "tug-of-war" at Puri, where Thou wilt have to deny my incessant prayers for Master's life. Must he, then, depart for higher duties at Thy behest?'

"In obedience to the inner command, I did not leave that night for Puri." *(Publisher's Note)*

station the following morning. Mejda anxiously asked me: "Gora, do you think he is still alive?"

"Certainly," I replied. "When we reach the ashram we will see that he is alive."

"Last night," Mejda continued, "I saw two lights hovering before me. I know Gurudeva has left his body."* Mejda wept profusely, and repeated again and again, "I should not have delayed coming to Puri."

When we entered the ashram and learned that our worst fears were true, we all broke down in tears. Sri Yukteswarji's form, seated in the lotus posture and leaning against the wall of his room, gave us the impression he was in deep meditation. Mejda was inconsolable.

We learned from Atulya Babu that when he was preparing the telegram to send to Mejda, Giriji Maharaj asked to see it. In Atul's prepared message he had used the phrase "seriously ill." Giriji asked him to change that to "never so ill." Mejda wept again and said that he would never excuse himself that he had come a day too late.

Later, Mejda asked Mr. Wright to remain in the room with Sri Yukteswar's body while we went to the nearby seashore to bathe in the ocean and offer prayers

* In *Autobiography of a Yogi,* Paramahansaji gives a full account of that experience: ". . . while the train roared toward Puri, a vision of Sri Yukteswar appeared before me. He was sitting, very grave of countenance, with a light on each side.

"'Is it all over?' I lifted my arms beseechingly.

"He nodded, then slowly vanished.

"As I stood on the Puri train platform the following morning, still hoping against hope, an unknown man approached me.

"'Have you heard that your Master is gone?' He left me without another word; I never discovered who he was....in diverse ways my guru was trying to convey to me the devastating news." *(Publisher's Note)*

before the funeral rites. Taking a dip in the sea is an act of piety engaged in by all pilgrims who come to the holy city of Puri. During our absence, Mr. Wright apparently had to leave the room for a brief time. When we returned, we saw that someone had removed the *navaratna* (a nine-jeweled bangle) from Sri Yukteswarji's arm. Mejda scolded his young disciple severely for the momentary lapse in his vigil.

We dug a large square sepulcher in the ashram garden and lined it with bricks and mortar, then covered the bottom with two feet of salt. The ancient solemn burial rites for swamis were conducted by Mejda, and we carefully lowered Sri Yukteswarji's body, still seated in lotus posture, into the crypt—his body facing toward the temple of Lord Jagannath.* When the tomb had been covered, we constructed on the site a temporary bamboo *samadhi mandir* (a shrine in memory of a holy person).

During the burial, Mr. Wright was taking motion pictures to preserve for posterity the last view of the great Guru's mortal form. Atulya Babu, in anguish over the loss of his guru, implored Mr. Wright, "Stop your camera, please. We have lost him forever. Never will we see him again!"

Before leaving Puri, Mejda summoned Sudhir, an ex-student of the Brahmacharya Vidyalaya in Ranchi, who had lovingly and faithfully served Sri Yukteswarji for many years. Mejda initiated him into *sannyas*. He gave Sudhir the ocher cloth of renunciation and the name Swami Sevananda, meaning "divine bliss through selfless service."

Mejda was the spiritual heir of Sri Yukteswarji, ap-

* The Lord in His aspect as "Ruler of the Universe." The ancient Jagannath Temple of Puri is considered one of the holiest shrines in India.

pointed as such by Giriji Maharaj himself. As Giriji had instructed him to do, Mejda took full charge of the Puri ashram under the Yogoda Satsanga Society of India. The society had been started by Sri Yukteswar and later organized and legally registered by Mejda. When Mejda was in Puri, he made Swami Sevananda the society's representative in charge of the Puri Yogoda Ashram. Giriji Maharaj had founded the ashram years earlier in his family name of Karar. But later, when he had bequeathed the ashram to Mejda, and the Yogoda Society became a registered entity, the ashram was called Yogoda Ashram. Swami Sevananda, at Mejda's direction, had the ashram legally registered in that name.

A few months after Sri Yukteswar Giri's *mahasamadhi,* Mejda returned to America. Our hearts were broken when he left us.

CHAPTER 13

The Last Years and an Ongoing Mission

Founding a Yogoda Center in Calcutta

After Mejda had returned to America in 1936, I traveled abroad to Vienna, in 1937, for an operation to remove a malignant tumor from my stomach. The operation was a success, and I returned to my family in Calcutta. In 1942 Father passed away in his residence at 4/2 Ram Mohan Roy Road. His death was an irreparable loss to our family. In his will, he bequeathed to Bishnu the house on Ram Mohan Roy Road. I was fortunate to receive the house at 4 Garpar Road, which had been consecrated by the devotion of our father and by Mejda's early *sadhana* there. Mejda wrote to me from America a few years later, suggesting that I start a meditation center there. He had written in his letters: "It is the place where I found God," and where "a worldwide movement has started which is continuously developing."

I began holding regular, weekly meetings. A large number of devotees responded. Every Tuesday evening we gathered in the drawing room. I read from the Bhagavad Gita and from Mejda's writings, and we had periods of meditation, *bhajan,* and *kirtan.* Swami Atmananda, from Yogoda Math at Dakshineswar, used to come with his party. After the center had been meeting for some time, Mejda wrote: "I cannot tell you what happiness it gives me that you have begun a Yogoda

Satsanga Center at 4 Garpar. If you will manage the center for three years, you will be entitled to a passage to America to visit our international headquarters in Los Angeles." By that time, Mejda was planning another visit to India, but those plans had to be postponed repeatedly. And then Mejda passed away suddenly. Our Yogoda Garpar Center had been running about four or five years when Mejda entered *mahasamadhi.* I was unfortunate not to have been able to go to America to see him there.

Mejda had bought a plot of land from Tulsida, at the rear of Tulsi's home, site of his early ashram there. Soon after Mejda's *mahasamadhi,* a small hall was constructed on that plot, and Swami Atmananda relocated the center from 4 Garpar to this new site. A devotee of Mejda's, Dr. Saroj Das, who was a renowned scholar of philosophy and a classmate of our cousin, Prabhas Ghosh, was placed in charge of the center.* We hold services there every Saturday. I open the meetings with recitation of the Sanskrit invocation, "Brahmanandam." Following a period of meditation, passages from Mejda's writings and the Bhagavad Gita are read. Some Yoga *bhajans* (devotional songs) are sung by me. And I close the meetings with the chanting of "Namo Namaste" (complete bowing down to God), and distribution of *prasad,* blessed sweets. We also observe the birth and *mahasamadhi* anniversaries of Mejda, and the birthday of Lahiri Mahasaya, and the autumnal equinox in memory of Sri Yukteswarji. Large crowds of devotees assemble on these holy occasions. In this way we have carried on, and fulfilled Mejda's wish for a center in Calcutta.

* Yogoda Satsanga Society of India, and, in particular, the Yogoda Garpar Center, sustained a great loss with the passing of the devout and faithful Dr. Saroj Das on March 2, 1978. *(Publisher's Note)*

A Samadhi Mandir for Swami Sri Yukteswar

In 1950, Mejda wrote to me: "Gora, remember when I was in India, I used to call you my secretary? I would like you to undertake construction of a temple over the burial site of my beloved Gurudeva, to whom I owe everything. If God wills, I wish to bring many devotees from America to spiritual India; but before we visit, I want a beautiful *samadhi mandir* constructed in his memory."

When Mejda had come to India in 1935, he had been impressed with the construction work I had supervised at 4 Garpar Road. I had added a third story to the building. He was able to look inside a person and see what capabilities were there. He saw I had an inherent ability for construction, so he entrusted me with building the *samadhi mandir* of Swami Sri Yukteswar.

Though I was having a difficult time making ends meet in supporting my family, and my sons were not employed, I wanted to fulfill Mejda's request. I left aside my artwork in Calcutta and went to Puri to undertake this task. I took Dhirajda with me. He was my second maternal uncle's eldest son, a retired accountant who had taken *sannyas* and the name of Swami Dhirananda.* Together we opened an account at the State Bank of India in Puri, with funds sent by Mejda from America for construction of the temple. Dhirajda maintained the accounts, and I supervised construction.

Swami Sevanandaji was in charge of the ashram, as assigned by Mejda. A Brahmin boy, Rabinarayan, had come to Puri as a tuberculosis patient; and when he was cured, Sevananda had allowed him to remain in the ash-

* Not to be confused with the Swami Dhirananda who was formerly Basukumar Bagchi, Mejda's childhood friend.

ram to assist with odd jobs and errands. Rabinarayan was a help to me in locating masons and the materials needed for construction of the temple. He often requested me to commend him and praise his work in my letters to Mejda. I did write to Mejda how much he had helped me and that he was a very nice boy.

Mejda was greatly concerned with all details of the plans and the work, and wrote many letters of inquiry in which he expressed his ideas. We didn't have a definite plan to start with; it evolved from inspiration as we progressed with the work.

Mejda wrote: "Be sure to put on top the golden lotus, which is our symbol." I went back to Calcutta, and with the help of an artist friend drew up plans for a five-foot lotus with individual petals, and a frame to hold the petals in place. We took the plans to Kansari Para, a village of coppersmiths, and had the lotus made of copper. When the temple was completed, I bolted the frame in place and attached the lotus petals. I also gave careful attention to completion of the inside of the mandir: construction of an altar and placement of a marble relief of the beloved *Jnanavatar,* and finishing touches provided by decorative mosaic tile. When the work was completed, I sent Mejda pictures of the temple, its interior, and the lotus made of copper. I included a complete set of drawings to show how the lotus was constructed and fitted together. When Mejda saw the pictures of the lotus on the temple, he wrote to me: "I am ever grateful to you. I have had lotuses made here in America, but they are not equal to the one you made. What I couldn't do in America, you have done there."

Anandamoyee Ma visited her ashram in Puri as we were finishing construction of the *mandir.* I went to her ashram to pay my respects. She had heard of our work and asked if I could loan her my mason to help with work on her ashram. Since our job was nearly completed, I sent her my principal mason. To express her gratitude, she had a feast prepared for us and showered us with loving care and attention.

A few days later, as we were beginning work on the floors of the veranda surrounding the temple, a telegram arrived from Swami Atmananda saying that Paramahansaji had left his body on March 7. Crushed by the news, in tears I prepared to return to Calcutta. A letter arrived, written by Mejda seven days before his *mahasamadhi.* The missive sent me some instructions. At the end of the letter, he said, "Life is ever ebbing away." I realized from these words that he had clearly foreseen his passing.

An earlier letter from Mejda, written about a month before, requested that we invest in some income property in Puri to help meet the expenses of the Puri ashram, all of which had been met with funds sent by Mejda from America, and from a monthly grant from Yogoda Math in Dakshineswar. Mejda wanted to insure that the sacred ashram and *samadhi mandir* would always be properly maintained. I had attempted to purchase some small houses to convert into rentals; but when struck down by the sudden blow of Mejda's passing, I had not the heart to remain in Puri. In addition, my family was faced with serious financial difficulty, as I had been involved with the Puri project for nearly a year and had not earned any income from my artwork. I returned to Calcutta. Only time could heal my anguish over the loss of my dear Mejda.

The Mahasamadhi of Paramahansa Yogananda

After Mejda returned to America in 1936, he had dedicated himself even more intensely to his Self-Realization Fellowship/Yogoda Satsanga Society mission of disseminating worldwide the ancient and universal soul-science of *Kriya Yoga,* as instructed by Mahavatar Babaji and his guru, Swami Sri Yukteswar. In 1942 Mejda built the Self-Realization Fellowship Temple of all Religions in Hollywood, California; followed, in 1943, by another temple in San Diego. In 1947 he established Self-Realization temple in Long Beach,* and in 1949 obtained a beautiful estate in Pacific Palisades on which he created the Self-Realization Fellowship Lake Shrine. There he constructed a "wall-less" temple dedicated to all religions. Some of Mahatma Gandhi's ashes were enshrined in the temple, which stands alongside the lovely lake that adorns this property. In dedicatory services in 1950, Mejda declared the site a World Peace Memorial. A large painting I had done of Mahatma Gandhi was hung above the Gandhi Shrine at the services. In 1951, Mejda completed construction of an auditorium and India Cultural Center adjacent to the Hollywood temple. The dedication services were attended by the Lieutenant Governor of California, Goodwin J. Knight, and the Consul General of India, Sri M. R. Ahuja.

Mejda's writings have inspired millions throughout the world. His spiritual classic, *Autobiography of a Yogi,* has been published in sixteen languages, and is used as a textbook in many universities. His other principal books are *Man's Eternal Quest* (lectures by Mejda), *The Science of*

* The congregation was subsequently transferred to a larger temple in nearby Fullerton, California, to accommodate the increasing attendance at services.

Religion, *Whispers from Eternity*, and *Metaphysical Meditations*. Tens of thousands have studied in their homes his *Self-Realization/Yogoda Lessons*.

Mejda breathed his last while attending, as a guest speaker, a banquet honoring India's ambassador to the United States, Sri Binay Ranjan Sen. The function was on March 7, 1952, in the Biltmore Hotel, Los Angeles. He concluded his address with words from his poem, *My India:* "Where Ganges, woods, Himalayan caves, and men dream God—I am hallowed; my body touched that sod." Lifting his eyes to the *Kutastha* center (spiritual eye), he entered *mahasamadhi*.

Sri Sri Daya Mata

Mejda had divine foresight. It was certainly evident in his choice of Sri Sri Daya Mata as his spiritual successor and leader of Self-Realization Fellowship/Yogoda Satsanga Society of India. He had trained her for this from an early age. Even her name is appropriate, for she is truly a mother of *daya,* compassion and love. Her mind is as pure as a child's, the equal of which I have never seen. She surrounds all whom she meets with divine kindness and love. Devotees from many countries who know her, and who have come on pilgrimage to visit Mejda's Garpar Road home, have said with one voice: "She is a real mother. Paramahansaji lives in her heart." I concur. I truly believe he resides within her, and it is for this reason that she is so graceful and kind, and always saturated with the presence of God. We cannot compare Daya Mataji with any other person; she is to be compared only with herself.

In 1958 Daya Mata and Ananda Mata* came to

* A faithful renunciant disciple of Paramahansa Yogananda since 1932, Ananda Mata is a Board member and officer of Self-Realization

(Left) Sri Sri Daya Mata and her sister, Sri Ananda Mata, photographed by the author during their visit to Calcutta in 1958. Daya Mataji is Mejda's spiritual successor, *Sanghamata* and President of Self-Realization Fellowship/Yogoda Satsanga Society of India. Both she and Ananda Mata have been disciples of Paramahansa Yogananda since 1931. As I developed this photo, the thought struck me: "Two blossoms on one divine stem." *(Right)* Daya Mataji in meditation.

The author, Sananda Lal Ghosh

With youngest sister Thamu, shortly

India to serve Paramahansaji's Yogoda work. Daya Ma and her party visited 4 Garpar one day; I took them to see a spiritual movie on the life of the great saint Sri Chaitanya. Prabhasda, Mejda's and my cousin, was also with us. We sat in the balcony. Towards the close of the inspiring movie, as Sri Chaitanya was singing in ecstasy, "Krishna, Krishna," Daya Mataji leaned back in her chair in *samadhi.* When the film ended, everyone left the cinema, but Daya Ma remained lost to this world in her deep meditation. The attendants came to turn off the lights. When they saw Mataji in ecstasy, they left a dim light on in the balcony and went downstairs to wait. Silently we sat with Daya Ma. It was almost an hour before she began to come out of her ecstasy; we escorted her downstairs. Seeing that the workers had been delayed, she asked them to excuse her. With one accord, they offered their *pranams* to her and said, "Our cinema hall has been blessed today. Great is our good fortune!"

Mejda lives on in Daya Mataji, in his work of Self-Realization Fellowship/Yogoda Satsanga Society of India, and in the hearts of the millions his blessings have touched.

As my own life draws nearer its close, I reflect on words Mejda wrote to me, and pray that I have lived in tune with them:

"This is a drama of God—play your part of sorrow or joy in the best way you can. As my brother, give your life in God's service, service of our gurus, and in spreading YSS in India. I am very proud of you...."

Fellowship/Yogoda Satsanga Society of India. She is also the sister of Sri Sri Daya Mataji.

Addenda

Biographical Notes About Mejda's Brothers and Sisters

Anecdotes About Mejda From Family Diaries

Letters to the Author From Paramahansa Yogananda

Notes from Paramahansa Yogananda's Discourses

Paramahansaji's Answers to Questions

Genealogical Chart

Biographical Notes About Mejda's Brothers and Sisters

Eight children were born to our parents, four sons and four daughters. Ananta, the eldest son, was born in Rangoon. The eldest daughter, Roma Shashi (Roma), and the second daughter, Uma Shashi (Uma), were born in Muzaffarpur. Mejda, the second son, was born in Gorakhpur. The third daughter, Nalini, was born in Calcutta. I, the third son, was born in Gorakhpur. Purnamoyee (Thamu), the fourth daughter, and Bishnu Charan (Bishnu), the fourth son, were born in Lahore.

Ananta (Barda: eldest brother)

Though often strict, and sometimes severe when disciplining us, our eldest brother was affectionate, with a soft and kind heart. He was quite young when Mother died. Realizing that his younger brothers and sisters would not have her guidance, and loving us with all his heart, he tried always to give us good training. From Father he acquired a penchant for thriftiness. On August 17, 1908, Barda passed the accountantship examination, and became an accountant for the Public Works Department. He was first assigned to Meerut, and then to other postings. In 1909, he was transferred to Gorakhpur, where he spent the remainder of his short life. Every year, during his vacation time, he came to visit the family in Calcutta.

After his death at thirty-one, I went to Gorakhpur to collect his personal belongings. Among them was his diary. Father and I were surprised to see how meticulously he had kept a record of his personal accounts and memoirs in that diary. Among the entries was mention of gifts of money to our sisters and additional financial help to them at the times of their marriages.

Barda took extremely good care of all his possessions. A bicycle that had been in his possession for almost twenty years looked as though it had been taken from the showroom only the day before. He was fond of singing and played the *esraj* well.

Because Barda was so thrifty, he had saved a goodly amount of his salary. These savings Father invested in government bonds for Barda's widow. Barda and Father had always consulted together on family matters, including investments.

Ananta was survived by his wife; a son, Gagan; and a daughter, Amiya.

Roma (Bardi: eldest sister)

Our eldest sister was nicknamed Tuni. She was as affectionate toward us as was our mother. In fact, it would not be too much to describe her as a goddess. She always bore a calm, smiling countenance; all her sorrows and sufferings she would quietly place in the hands of God. Bardi devoutly worshipped, and always remembered, the Lord as Divine Mother. While we were living in Lahore, Bardi was married to Sri Satish Chandra Bose of Calcutta. Her father-in-law, Dr. Keshab Chandra Bose, was an atheist. And her husband, our eldest brother-in-law, held his father's atheistic views. Bardi kept pictures of Kali and Lakshmi in one corner of her room, and daily offered her devotions to the Divine Mother represented in these forms. Her husband constantly ridiculed her devotion to the Lord, for which reason Bardi sought Mejda's help in softening her husband's harsh attitude. The success of this endeavor through divine intervention is recounted in Mejda's *Autobiography of a Yogi*.

That Bardi herself actually communed with Divine Mother I have no doubt. Many were the times I stood by her side when she was immersed in prayer. She never noticed I was there, for she was completely absorbed in another world. As quiet words of prayer came from her lips, tears of joy ran down her cheeks. Even now, as I recall her thus, tears well up in my own eyes.

Bardi lived with her husband in her father-in-law's house at 4 Girish Vidyaratna Lane, not far from our Garpar Road home. Because Bardi was like a mother to me, during my youth I often went to her house in the evenings. She taught me one of her favorite songs. In my boyhood, I had a very sweet voice, so she would ask me to sing the song for her as we sat out on the roof of her house looking up at the sky:

> O thou blue sky,
> Under blue cover
> Hast thou hidden my beloved Lord?
> Open thy cover,
> Let me discover
> My beloved Lord
> In thy heart of hearts.*

As I sang, she gazed at the sky; soon tears would roll

* These words are as translated by Paramahansa Yogananda in his original adaptation of the Bengali song, and appear with the music in his *Cosmic Chants*. *(Publisher's Note)*

down her cheeks. She told me: "Look at the sky. You will see the lustrous image of God hidden behind the expansive blue canopy. The twinkling stars are tiny holes through which His light is visible."

Often she told me that by concentrating on the infinite sky or the vast expanse of the sea one's consciousness becomes expanded.

Another instruction she gave me was in the form of verse:

> Once I had no shoes, my feet were bare.
> I yearned for a pair of shoes so fair.
> But one day I saw a man who had no feet;
> My desire for shoes was no longer there.

She told me: "Always compare your needs and sorrows with the greater tribulations of others; your own will then seem as nothing."

Her instructions, in Bengali verse, on the ever-changing states of happiness and sorrow have strengthened me in time of need; helping me to bear the loss of two sons, and of finances, and to endure other troubles in my life:

> In this world
> In cyclic rhythm—
> Like day and night—
> Weal and woe forever move
> In the life of man.
> No one is happy forever;
> None lives forever in pain.
>
> When you are happy, remember
> Let it not be in reckless abandon;
> That joy cannot live forever,
> Pain and sorrow must needs be endured.
> Even he whom you think to be happiest,

You know not his silent grief—
How many nights he spends sleepless,
Bathed in his tears.

When
In darkest hour of trouble
You do not lose heart,
Then by the grace of God
The night of misery will pass
And the dawn of happiness
Will come again.

One day I went to our house at 4/2 Ram Mohan Roy Road and saw that her son, Ramgati, was waiting outside in a hired carriage. He was calling her: "Come quickly, Mother. The driver doesn't want to wait any longer." I went into the house and found Sister in a small storeroom dusting off photographs of Father and Mother. I asked her if she was planning to take them with her to her house. "No," she replied so sweetly. "These photographs of our dear parents, through whom we all have become well established in life, have been neglected. I am cleaning them, and then I will hang them in a proper place." Hearing her words I was wounded at heart, and felt ashamed. Truly, we had all had very blessed and happy lives only because of the love and sacrifices of our parents. I bowed my head and asked her forgiveness that we had treated their photos with disrespect. Then I told her that her son was calling her to hurry.

"Let him call," she replied. "This is my last work in this house, and I must finish it." I did not understand then that she would never come again. In a few days she left her body.

On the day of her demise, Bardi invited Bishnu's wife and Bishnu's son-in-law, Buddha, to come to her house for dinner. They all dined together and enjoyed the evening. They left Bardi's home about ten p.m. At the time, Bardi appeared quite well. About midnight we received a telephone call at our house from Ramgati; he said that his mother had passed away at 11:30. We went at once to her house by car. We saw her body lying on the bed; her face was smiling. Both her hands were resting on her chest. In one she was holding a *japa mala* (prayer beads); in the other, she clasped a copy of the Bhagavad Gita.

Her husband told us that when he went to bed, Roma was massaging his feet and legs to help him sleep —which she often did. Suddenly, she said, "I must go. Someone is calling me." She rushed from the room and went upstairs to the prayer room. Picking up her prayer beads and the Gita, she came back to her husband and bowed at his feet. In the next moment she passed away.

Bardi looked as though she were sleeping peacefully. When, years later, I saw the photograph of Mejda's beatific smile as he lay in state on his bed at the Self-Realization international headquarters after his *mahasamadhi,* I was instantly reminded of Bardi's blissful expression.

A few days before her passing, Bardi had purchased a red-bordered *sari,* vermilion powder, and "lac-dye" (a red coloring used to paint the feet). In India it is customary to dress a deceased married woman in a red-bordered *sari,* to place a spot of vermilion powder on the forehead at the place of the spiritual eye, and to put lac-dye on the feet. Bardi gave these items to her daughter-in-law, with the words, "Bouma, keep these with you. They might be needed suddenly, perhaps even late at night." Although her daughter-in-law protested, Roma insisted she hold the items in readiness.

We never knew how Bardi foresaw the moment of her passing. When she left us, we felt we had lost our mother for a second time. Even now, so many years later, I am overwhelmed by the feeling of her affection. She was always tranquil; her manner, mild. Seldom have I met another of equal piety. Roma was survived by her husband, one son, and four daughters.

Uma (Mejdi: second eldest sister)

Our elders called our second sister Muni. We juniors called her Mejdi, our second elder sister. She had the simplicity of a child and a beautiful, smiling face. She liked to call me Sontu. (She couldn't call me "Gora," as the name of her grandfather-in-law was Gorachand. In India it is a discourtesy to speak the first names of elders; a title is always used instead when addressing them or speaking of them).

Uma married Sri Satya Charan Basu Mullick, the grandson of the famous and wealthy contractor, Sri Gorachand Basu Mullick. She was survived by three sons and a daughter. Her second son, Bijoy Mullick, became a renowned gymnast and singer of devotional songs. He was given the title *Kirtan Sagar,* "Sea of *Kirtan.*" Uma had two other sons: Bishu, the eldest, and Binu, the youngest. She had one daughter, Rani.

Nalini (Sejdi, third elder sister)

Nalini was born three years before I was. Since we often played together, I at first called her Nali, the nickname by which our elders addressed her. One day

Father scolded me for doing so, and asked me to address her by the proper title of respect, Sejdi (third elder sister), since she was older than I.

Sejdi married Dr. Panchanon Bose. The ceremony took place in our Garpar home. Not long after Nalini was married, she had a near-fatal attack of typhoid while Mejda was on his trip to Japan. He returned to find her in a coma at death's door. For one week he stayed at her bedside and applied various yogic methods of healing. To the amazement of the doctors she recovered, but her legs remained paralyzed. She was confined to a wheelchair. In her dejected state, she wept bitterly. Mejda, deeply moved by her sorrow, visited her every evening for several weeks and continued to apply healing techniques. He also sought the divine intercession of his guru, Swami Sri Yukteswar, who foretold she would recover in one month. In exactly a month's time, she was completely well. Her physician-husband and our entire family could hardly believe her miraculous recovery. Some years earlier, shortly before Mejda cured Sejdi of chronic thinness, she had become his faithful disciple. After this second healing, Sejdi was even more deeply devoted to Mejda and followed implicitly all of his spiritual injunctions. She often secretly sent money to Mejda for his spiritual activities, hiding it in her harmonium box when he asked to borrow the instrument. She also gave generously to Bishnu. Nalini had two daughters, Annapurna and Minu.

Myself, Sananda

As related earlier, I was born on March 13, 1898, in Gorakhpur, in the same room of our house in which Mejda was born. I was named Gorakhnath Ghosh, after the famous saint, Gorakhnath of Gorakhpur. My nickname was Gora. When I was admitted into the Hindu School in Calcutta, with Father's approval Ananta named me Sananda Lal so that the names of us older brothers would have a similarity: Ananta, Mukunda, Sananda. I remember that all the way home from school on that first day I kept saying to myself: my name is Sananda Lal.

While in class seven of the Hindu School, I enrolled in an art course. This was the first training I received in drawing. Our mother had exceptional talent, and I inherited from her the ability to draw and a deep appreciation of art. The pictures I painted in class were highly praised by my teachers and others. One picture, of Krishna, was mounted and hung in the school. That was my first official recognition as an artist.

When I was about twelve years old, Mejda gave me his box camera. Later, when I entered college, I purchased a more professional camera, and so enjoyed taking pictures that photography became my hobby. As my ability developed, and demand for my pictures grew, I decided to make photography my livelihood. I had always felt an inner urge to go in this direction, so I was enthusiastic with my work. And, without any further training in art, I became proficient at painting photographs in oil.

Throughout our childhood I was Mejda's close companion. From his Sanskrit tutor, Shastri Mahasaya, I learned the sacred meditation technique of *Kriya Yoga*. When I went with Mejda to Serampore, I was also initiated into *Kriya* by Swami Sri Yukteswar. I practiced it at home. Years later, after the death of our father, and with Mejda away in America, I went to Puri and took initiation in the higher *Kriyas* from Sri Bhupendra Nath Sanyal, the last living disciple of Lahiri Mahasaya.

I have painted hundreds of pictures of Paramahansaji in various poses. Many of these were sent to Self-Realization centers around the world. I was honored when Mejda chose my painting of Mahatma Gandhi to be displayed at the dedication of the Mahatma Gandhi World Peace Memorial at the Self-Realization Fellowship Lake Shrine in Pacific Palisades, California—at which time a portion of the Mahatma's ashes were enshrined in the wall-less outdoor temple. Today that painting hangs in the India Hall of Mejda's Self-Realization Fellowship Ashram Center in Hollywood, California.

Later, I painted a portrait of Rabindranath Tagore in standing pose. This canvas was acclaimed throughout India and in many foreign countries. The great poet kindly sent me a letter of commendation. I have continued with my painting to this day. My desire is to help spread the spiritual message of Paramahansaji throughout the world through my art. I will endeavor to do this until I die.

Of my immediate family, only my second son, Sriman Harekrishna Ghosh; my only daughter, Srimati Shephali Mukherjee; and a grandson, Sriman Somnath Ghosh, are living. My first son died in infancy. My third son, Shyamsundar, at the age of twenty-four, was fatally wounded by a stray bullet during an uprising in Calcutta in December 1946.

Thamu

Thamu, three years younger than I, was born in Lahore. When our mother passed away, I was six; Thamu was two. From an early age she showed remarkable aptitude at household management. When she was twelve, she began serving Father as his little secretary: she was economical and kept careful track of all expenses, and maintained the household accounts for Father. Daily she brushed his office clothing and attended to many of his needs. Though she was so small — and quiet — she extended her care to all of us.

Thamu married Sri Arindam Sarkar, M.Sc., of Serampore. Sri Sarkar was an employee of the Bengal-Nagpur Railway, and through his diligent services became Personal Assistant to the Agent. Thamu and Arindam had one son and four daughters. Arindam was a benevolent man and often helped others get employment. He himself was due for a promotion when he passed away suddenly from a heart attack. His son was still an A.B. student in college. The family had hoped he would get a job with the B-N Railway on graduation, through the help of his father, but Providence ruled otherwise. Thamu is still living, but her health is not good.*

Bishnu

Mother passed away when Bishnu was only ten months old. His health suffered because he could not have Mother's nourishing milk nor her loving care. Consequently, he was frail. Later, when Mejda founded the Brahmacharya Vidyalaya in Ranchi, he enrolled Bishnu in the first session of the new school because the climate in Ranchi is so healthful. From Mejda, Bishnu learned yoga exercises; and through Mejda he was fully cured of his debility. He returned to Calcutta to enter the Hindu School.

* Thamu passed away on April 25, 1978, at the age of seventy-seven. *(Publisher's Note)*

I was in excellent health and exercised regularly. I urged Bishnu to join me, and coached him daily. He applied himself diligently and in time developed a marvelous physique. He obtained a bachelor of science degree in college, and passed his examinations in law. He practiced law for a while. But his interest lay in physical culture and *Hatha Yoga,* and so he decided to devote himself to this as a full-time career. He opened a school, which immediately attracted many young people. He and his students soon became known throughout India; they even traveled abroad to America and Europe to give exhibitions. While in the United States Bishnu lectured at Columbia University. In London he served as one of the judges in the Mr. Universe competition; he was the first and only one from India given that distinction. Later, in his own home in Calcutta, he founded the Ghosh College of Physical Education. A very wealthy philanthropist of India, Sri Jugal Kishore Birla, was so highly pleased with his work with India's youth that he purchased land at Ballyganj and constructed for Bishnu a large gymnasium. It was called Bajrang* Gymnasium. To this day, I have served as one of its trustees.

On one occasion, tourists from Japan saw Bishnu's performance and were so impressed with his method of physical training that they founded a *Hatha Yoga* center in Japan patterned after his system. The yoga method of physical culture is very popular now in Japan. Karuna, Bishnu's youngest daughter, is presently running one of his physical culture centers there.

* Vajranga is a name for Hanuman, the monkey-devotee of Lord Rama, noted for his devotion and great strength. The name comes from *Vajra,* the weapon of the god Indra, suggesting that Hanuman's body is powerful like the *Vajra.* (Bengalis often transliterate the Sanskrit *v* as *b,* and drop silent, or near-silent *a*'s. Thus, Bajrang instead of Vajranga.—*Publisher's Note)*

Bishnu was married at our Garpar home to Ashalata Roy, daughter of Sri Rasik Roy. They had one son, Bishwanath; and two daughters, Abha and Karuna. Bishwanath was one of Bishnu's finest students. He has often taken his own troupe of performers to Japan. In one competition, he won the gold cup, bringing honor to himself and to India. Unfortunately, Bishnu died suddenly on July 9, 1970, and never learned of his son's lustrous success.

Bishnu worked devotedly to teach physical culture to the common man of India. His dedication fired the enthusiasm of India's youth: he attracted a large following and left a heritage that still lives today.

Anecdotes About Mejda from Family Diaries

From the diary of my wife Parul:

Parul wrote: "In 1920, on the day Swami Yoganandaji left India for America, I along with others offered *pranams* to him. He blessed me, saying: 'Ma, do not grieve about the loss of your son. You will be a mother again soon; your child will be a son, and he will live. But put this *shanti taga* ("peace thread") on him as soon as he is born. Put it on with your own hands, and do not remove it before he is sixteen years old.'"

Mejda returned from America when our son was sixteen; with his own hands he removed the amulet.

I had lost my first son because my wife was seriously ill for a prolonged period after his birth, and he could not have her milk. He was sickly and never recovered his health. He died before his second birthday. At the time, Mejda was at his school in Ranchi. My wife and I, and my father-in-law, each wrote to Mejda asking for his prayers. But Mejda did not reply. When the child died, I wrote to Mejda telling him the sad news. Then Mejda broke his silence. He wrote: "I knew from the beginning that the Lord would take away your son, so to spare you the mental agony of living with this thought, I refrained from writing."

Later I asked Mejda how he knew the child would not live. He told me: "One day while I was drawing water for my bath from the tank in the courtyard, our elder sister-in-law came to me and said, 'Brother, you will soon be an uncle.' Not realizing what she was hinting at, I raised my eyebrows, questioningly. 'What do you mean?' I asked. 'Gora will soon be a father,' she told me happily.

"In that moment, like a cinema scene before me, I saw a dead child. 'But not for long,' I said. Our sister-in-law rebuked me. 'How can you utter such an evil prophecy? The child hasn't even been born yet!' I told her, 'You will see.'"

From Thamu's diary:

We younger ones in the family loved Mejda deeply. Our youngest sister, Purnamoyee, whom we called Thamu, especially respected Mejda and was wholly devoted to him; and she received from him his sweetest love and affection. In her diary she wrote that though he called her "Thamo" in front of the other family members, he often lovingly called her "Mathu"* when they were alone.

Thamu wrote: "I once had a very high fever and my whole body was wracked with pain. I had a headache that was almost unbearable. I didn't want to worry Father, so I said nothing. I helped him get ready for the office as usual: I brushed his clothes and saw that he had everything he needed. As soon as he left the house, I managed just barely to reach my room and lie down. I placed a cover over me and clasped my hands to my chest, praying to God that He would cure my fever and pain. I asked Him to spare Father any worry for me.

* "Mathu" was coined by Paramahansaji through a semi-inversion of "Thamu," so that there was an affectionate emphasis on "Ma" (mother) in addressing her.

"I heard Mejda coming downstairs, and for a moment he glanced into my room. As I continued my silent prayer, I dozed off to sleep. Suddenly I was awakened by a gentle touch on my forehead. I opened my eyes; Mejda was standing over me with a sweet expression of compassion.

"'I thought you had gone out,' I said to him. 'When did you return?'

"'Oh, my sister, you are feeling so much pain. I knew you were praying to God to take away your pain so that Father would not have any worry. So I came back. Just go to sleep now.'

"Mejda stroked my forehead. His touch was so soothing, I soon felt the pain slipping away; I drifted off to sleep. I didn't awaken until early afternoon. When I got up, I discovered that the fever and all pain had vanished."

Another entry in Thamu's diary reads:

"One day Roma, Nalini, Ananta's wife, and I were listening to Mejda talk of God. Suddenly he looked at me and said, 'You will not have to wait very long.' His comment surprised us and we wondered what he meant. I thought: 'Is my death near?'

"Reading my mind, Mejda burst into laughter. He affectionately patted me on the back and said, 'No, not that! You will soon be bound for your father-in-law's house.' No plans for my marriage had yet been made. I blushed and bowed my head. Yet we were all excited, for every young girl looks forward to her marriage. We asked him how soon, how many days? He didn't answer. But I began to count the days. Within two months I was married."

About her dedication to Mejda, Thamu writes:

"Mejda meditated daily in the small attic room on the third story of our house. One evening he called me to his meditation room. He taught me to pray to God, and through the blessing of his touch I saw the light of the Lord. From that time I began to devoutly worship God. And though I was only ten years old, a deep reverence for Yoganandaji was added to my sisterly love for him."

On another page of Thamu's diary:

"I had beautiful hair. One day Yoganandaji touched my hair gently and said, 'Your hair is truly beautiful. Would you be sorry if I cut it all off?' I remember I replied, 'No, of course not. It would grow back.' Then Yoganandaji asked me, 'Would you pull your own hair out by the roots?' I told him, 'Yes.' With that, I curled some of my hair around my hand and began to pull at it with all my strength. 'Stop!' Yoganandaji cried. 'You pass my test!'"

Thamu also experienced Mejda's extraordinary mental powers, as had I. She writes:

"Yoganandaji called me to his meditation room one evening. Jitenda and Basuda, who were his friends and devotees, were there with him. Yoganandaji asked me to sit beside him. He touched my head and body, and I suddenly lost conscious awareness. He then asked me the names and addresses of all the boys who were at that moment playing football on the field of the Calcutta Deaf and Dumb School across the street. Later, I learned that I had answered correctly in every detail."

On another page Thamu wrote:

"On the same football field, a boy had hung his expensive coat on a branch of a nearby tree so that he could play with the other boys. Someone took the coat.

Distressed, the boy came to Yoganandaji for help. Yoganandaji asked me to say where the coat could be found. I didn't know the answer, but I said, 'At 7 Garpar Road.' The stolen coat was recovered from that house."

From Roma's diary:

"I had prayed to Mother Kali since childhood; I neither knew nor worshipped any other deity. Father had a book of songs written to the Divine Mother by Sri Ram Prasad. Mother often sang from that book at noontime before lying down to rest. While she was sleeping I would read from the book. As a result I felt my devotion for Kali increase day by day. At that time I was only six or seven years old, but I used to regularly meditate in a quiet dark room.

"Our second brother, Mukunda (now Swami Yogananda Giri), was only one-and-a-half years old when this incident took place. Even at that age he was beginning to talk. He used to follow me about, and was obedient to me, though I don't know why. Of all the family members, after Mother, he loved me and Father most. When I sang praises to Kali from Ram Prasad's book he listened with rapt attention. I did not know then that I was sowing seeds of love for Divine Mother in the devotionally fertile soil of his heart.

"One Sunday afternoon during the summer, Father lay down in the drawing room to take his usual rest after lunch. When he got up he saw Mukun sitting on the staircase leading to the second story, his tiny legs sticking straight out in front of him, his head bowed low. In a loud voice, Mukun was singing the name of Kali. In astonishment, Father called to Mother to come and see Mukun, but he cautioned her not to distract his attention.

"'Where did Mukun learn this song to Kali?' Father asked Mother. 'We usually chant the name of Lord Krishna; how has he come to learn the name of Kali?' Then each of them went about their tasks. I knew I was responsible, and from a hiding place I continued to watch Mejda. I felt fearful that he was singing so seriously at such a young age. I vowed I would never sing in his presence again."

Letters to the Author from Paramahansa Yogananda

In the typeset copy beneath the reproduction of each of the following letters, italics indicate a translation of the Bengali script in the original letter. *(Publisher's Note)*

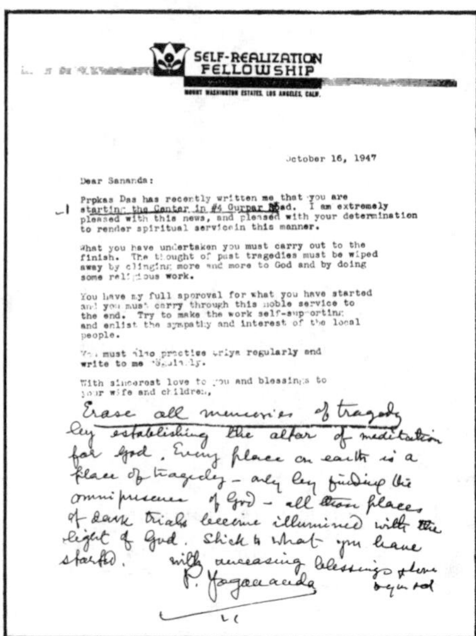

SELF-REALIZATION FELLOWSHIP
MOUNT WASHINGTON ESTATES, LOS ANGELES, CALIF.

October 16, 1947

Dear Sananda:

Prpkas Das has recently written me that you are starting the Center in #4 Gurpar Road. I am extremely pleased with this news, and pleased with your determination to render spiritual servicein this manner.

What you have undertaken you must carry out to the finish. The thought of past tragedies must be wiped away by clinging more and more to God and by doing some religious work.

You have my full approval for what you have started and you must carry through this noble service to the end. Try to make the work self-supporting and enlist the sympathy and interest of the local people.

You must also practice Kriya regularly and write to me regularly.

With sincerest love to you and blessings to your wife and children,

Erase all memories of tragedy by establishing the altar of meditation for God. Every place on earth is a place of tragedy – only by finding the omnipresence of God – all those places of dark trials become illumined with the light of God. Stick to what you have started. With unceasing blessings & love to you and all

P. Yogananda

Prokas Das has recently written me that you are starting the Center in #4 Gurpar Road. I am extremely pleased with this news, and pleased with your determination to render spiritual service in this manner. / What you have undertaken you must carry out to the finish. The thought of past tragedies must be wiped away by clinging more and more to God and by doing some religious work. / You have my full approval for what you have started and you must carry through this noble service to the end. Try to make the work self-supporting and enlist the sympathy and interest of the local people. / You must also practice Kriya regularly and write me regularly. / With sincerest love to you and blessings to your wife and children. / Erase all memories of tragedy* by establishing the altar of meditation for God. Every place on earth is a place of tragedy—only by finding the omnipresence of God—all those places of dark trials become illumined with the light of God. Stick to what you have started.

With unceasing blessings and love to you and all

* The "tragedy" referred to was the death of Sananda's son Shyamsundar. See page 248. *(Publisher's Note)*

3880 San Rafael Avenue
Los Angeles 31, California
Mt. Washington Estates

April 6, 1949

Sri Sananda lal Ghosh
Yogoda Sat-Sanga Center
4, Gurpar Road
Calcutta, India

Dear Sananda:

It has been physically impossible to write letters as I wanted to do. Really I work fourteen to fifteen hours a day and it doesn't seem I can catch up with all my work.

(I am pleased that you liked the pictures of you and your family and the students . I am extremely proud of you that you have kept the name of my guru in the good old Gorpar Road homestead wherein I was brought up and carried on my spiritual activities first.)

(Aren't you happy to see that from the very place which you are occupying now a world-wide movement has started which is continuously developing.)

Please keep it confidential that if God wills, by the end of this year I propose to visit India.

Please forget the past memories of tragedy. (On the dark back ground of tragedy God has built through you this wonderful Center which will immortalize your name and purify you and many generations behind you and ahead of you with God's and the Guru's blessings.)

Cling to the skirt of the Divine Mother and to her bosom in a stronger way no matter how she beats you or tests you.

Yogananda

It has been physically impossible to write letters as I wanted to do. Really I work fourteen to fifteen hours a day and it doesn't seem I can catch up with all my work. / I am pleased that you liked the pictures of you and your family and the students. I am extremely proud of you that you have kept the name of my guru in the good old Gurpar Road homestead wherein I was brought up and carried on my spiritual activities first. / Aren't you happy to see that from the very place which you are occupying now a world-wide movement has started which is continuously developing. / Please keep it confidential that if God wills, by the end of this year I propose to visit India. / Please forget the past memories of tragedy. On the dark background of tragedy God has built through you this wonderful Center which will immortalize your name and purify you and many generations behind you and ahead of you with God's and Guru's blessings. / Cling to the skirt of the Divine Mother and to her bosom in a stronger way no matter how she beats you or tests you.

April 19, 1949

Sananda lal Ghosh

Dear Sananda:

I have your letter written January 22nd and am very glad to hear from you. I should have written much sooner but have been extremely busy looking after affairs here and seeing people all day long-day in and day out. I long for solitude but this seems to be my life for the present.

Yogananda

I have your letter written January 22nd and am very glad to hear from you. I should have written much sooner but have been extremely busy looking after affairs here and seeing people all day long—day in and day out. I long for solitude but this seems to be my life for the present. / I wrote you a letter recently. I hope you have received it. Love God in spite of His test—everybody belongs to Him. This is His play—work for His drama good or bad—trying to love Him and concentrate on Him—*life is not only "Nothing belongs to anyone"*—we must learn to love all as we love those with whom we are born and know we all belong to God. Then everybody becomes our own. / I am so proud of you that you are carrying on such a good work at 4 Gurpar, my *pith* [place] where I found God. It was written in my name and I transferred to you if you remember, knowing someday you will be heart and soul with me. Do you remember I used to call you my secretary.

Beloved Sananda, Oct 12th 1949
Please come out of your sorrow.
This is a drama of God – play your
part of sorrow or joy in the best way
you can.
(As my brother give your life in God's
service – service of the Gurus and in
spreading YSS in India.)
I am very proud of you that
the same old homestead of my
साधना on 25th September saw a great
celebration with लुचि etc.)
– very sincerely yours
Yogananda

Please come out of your sorrow. This is a drama of God—play your part of sorrow or joy in the best way you can. / As my brother give your life in God's service—service of the Gurus and in spreading YSS in India. / I am very proud of you that in the same old homestead of my *sadhana* on 25th September saw a great celebration with *luchis,** etc.

Very sincerely yours

* A light puffed Indian bread, of which Paramahansaji was very fond. After special religious functions, food is often served to those who attended; thus Paramahansaji's quip about celebrating with *luchis*. *(Publisher's Note)*

SELF-REALIZATION FELLOWSHIP
3880 San Rafael Avenue
Los Angeles 65, Calif.
U. S. A.

November 17, 1949

Sananda Lal Ghosh
4, Garpar Road
Calcutta 9, India

Dear Sananda:

Thank you so much for your letter of October 27th. The sincerity of your words touched me very deeply.

The Board of Reconciliation and Recommendation can act as a great boon in co-ordinating YSS in India. And I was especially pleased to read your interpretation -- to revitalize the entire organization. That is exactly what the new Board of R and R can help greatly to do.

Being on the Board of R and R will give you the greater opportunity to serve our great Universal cause and I humbly join with you as we turn our minds to God, Babaji, Sri Sri Lahiri Mahasaya and my beloved Guru, Srijukteswar and all the Great Ones who are giving us our renewed energies and inspirations to make our plans and carry them out.

My love and unceasing blessings always,

R Yogananda

Thank you so much for your letter of October 27th. The sincerity of your words touched me very deeply. / The Board of Reconciliation and Recommendation* can act as a great boon in co-ordinating YSS in India. And I was especially pleased to read your interpretation—to revitalize the entire organization. That is exactly what the new Board of R and R can help greatly to do. / Being on the Board of R and R will give you the greater opportunity to serve our great Universal cause and I humbly join with you as we turn our minds to God, Babaji, Sri Sri Lahiri Mahasaya and my beloved Guru, Sriyukteswar and all the Great Ones who are giving us our renewed energies and inspirations to make our plans and carry them out.

My love and unceasing blessings always

* An administrative committee formed by Paramahansaji. It was in existence for only a short time and was then dissolved. *(Publisher's Note)*

December 23rd, 1949

Dear Sananda:

I am proud of all that you are doing in God's name to spread the work of Yogoda Sat-Sanga. God will ever bless you if you keep on striving to please Him as you are doing.

Unceasing love,

Paramahansa Yogananda

I am proud of all that you are doing in God's name to spread the work of Yogoda Sat-sanga. God will ever bless you if you keep on striving to please Him as you are doing.

Unceasing love

I am very glad to receive your letter. The more God beats you, the more you should cling to Him with both arms. You have gladdened my heart very much by holding satsanga at 4 Garpar, by selfless service to the work of God, by upholding the greatness of Gurudeva [Swami Sri Yukteswarji], and by preserving the family's prestige. Tell Thamu that I am surprised and hurt by not receiving a letter from her. Even if you do not get my reply regularly keep on writing. Working for 14 to 17 hours daily for the great cause of God and Guru — this is the most worthwhile way of laying down one's life.

July 17, 1950

Sananda lal Ghosh
4 Gurpar Road
Calcutta 9, India

Dear Gora:

I have received your letter written June 28th and am glad tohave the information which you sent.

Nagen Babu has just left here and brought with him the four paintings. They are most wonderful and will hang in our newly-constructed India House. I am very proud of your work on them.

I have received your letter written June 28th and am glad to have the information which you sent. / I am glad you are in Puri with Nirvanananda and at last are repairing the Hall (left unfinished by Guruji) and creating a temple over his grave. This makes me very happy. I hope you keep the lotus design. I like to know when building will be finished. / Nagen Babu has just left here and brought with him the four paintings. They are most wonderful and will hang in our newly constructed India House. I am very proud of your work on them. Everybody is astonished at your ability to paint. Such oil painting is indeed classical. They will be immortalized in America in the India House newly created at Los Angeles with an auditorium of 300 people and India Cafe*—right in the heart of Hollywood. We have 72 centers in the world. New institutions are cropping up all the time. / How is your family and building at home. With love to you that you have turned towards God. Keep going towards Him more and more.

With unceasing blessings
I remain very sincerely yours

* The restaurant, featuring many of Paramahansaji's unique recipes, was phased out in 1969 when the facilities and personnel were needed for the expanding congregation and activities of the Self-Realization Hollywood Temple nearby. ***(Publisher's Note)***

Ananta Lal Ghosh, our eldest brother

Roma Shashi, our eldest sister

Satish Chandra Bose, husband of Roma

Uma Shashi, our second sister, as a young girl

Satya Charan Basu Mullick, husband of Uma

Nalini Sundari, our third sister

Dr. Panchanon Bose, husband of Nalini

Purnamoyee (Thamu)

Arindam Sarkar, husband of Thamu

Bishnu Charan Ghosh
Our youngest brother

The author and wife Parul
at marriage ceremony, 1914

Mahavatar Babaji, guru of Lahiri Mahasaya, and Lahiri Mahasaya (1828–1895); from paintings by the author.

Lahiri Mahasaya
as a young man

Tincouri Lahiri
Son of Lahiri Mahasaya

Ducouri Lahiri
Son of Lahiri Mahasaya

Satyacharan Lahiri
Grandson of Lahiri Mahasaya

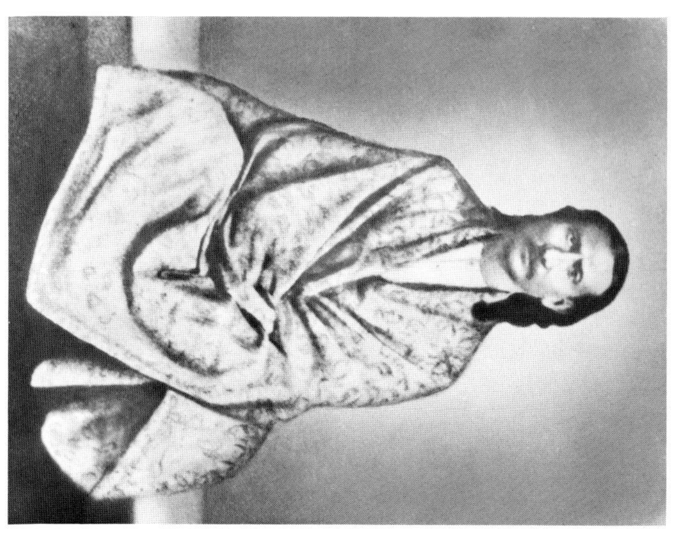

Temple dedicated to Lahiri Mahasaya, Bhagalpur, Bihar

Bhupendra Nath Sanyal
Disciple of Lahiri Mahasaya

Trailanga Swami
A great saint who had mastered the yoga *siddhis* (divine powers); a contemporary and friend of Lahiri Mahasaya

Mejda's first meeting with the ecstatic saint Anandamoyee Ma and her ascetic husband, Bholanath *(left),* in Calcutta. Of the "Joy-permeated Mother" Mejda wrote: "Whether amidst a crowd...or sitting in silence, her eyes never looked away from God." Inset is a painting by the author.

Mejda at age of six; from a painting by the author

Mejda in yoga posture, 1916; from a painting by the author

Altar at family home in Ichapur, showing ancestral deities Goddess Chandi *(left)* and a sacred black stone symbolizing Narayan *(right)*

Mejda's bedroom in our Calcutta home at 4 Garpar Road

Doorway to Mejda's room where Mahavatar Babaji came to him to bless his mission to the West

A plaque I made and installed on the outside of our family home to honor Mejda and his worldwide mission

Composite photo depicting the author on Mejda's motorcycle, with Sri Yukteswarji in the sidecar

Mejda driving motorcycle, 1916. Behind him is N.N. Das, and in the sidecar, Tulsi Bose. (Regrettably, deterioration of this photo-painting has distorted Mejda's face.)

The author's family: *(seated)* myself and my wife Parul. *(Standing, left to right)* my daughter-in-law Anjali, my daughter Shephali, and my son Harekrishna, Calcutta, 1949

Yogoda Meditation Center at 4 Garpar Road, Calcutta, 1949

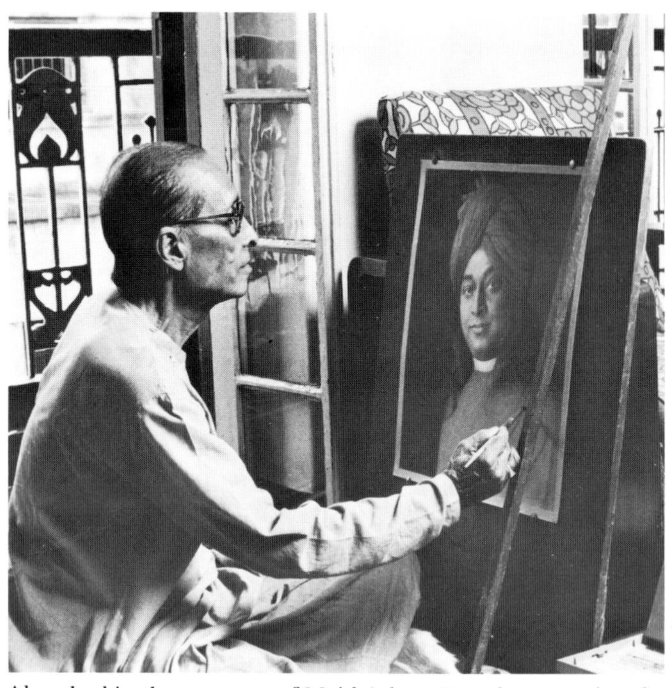

Absorbed in the memory of Mejda's love, I am here putting the finishing touches on one of my paintings of the Premavatar ("Incarnation of Divine Love").

SELF-REALIZATION FELLOWSHIP
3880 San Rafael Avenue
Los Angeles 65, Calif.
U.S.A.

August 29, 1950

Dear Sananda,

I am very glad of the good work you are doing at Puri.
Have you started any work on Gurpar.
I am very glad your daughter was spared from disease.

With boundless love and blessings

P.S. Your picture of Gandhi is most excellent — praised by eminent artists here. It will permanently find its place in our new most gorgeous "million dollar" SRF Lake Shrine, with ocean, lake and mountain, donated to us.

With blessings

December 27, 1950

Sananda lal Ghosh
#4 Gurpar Road
Calcutta, India

Dear Sananda:

I am so pleased that you are overseeing the work on Master's shrine at Puri. Be sure to put on top the golden lotus, which is our symbol, and write to me how the work is coming along. What about the lotus on top of temple.

How is your family? Please remember me to them. And how are you getting along?

With love & blessings to you & Prokas, Prabhas & all

Very sincerely yours

P. Yogananda

I am so pleased that you are overseeing the work on Master's shrine in Puri. Be sure to put on top the golden lotus, which is our symbol, and write to me how the work is coming along. What about the lotus on top of temple. / How is your family? Please remember me to them. And how are you getting along? / With love and blessings to you, Prokas, Prabhas and all.

Very sincerely yours

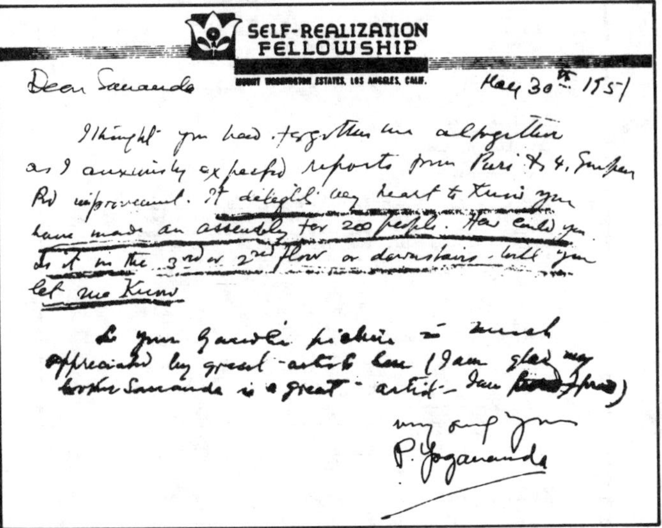
SELF-REALIZATION FELLOWSHIP
MOUNT WASHINGTON ESTATES, LOS ANGELES, CALIF.

Dear Sananda May 30th 1951

Very sincerely yours
P. Yogananda

I thought you had forgotten me altogether as I anxiously expected reports from Puri & 4 Gurpar Rd improvement. It delights my heart to know you have made an assembly for 200 people. How could you. Is it in the 3rd or 2nd floor or downstairs. Will you let me know. / Your Gandhi picture is much appreciated by great artists here (I am glad my brother Sananda is a great artist—I am proud).

Very sincerely yours

SELF-REALIZATION FELLOWSHIP

Telephone: CApitol 0212 | 3880 San Rafael Avenue, Los Angeles 65, Calif. U.S.A. | Cable: "SELFREAL"

November 14, 1951

Sri Sananda Lal Ghosh
4 Garpar Road
Calcutta, 9, India

Dear Sananda,

Thanks for your recent letter and greetings from you and family. I am very happy to know about the silver lotus. I hope that it won't be too long before I receive the glad tidings that Gurudeva's Samadhi-pith in Puri is finished. From time to time I receive letters from over there asking about it.

Thanks for your recent letter and greetings from you and family. I am very happy to know about the silver lotus. I hope that it won't be too long before I receive the glad tidings that Gurudeva's Samadhi-pith in Puri is finished. From time to time I receive letters from over there asking about it. / Your trouble is you don't write to me and inform me about the happenings and building at Gurpar Road in which I am so interested. Please, send me a photograph of the hall with the people and yourself there. Tell N. N. Das to take a flash light picture. Please let me know if the hall is in the 1st floor, or 2nd or 3rd floor and how you made it.

With love to you & all
Very sincerely yours

SELF-REALIZATION FELLOWSHIP
3880 San Rafael Avenue,
Los Angeles 65, Calif.
U.S.A.

Telephone:
CApitol 0212

Cable:
"SELFREAL"

December 26, 1951

..ar Sananda,

I am glad that you are going ahead with the work on the temple and that you will be sending weekly reports to Premanandaji and that you are making a sketch of the plan. I am looking forward to seeing the sketch. I am awfully delighted you made those nice lotuses of varnished silver or stainless steel. Unless it is varnished every six months with colorless shellac the sea will rust them. We do it varnish our lotuses by the sea & thus save them. Please never give in to anger "[illegible]

[illegible]

I am glad that you are going ahead with the work on the temple and that you will be sending weekly reports to Premanandaji and that you are making a sketch of the plan. I am looking forward to seeing the sketch. I am awfully delighted you made those nice lotuses of varnished silver or stainless steel. Unless it is varnished every six months with colorless shellac the sea will rust them. We do varnish our lotuses by the sea and thus save them. /Please never give in to anger. *"Passion and anger become slaves to great souls"* [a Sanskrit sloka rendered into Bengali]. *Have complete faith in God. Regard your own family and all others as belonging to God — as His own Self. Behave very well with them, and practice respect and God-love for all. You are good-hearted. Even though you are suffering, don't allow any place for anger within your heart. Nothing could cause greater unhappiness and be more sinful than that. I have undergone many sufferings but have not allowed anger to enter my heart. God gives happiness if you use sweet words.*

January 30, 1952

Sananda Lal Ghosh
c/o Puri Ashram
Puri, India

Beloved Sananda:

I have received your recent letters about going to Puri and of the progress of the building of the temple there. I cannot begin to tell you how much this means to me. The work that you all are doing is of utmost importance -- and God will ever bless you for it.

The enclosed letter is for your information. When Prokas comes to Puri, please look into the matter fully and send me complete information about your findings. Please let Robinarayan see the enclosed letter also.

With love
Very sincerely yours
Paramahansa Yogananda

I have received your recent letters about going to Puri and of the progress of the building of the temple there. I cannot begin to tell you how much this means to me. The work that you all are doing is of utmost importance—and God will ever bless you for it. / The enclosed letter is for your information. When Prokas comes to Puri, please look into the matter fully and send me complete information about your findings. Please let Robinarayan see the enclosed letter also.

With love

Very sincerely yours

Feb 25th–1952

Dear Sananda

My joy knows no bounds for my brother is such an artist — builds a better lotus than I built in America — Indeed it is very artistic.

I am very proud of you & grateful to you that my Guruji's Samadhi Mandir is so beautifully done I owe everything to Guruji

With deepest love to you and all
Very sincerely yours
P Yogananda

My joy knows no bounds for my brother is such an artist—building a better lotus than I built in America. Indeed it is very artistic. / I am very proud of you and grateful to you that my Guruji's Samadhi Mandir is so beautifully done. I owe everything to Guruji.

With deepest love to you and all
Very sincerely yours

Rev Sanandalal
Dear one, Feb 28th 1952

Thank you for your letter and wonderful photographs. Please send photographs without the building platforms. The lotus is extremely wonderful befitting my artistic brother

I long for photographs – please take photographs of Yogoda Math from all sides

I again say the lotus is beautiful & the temple very wonderful I will soon the $100/

[illegible]

P Yogananda

Thank you for your letter and wonderful photographs. Please send photographs without the building platforms. The lotus is extremely wonderful befitting my artistic brother. / I long for photographs—please take photographs of Yogoda Math from all sides. / I again say the lotus is beautiful and the temple very wonderful. I will soon [send] the $100. / *As you behave with others in a good manner, similarly you should behave with Parul and other family members. Life is ever ebbing away—therefore you should extend hearty sincere behavior and sweet words to all.*

Blessings and love

Discourses of Paramahansa Yogananda

*I made notes from many of Mejda's discourses. The following is some of his invaluable advice.**

What Is "Nishkama Karma"?

In meditation, the *kriya,* or action, performed by the yogis in the cerebrospinal *chakras,* from the *muladhara* (at the base of the spine) to the *ajna chakra* (in the medulla and point between the eyebrows), is *nishkama karma:* action that is free of desire, and therefore free of karmic result. By such action the mind becomes purified, and this produces *atma-jnana,* soul knowledge or Self-realization. Without Self-realization, none can attain the bliss of Brahman, Spirit.

Man's right is to act; but he has no right to the fruits of his actions.† He must learn to work without desire for the results. Such work is called *nishkama.*

* These notes from Paramahansa Yogananda's discourses were recorded in Bengali by Sananda Lal Ghosh. In rendering them into English, many key Sanskrit words and philosophical terms have been retained, that the reader might enjoy something of the flavor of expression that would have characterized Paramahansaji's talks given in India. Parenthetical translations or explanations of the Sanskrit have been added to enable the Western reader to readily understand the text without repeated referral to footnotes. *(Publisher's Note)*

† "Thy human right is for activity only, not for the resultant fruit of actions. Do not consider thyself the creator of the fruits of thine activities; neither allow thyself attachment to inactivity." — Bhagavad Gita II:47.

Another name for *nishkama karma yoga* is *buddhi yoga:* union with Spirit through *buddhi,* purified or divine intelligence. Failure to use intelligence in the performance of material duty brings unsatisfactory results. Similarly, *buddhi* must be applied to one's *sadhana* (spiritual practices), or those actions will yield imperfect results. Persons who are filled with desire bear the burden of desire, which is worry and disappointment. So real yoga is the ability to work with *buddhi,* or purified intelligence, which is capable of producing perfect results without creating a desire for those results.

Single-pointed concentration, even on a trivial matter, gives control of the mind. The natural distractions of the body and sensory stimuli are subdued. When the mind becomes concentrated in the *sahasrara* ("thousand-petaled lotus," the highest center of spiritual awakening in the brain), the consciousness transcends the delusive perceptions of the universe and reattains divinity, oneness with God or Cosmic Consciousness. This union is called *nirvikalpa samadhi.* With the dissolution of ego consciousness, there is no longer an "enjoyer" to receive the results of past and present good or bad actions. Thus the *karma* of an enlightened soul is destroyed.

When the *jiva* or the little self merges with the *Paramatman* or Great Self, duality no longer exists, only the eternal One. Past and future become the ever-present Now. With the intelligence fixed in God in *samadhi,* one attains *tattva-jnana,* or realization of the true nature of the universe as a manifestation of Spirit. When, through *samadhi,* the yogi has transcended desire for and attachment to the objective world, then, whether he is in the waking state, or dreaming, or in deep sleep, he remains ever conscious that no difference exists between the created and the Creator, between himself and the Supreme Being.

The State of a Jivanmukta, a Soul that Is Liberated While Still Incarnate

"He whose consciousness is not shaken by anxiety under afflictions nor by attachment to happiness under favorable circumstances; he who is free from worldly loves, fears, and angers — he is a *muni* (one who can dissolve his mind in God) of steady discrimination" (Bhagavad Gita II:56). Remaining in the world, but not of it, such an illumined soul is neither anxious nor sorrowful, nor does he desire pleasures of the senses. He is a *muni,* one whose mind is interiorized, established in the omniscient *Paramatman,* Supreme Being. He perceives the blissful Brahman as permeating everything; therefore, there is no scope in him for human passion, fear, and anger. This state is known as *jivanmukti,* "freed-while-living."

One who is a *jivanmukta* is unmoved by birth or death; and, unlike the deluded man, he is neither elated by gain nor made sorrowful by loss. He remains impervious to the constant flux of duality.

To know the bliss of one's true soul nature, the mind has to be kept turned inward. When the outward flow of consciousness and energy that enlivens material sense perceptions is reversed (through yoga), the origin of the senses in the spinal *chakras* is experienced. This produces an extraordinary enjoyment of smell, taste, touch, sight, and hearing. Each of the five senses is perceived as manifesting from the action of the primal creative vibration as it operates in the five lower *chakras.* Withdrawing the energy and consciousness into the spine, and upward through the *chakras,* each sense merges successively into the one in the next higher center, until only the creative vibration, *Aum,* the source of the senses, remains. Being attracted by this sound, which is the manifestation of God as the Creator, the soul becomes wholly concentrated on *Paramatman.* As an owl sees clearly at night, but not in daylight, so the knower of Brahman beholds God alone, and has the eyes of his consciousness closed to the delusive sense objects of creation. He sees God everywhere, and that everything is God. Naught exists for him but the omnipresent Spirit within and beyond matter. This is the ultimate experience of a realized soul. It indicates attainment of the state of *jivanmukti.*

Worldly Attachments

"Brooding on sense-objects causes attachment to them. Attachment breeds craving; craving breeds anger.

"Anger breeds delusion; delusion breeds loss of memory of the Self. Loss of right memory causes decay of the discriminating faculty. From that the annihilation (of spiritual life) follows" (Bhagavad Gita II:62–63).

When the sky of the mind is thus clouded by delusion, the light of divine wisdom cannot penetrate to illumine the consciousness.

Karma Yoga and Jnana Yoga

To put the mind in *prana* in the practice of *pranayama* is (interior) *karma yoga,* and to put the mind in the mind in meditation is (interior) *jnana yoga.* Thus, to put the mind in *prana* means to do a *Kriya. Kriya Yoga* is inner or esoteric *karma yoga,* or God-uniting action of *pranayama,* life-energy control. During the practice of *Kriya,* when done according to the guru's instructions, the *prana* (and therefore the mind or consciousness) withdraws from the senses and pierces the cerebrospinal *chakras* as it is drawn upward and becomes settled at the top of the *sushumna* (the astral spine that extends from the base of the spine to the door of Spirit in the brain).

To put the mind in the mind (in interior *jnana yoga*) means to try to know the *tattva* (attain realization) through *shravana* (hearing), *manana* (thinking), and *nididhyasana* (concentration); i.e., the mind is fixed at the *ajna chakra,* and is "concentrated" on "hearing" and "thinking of," or contemplating, the *nada* (sound of *Aum*) that has its source in Brahma in the *sahasrara.*

When the consciousness penetrates the *ajna chakra,* and becomes fixed on *nishkriya Brahmapada* (the place or state of Brahma who is beyond active creation), the yogi attains *nishkama,* the inactively active state of desire-free consciousness. So long as there is movement of the *prana,* there is *karma,* or action. But when the yogi has taken refuge in *para-pada* (the "highest place" of consciousness), breath and all other mortal activities of the body are suspended in that state of *samadhi.* He becomes *nishkarma siddha,* one who has attained divine illumination in the action-free state.

While practicing *Kriya,* when the mind becomes enchanted in listening to *nada,* the sound of *Aum,* a divine nectar-like current flows from the *sahasrara.* Through the performance of *Kechari Mudra,* touching the tip of the tongue to the uvula or "little tongue," (or placing it in the nasal cavity behind the uvula), that divine life-current draws the *prana* from the senses into the spine and directs it up through the *chakras* to *Vaishvanara*

(Universal Spirit), uniting the consciousness with Spirit. The entire body is thereby spiritualized and energized. As a result, a perceptible glow may emanate from the body.

The yogi, sitting in a secluded place, should close his ears with his hands and perform *pranayama*. Listening in the right ear, the devotee will hear various sounds emanating from the cerebrospinal *chakras* as he lifts his consciousness up the spine. First he will hear a sound like a buzzing bee in the *muladhara*, and then a flute in the *svadhishthana*, and then a harplike sound in the *manipura chakra*. Advanced spiritual awakening begins when he has raised his consciousness to hear the sound of the dorsal center, a gong-like bell sound in the *anahata chakra*. By concentrating on this sound the devotee will ultimately hear the sounds of the still higher *chakras*, until they merge in the ultimate pure sound of *Aum*. As the devotee continues to meditate, he will perceive a divine light at the *Kutastha*, or in the region of the twelve-petaled lotus of the heart *(anahata chakra)*. This light is *Parabrahman*, the Supreme Lord. When the yogi's mind is attuned with Brahman, he finds emancipation and is merged with the Infinite.

Karya and Karma

The outflowing of the life-current, *prana prabhava*, that keeps the mind active in the senses — perceiving, experiencing, and desiring matter — is called *karya*. When *prana prabhava* flows inward, from the senses toward the soul, that inflowing action is called *karma*.* *Karya* is external action; *karma* is internal action.

* *Karma* comes from the root *kri*, "to do," and thus has the general meaning of "action." In a broader sense, it applies also to the *effects* one

In order to explain *karma,* it is necessary to describe its three differentiations: *karma, vikarma,* and *akarma.*

1) *Karma* is the movement of life energy from the senses toward the soul, ultimately uniting the *jivatman* (soul) with *Paramatman* (the Supreme Being or Spirit).
2) *Vikarma* is action that transgresses divine cosmic law. It causes the soul to reincarnate again and again. It is the initiation of actions whose results will have to be reaped in the present or a future lifetime.
3) *Akarma* is cessation of action. This occurs when the ego consciousness merges in the Self. The stillness that comes in this state of *atma chaitanya,* soul consciousness, is *akarma* or *nishkarma.* In other words, after the *prana* has moved through the subtle nerves of *ida* and *pingala* and has ascended the *sushumna,* or astral spine, and the soul becomes united to Spirit, the state of *akarma* (motionlessness) is reached. In this union, there is no ego consciousness, nor does the world of duality exist. This is the state of *nirvana*—not "nothingness," as many have mistakenly interpreted it, but Absolute Consciousness.

Karma helps to free the *sadhaka* (spiritual aspirant) from *maya* (delusion) and to draw him toward soul consciousness. *Vikarma,* conversely, tries to pull him outward toward the senses, toward matter attachment. When *Kriya Yoga* is practiced regularly, the force of *vikarma* is gradually weakened. As *karma* becomes stronger, and

---

reaps from his actions. In the context above it takes on one of its specialized meanings, "religious rite, or spiritual action" as opposed to "material action" or *karya,* which also comes from the same root, *kri.* *(Publisher's Note)*

vikarma loses its power, short periods of *samadhi* are experienced. The duration of these periods gradually extends as *vikarma* is overcome. When the meditating devotee is able to remain in *samadhi* for long periods of time, ego consciousness is destroyed, and the soul becomes established in Spirit. Then, even when the yogi engages in outward activity, he is not affected by *vikarma*. He is no longer bound by the law of cause and effect; he is as unaffected by his actions as though no action had been performed. To him, there is no longer any difference between *karma* and *akarma*. He is inactively active and actively inactive. This is the state of the *jivanmukta,* one who is liberated while living. In this *jnana,* pure knowledge or illumination, *karma* ceases.

Manas (Mind)

The mind is superior to the senses. Whatever the mind decides, whichever way it leads, the senses will follow. Since the senses obey the mind, purification of the mind automatically purifies the senses. Therefore, if the mind is lifted from the *muladhara chakra* to the *sahasrara* and is attuned with the soul, the inferior qualities of the mind become spiritualized; and together with this, the grossness of the senses diminish. And when ultimately the mind merges with the soul, the mind and senses become one with Brahman. This is natural law. It will happen automatically, without conscious effort, if one faithfully practices the *pranayama* of *Kriya Yoga,* and observes the laws of right behavior.

When the mind is purified by being united to the all-knowing wisdom of the soul, the *sadhaka* can know all there is to be known by turning his queries to the *jnana* within. These subtle transformations of the consciousness, which free the soul from all worldly ties, result from the *sadhana* given by realized souls who come to inspire and guide God-seeking devotees by revealing the truth behind the seeming. As doubts are dispelled (by the wisdom of the great ones, and by personal experience of truth) the *sadhaka* attains perfect knowledge. Lord Krishna says in the Bhagavad Gita that God is beyond the mind *(manas)* and intelligence *(buddhi)*. If the devotee merges these two in Him, he becomes one with the Lord. Devotion comes from *karma* (righteous action), and from devotion comes knowledge, realization.

Kutastha (Spiritual Eye)

When the yogi converges the gaze of the two eyes at the *Kutastha* (the point between the eyebrows) and concentrates deeply, a light will appear. In the center, a dark spot or area will form, which is known as the *bhramari guha.** It is surrounded by luminous rays (a manifestation of the creative vibration of *Aum*), and protected by two powerful forces, *avarana* (a veil-like power)† and *vikshepa* (a scattering power). As the devotee tries to concentrate on this manifestation, it vanishes: *vikshepa* deflects his gaze and scatters his attention; and *avarana* casts a veil of delusion over his perception. The practice of *brahmacharya* (self-control), adherence to a pure diet,

* Literally, a cave *(guha)* that is filled with honey (*bhramari,* relating to or belonging to a bee, *bhramarin,* made of honey); hence, the receptacle of *amrita,* the divine nectar of immortality. *Bhramari* is also a name of Durga, an aspect of the Lord as the Divine Mother. It also means "revolving," referring in this context to the spiritual eye, whose light appears to revolve as it deepens into a luminous tunnel of gold and blue, in whose center is a white star that leads to Cosmic Consciousness. *(Publisher's Note)*

† *Varana,* from *vri,* to cover, screen, veil, conceal; the prefix *a* meaning compared to, or like (a veil).

detachment from worldly objects, endurance with evenmindedness, and *Kriya Yoga pranayama* increases the power of *sattva* (the spiritual or elevating quality) in the yogi. This creates a great power at the *Kutastha,* which enables the yogi to penetrate the darkness of closed eyes. Then as he looks at the *bhramari guha,* the powers of *avarana* and *vikshepa* decrease, and the mouth of the "cave" opens wide, revealing the inside. The golden luster increases a thousandfold; the dark area becomes the brilliant blue of *Kutastha Chaitanya* (universal consciousness, the Christ or Krishna* Consciousness); and in its center, the bright starlight of Cosmic Consciousness. (This triune light is the spiritual eye through which Spirit is perceived, and through which the consciousness passes to reunite with God.) With the annihilation of *avarana* and *vikshepa, dharma tattva* (the true nature of the Divine Principle that upholds all creation) is realized.

Without surrender to God through the knowledge that He alone is the Doer, it is not possible to reach Him. When the sense-bound soul merges with God, the organs of the enslaving senses are automatically constrained and rendered powerless.

When *Kriya Yoga* is performed correctly, bliss is felt within; great fulfillment and satisfaction come to the devotee. But if *Kriya* is performed incorrectly, no satisfaction accrues and the devotee may develop an aversion or disgust. But such irritation and discouragement should not be allowed to take hold, for they are the devotee's enemies, and great obstacles in his path to Self-realization. If the devotee perseveres in spite of any difficulty, he will find soul satisfaction. Then no restlessness

* Christ and Krishna are titles, denoting one who manifests the universal consciousness of Spirit omnipresent in creation. *(Publisher's Note)*

of body or mind can create any obstruction to his practice of yoga.

Svadharma and Paradharma

Sva means "self." The true self is the *atman,* the soul. What is the soul? It is *sat-chit-ananda:* ever-existing, ever-conscious, ever-new bliss. *Dharma* means eternal laws or principles of righteousness, existence, order—and the duty to uphold these principles. *Svadharma* thus consists of the divine laws and duties to which the soul adheres.

Para means "opposite." *Paradharma* is that which is opposed to *dharma.* As *dharma* is the aggregate of truth, reality, so *paradharma* is *maya,* delusion, which cloaks the true nature of the soul and binds it to the three *gunas* and twenty-four *tattvas* of creation,* producing, instead of soul bliss, ego consciousness with its limited sense perceptions.

In short, *svadharma* is the way of the soul: eternal, blissful truth-realization; and *paradharma* is the opposite, the way of the senses: mortal ignorance.

The Gita says: "It is better to die performing one's own duty *(svadharma);* the duties of others *(paradharma)* are fraught with fear (and danger)" (III:35). It is better to follow the lawful duties of the soul, for thereby comes salvation. If one dies performing sense activity, he is subject to the recurring cycles of birth and death.

* Three *gunas* (qualities of nature): *sattva* (elevating), *rajas* (activating), *tamas* (obstructing or dissolving). The twenty-four *tattvas* (the subtle "that" which is behind their corresponding manifestations in creation) are ego *(ahamkara); buddhi* (intelligence); *manas* (mind or sense consciousness); *chitta* (feeling, consciousness); five senses or instruments of knowledge; five instruments of action; five elements (earth, water, fire, air, ether); and five *pranas,* cosmic life-forces (crystallizing, metabolizing, assimilating, circulating, eliminating). *(Publisher's Note)*

In the Gita, Arjuna asks Lord Krishna, "By what force is a man often compelled, as it were, to perform evil?" (III:36). A devotee may find that his *Kriya Yoga* is being done well, and that the attention is fixed on the *Kutastha.* But suddenly the mind is forcibly dragged from its state of concentration, and he becomes restless. He asks himself: "Why did this happen? Who did it?"

Kama (desire) is the driving force of action in the material world. When desire is obstructed, wrath wells up; desire becomes anger. Desire is a result of *raja guna* (the outgoing activating quality of nature), and because it is insatiable, it brings sorrow. Material desire is never satisfied, even if those desires are fulfilled, for sense pleasures are not lasting. Until the mind becomes established in the *ajna chakra,* through practice of *pranayama, kama* continually drags the consciousness toward matter, often working so subtly that the devotee doesn't realize he has "fallen." In this descent of consciousness, *atma* becomes *manas* (mind or sense consciousness), subject to restlessness. When the consciousness descends below the *anahata chakra,* the heart center, it becomes concentrated in the three lower *chakras (manipura, svadhishthana,* and *muladhara),* and the sense-instigating activities of these centers give rise to desire. "As fire is covered by smoke, as a looking-glass is covered by dust, as an embryo by the womb, so it (the Self) is enveloped by desire....The constant enemy of wise men is the unquenchable flame of desire, which conceals wisdom" (Bhagavad Gita III: 38–39). Thus does the enemy, insatiable desire, prevent sense-enslaved beings from attaining *atma jnana* (divine soul wisdom).

To unite the knower, knowing, and That which is to be known is the ultimate objective. The knower is the *jiva* (sentient soul), the knowing is the comprehending power of the soul, and That which is to be known is the *Paramatman,* God. Knowledge of God gained through reading scriptures and through external forms of worship is objective or indirect knowledge. That which is gained through *laya,* the merging of Self with Brahma in yoga meditation, is subjective knowledge, or direct perception.

Desire is the perennial enemy of the knower. It is like fire. Fire illuminates other objects, but itself is not light. It cannot burn without the help of something to ignite it, and to feed it. So long as fire has something to consume, it will continue to burn. An endless heap of material cannot satisfy its appetite. Rather, the flames spread further. Similarly, *kama* torments the mind and increases longing for and attachment to worldly objects. But as a fire dies automatically when the objects it is feeding upon are consumed, so also desire is extinguished when it is no longer fed by attraction to material things.

Senses, mind, and intellect—these three are said to be the seat of desire. Through the lure of the senses, desire clouds the intellect and deludes the mind. As sentient beings, we have a natural affinity for objects of the senses, for it is desire for these that has caused us to take rebirth. As wet wood does not readily catch fire, neither does a mind or intellect filled with desires become illumined with *jnana* (pure knowledge). But when the senses are controlled, desire begins to dry up, and mind and intellect come under the control of the wisdom of the soul.

Vijnana is that knowledge, or Self-realization, that comes through *shravana* (hearing scriptural truth), *ma-*

nana (contemplating or perceiving it), and *nididhyasana* (concentrating on it until one becomes one with that truth).

Bhagavan Krishna said: "Sanctified by asceticism and wisdom, relinquishing attachment, fear, and ire, engrossed and sheltered in Me, many men attain My nature" (Bhagavad Gita IV:10).

Jnana, or true knowledge, is the soul's realization of "*Aham Brahmasmi* (I am Brahma)," or "*Tat tvam asi* (Thou art That)." And when one sits erect in meditation posture and directs the pranic current to the *Kutastha* (between the eyebrows), that is true *tapasya,* spiritual austerity or practice that masters the divine power within. Many souls, purified by *jnana* and *tapasya,* give up all worldly attachment, fear, and anger, and realize the blissful Lord.

As a man thinketh, so is he. Whatever way the devotee thinks of himself — free, in bondage; attached, nonattached; restless with passion, or free of all desire — that is the consciousness the body-identified soul adopts. If a devotee practices *sadhana* with the firm resolve that he will be free in this life, can there be another world for him after death? No. Merging in Spirit, there is no death for him. He becomes ever-living, everywhere present. Pursue your path to knowledge fearlessly. Destroy all obstacles. Think of your self as the Self.

If a white object is seen through colored glass, the object appears the same color as the glass. Similarly, men judge the nature of God according to their own level of development. Noticing that some people are happy and others are sad, the man lacking wisdom blames God as unjust. But God has not created the sorrow and destruction in this world. Then how to answer the question,

"What is the cause?" The scriptures say: "The actions of *jivas* (body-identified souls)." All the disparities in this world are the result of good or evil actions initiated by human beings of varied natures. As the rain cloud is the common cause of the growth of various grains, so Ishvara is the *sadharan-karana* (common cause) of all *devas* (gods) and human beings. But as the cloud does not make the grain good or bad, so the differences in beings comes from *asadharan-karana,* an uncommon (or individual) cause: their own individual actions.

If God appears to show special favor to His devotees, it is not because He is partial. It is the devotion of His devotees that attracts Him. Those who see God in all things, in all people, in all conditions; whose thoughts and feelings are fixed on Him alone; and who, saturated with devotion for God, consider Him to be the only worthwhile good, "...such supremely engrossed devotees are extremely dear to Me" (Bhagavad Gita XII:20). When we look into a mirror we see our reflection. If we turn our faces away from the mirror, we no longer see the reflection. If we turn our faces away from God, we cannot expect to see Him, or attract His grace. Lord Krishna says: "He who perceives Me everywhere, and beholds everything in Me, never loses sight of Me, nor do I lose sight of him" (Bhagavad Gita VI:30). A person's condition in this life reflects his actions in previous lives. One reaps what he has sown. Whether he is rich or poor, pious or ignorant, depends on the forces he himself put into motion in prior incarnations. God remains forever impartial; His grace is available to all.

As the *Kriya Yogi* lifts *prana,* life energy, up the spine through the innermost channel of *Brahmanadi,* toward the *ajna chakra,* if the consciousness remains centered on

God and does not become waylaid by fascination with the lesser spiritual experiences in the *chakras,* the blissful impact of increasing realization of the Divine is such that it eclipses all worldly desires and attractions. The mind ultimately becomes firmly centered in *Taraka* Brahman,* or Cosmic Consciousness. The yogi attains peace unsurpassable, forever anchored in Brahman. Know this to be a never-failing truth.

The scriptures say: "How can *Parameshvara* (Supreme Spirit) have any desire, when all things reside in Him; He is *apta-kama Purusha* (the Being in whom all desires are fulfilled)." God did not create the universe out of any necessity; it is merely His *lila,* divine play. When *jiva,* the sentient soul, understands *atma tattva,* the true nature of the soul, it realizes its oneness with *Parameshvara* and attains liberation.

What Causes Death?

The centers of *prana* and of *apana* (two of the *vayus,* or vital airs) are, respectively, in the *ajna* (point between the eyebrows) and the *muladhara* (coccyx). *Prana* moves up the spine to the *ajna* and draws breath into the body; *apana* moves down the spine to the coccyx and forces the breath out. In ordinary consciousness, their powers balance each other, and so inhalation and exhalation remain constant. But when the *apana* current overpowers the *prana* current, *apana* pulls the breath from the body permanently, and death ensues.

"As fire reduces to ashes all wood, even so, O Ar-

* *Taraka,* "star" or "pupil of the eye"—a reference to God or Cosmic Consciousness experienced when one's consciousness penetrates the star in the center of the spiritual eye, doorway to Cosmic Consciousness. *(Publisher's Note)*

juna, does the flame of wisdom consume all *karma*" (Bhagavad Gita IV:37).

Karma is the objective cause of birth and death. *Karma* is of three types: *prarabdha, sanchita,* and *kriyamana.*

Prarabdha karma is that which is yielding fruit in the present life, i.e., the body and its conditions resulting from past-life actions.

Sanchita karma is that which is accumulating, but will not yield fruit until a future lifetime.

Kriyamana karma means future action, or *karma* not yet started.

As wood is reduced to ash by fire, so *prarabdha karma* and *sanchita karma* are destroyed when the devotee becomes Self-realized. Past and present *karma* thus destroyed can no longer govern or overwhelm the devotee. When he reaches this illumined state, *kriyamana karma* (any action he performs thereafter) cannot have any effect on him, just as water rolls off a lotus leaf.

Bhagavan Krishna said: "The mind of the liberated being is unattached, enveloped in wisdom. No *karma* pursues any of his actions, which he performs only as *yajna* (sacrificial rite)" (Bhagavad Gita IV:23). When the yogi's activity is directed inward in meditation, and he concentrates his life force and consciousness in the cerebrospinal centers (the true *yajna* or sacrificial rite) he overcomes ego consciousness and becomes established in the Self, the soul. The effects of all *karma,* no matter how evil, are thereby destroyed automatically. If one does not destroy *karma* by this inner activity, he is subject to the effects of good and bad actions. To remain in this karmic bondage is a sin against the Self. The mind of the wise remains fixed in the *sahasrara,* which is beyond duality; the effects of *karma* cannot touch that exalted being.

He who is full of faith, who performs right action, and who has control over his senses gains true knowledge and bliss. The Self-realization achieved through this *raja yoga* (the sovereign path), is the greatest of all knowledge. It brings direct spiritualizing results: when one gains this immutable Self-knowledge, he is no longer affected by *prarabdha* or *kriyamana.* Being thus freed from the bonds of delusion, he becomes successful in finding God through his Self-realization. This supreme knowledge is therefore the best, and holier than the holy. "This knowledge is the king of sciences, the royal secret, the peerless purifier, the imperishable enlightenment, and the essence of *dharma* (man's righteous duty). Through ways (of yoga) that are easy to perform, this truth is knowable by direct experience" (Bhagavad Gita IX:2).

Samshaya (Doubt)

"The ignorant, the man lacking in devotion, the doubt-filled man—all must perish. The unsettled individual has neither this world (earthly happiness), nor the next (astral happiness), nor the supreme happiness (God)" (Bhagavad Gita IV:40).

Doubt comes from ignorance in the mind. It is a great cause of suffering, and therefore must be banished! It is within the individual's power to remove doubt from his mind through *purushakar* (the free-will action of the soul). If one doesn't make this effort himself, no one else will be able to help him.

When *kundalini* is awakened through *raja yoga, shud-*

dha buddhi (pure understanding) manifests; everything worthwhile is known through direct perception, and doubt is vanquished. *Kundalini* is the subtle energy lying dormant in the *muladhara chakra.* Through guru-given *sadhana, kundalini* is awakened and ascends the *sushumna,* freeing the consciousness from the senses and worldly attachments and uniting the self with the Self. This process is known as *dhyana,* meditation.

What Is Yoga?

O *sadhaka* (devotee)! the path of yoga is not found in the heavens, neither on the earth, or beneath it. The path lies within. Yoga is union of *jivatman* (the sentient soul) with *Paramatman* (Spirit), of *nara* (man) with *Narayana* (his Creator). Obstacles on this inner path are lust, anger, greed, delusion, arrogance, and conceit. The yogi unites his soul with God when he overcomes these obstacles through the practice of yoga meditation and ascends to Self-realization by way of the Eightfold Path of Yoga: *yama, niyama* (proscriptions and prescriptions of right behavior), *asana* (posture), *pranayama* (life-energy control), *pratyahara* (interiorization of the mind), *dharana* (concentration), *dhyana* (meditation), and *samadhi* (union).

"O Arjuna, remaining immersed in yoga, perform all actions while forsaking attachment (to their fruits). Be indifferent to success and failure. Mental evenness during all states of activities (whatever the result) is termed yoga" (Bhagavad Gita II:48). Fix your attention on the *Kutastha,* and always dwell in *chidakasha* (the inner realm of consciousness). Do not look for results of your actions, even of your spiritual action of meditation. Eventually (in the *samadhi* state), the breath becomes calm and, finally, stilled. Mind also shall become pure consciousness when it penetrates *kuta* (the place in the forehead which is the seat of the spiritual eye) and becomes merged in *vindu sarobar* (that mystical dot, the center of the spiritual eye, which is the opening to the divine reservoir of Cosmic Consciousness in the *sahasrara*). This mental poise is known as yoga. This state cannot be defined by words.

Yogarudha

The senses of the advanced yogi perform their functions in his body, but he does not feel identified with them. He realizes his true self as the taintless soul. In that awareness, all bodily and material attachments dissolve automatically. This is the state of *yogarudha* (fixed in yoga).

Practice Yoga According to the Guru's Instructions

Sit erect on an *asana* (meditation seat) of *kusha* grass, covered with a deer skin, on top of which has been placed a silk cloth.* This *asana* insulates the body so that the powerful life current generated in the spine by the practice of *Kriya* is not drawn outward by the pull of the earth's magnetism.

To attempt to raise the life current through the *chakras* by unscientific methods taught by unenlightened teachers can cause bodily harm. An advanced yoga technique such as *Kriya* should be practiced under the blessing of a true guru's instruction. Mere book knowledge of *Kriya* without the blessing of the guru may lead

* *Kusha* grass and deer skins are common *asanas* in India. Paramahansa Yogananda taught, however, that a woolen blanket or cloth covered with a silk cloth provides similiar insulation. *(Publisher's Note)*

to difficulties. But *Kriya* instruction given by the guru and blessed by his inner guidance bestows the highest benefits, regardless of one's age and health.

Yoga exercises, including *Kriya Yoga,* should be performed in a well-ventilated room of moderate temperature; avoid extreme cold during *Kriya* practice.

After practicing *Kriya,* sit long in meditation to enjoy the peace and bliss produced by *Kriya.* To get up immediately after *Kriya* is like kicking over the pail and spilling the milk you have just drawn from the cow.

The Dream State Versus the Waking State

According to the scriptures, so long as we are engaged in worldly thoughts and activities, be it day or night, we are in the "dream state." But whenever our time is spent thinking of God and contemplating the transitoriness of this world, we are in the "waking state." "That which is night (of slumber) to all creatures is (luminous) wakefulness to the man of self-control. The seeming state of wakefulness of the ordinary man is perceived by a sage to be, in reality, a state of delusive sleep" (Bhagavad Gita II:69).

The True Wealth

The only person of true wealth is he who has acquired Self-realization. Money and property do not make a man rich, for at death not a farthing can be carried with him — everything has to be left behind. Thus, money and property are not our real wealth. Knowledge of the Self is the only possession that remains with us permanently. The man of Self-realization is unmoved by gain or loss, sorrow, disease, or death, because he has That which no other gain makes greater.

This yoga, or God-union, is defined as *chitta vritti nirodha.** Yoga must be practiced with unswerving perseverance, with complete dedication. When the Goal is attained, there is nothing more to acquire. The yogi has reached *kaivalya, nirvana,* complete liberation of the soul.

It is through meditation that the yogi realizes Brahman; no other gain, no joy, no knowledge surpasses that which comes in oneness with God.

The Yogi

Lord Krishna says in the Bhagavad Gita: "The yogi is greater than body-disciplining ascetics, greater even than the followers of the path of wisdom *(Jnana Yoga)* or of the path of action *(Karma Yoga);* be thou, O Arjuna, a yogi!" (VI:46). So he who is wise becomes a yogi.

The Six Chakras in the Cerebrospinal Axis

The subtle centers of life and consciousness in the cerebrospinal axis contain the five *tattvas* (elemental vibrations of matter), which, when awakened, allow human consciousness to express universal consciousness. *Prithivi tattva* (the earth vibration) is manifested in the coccygeal center *(muladhara chakra); apas* (the water vibration) in the sacral center *(svadhishthana chakra); tejas* (the fire vibration) in the lumbar center *(manipura cha-*

*Patanjali's *Yoga Sutras* I:2: "...'neutralization of the alternating waves in consciousness'...which may also be translated as 'cessation of the modifications of the mind-stuff.' *Chitta* is a comprehensive term for the thinking principle, which includes the pranic life forces, *manas* (mind or sense consciousness), *ahamkara* (egoity), and *buddhi* (intuitive intelligence). *Vritti* (literally 'whirlpool') refers to the waves of thought and emotion that ceaselessly arise and subside in man's consciousness. *Nirodha* means neutralization, cessation, control." —*Autobiography of a Yogi,* "I Become a Monk of the Swami Order," by Paramahansa Yogananda. *(Publisher's Note)*

kra); vayu (air vibration) in the dorsal center *(anahata chakra); akasha* (ether vibration) in the cervical center *(vishuddha chakra); buddhi tattva* (super-ether vibration)—in which thoughts and life energy move—in the medullary and *Kutastha* center *(ajna chakra);* and *Samashti* or *Hiranyagarbha* (the Cosmic Being or Brahma, the Creator) in the thousand-petaled lotus *(sahasrara chakra),* the creative dynamo enlivening all the functions of the lower centers.

The three qualities of Nature—*sattva* (elevating), *rajas* (activating), and *tamas* (obstructing), referred to collectively as the *gunas*—are expressed in varying proportions in the five elemental vibrations of earth, water, fire, air, and ether. *Sattva* is manifested when the consciousness remains centered in the spiritual eye. *Rajas* is expressed when the mind is in the dorsal center; and *tamas,* when the mind is concentrated in the lower three centers: lumbar, sacral, and coccygeal.

MAYA (DELUSION)

In the Bhagavad Gita, Lord Krishna says: "It is difficult indeed to go beyond (the influence of) My divine cosmic hypnosis *(maya),* imbued with the triple qualities. Those who take shelter in Me become free" (VII:14).

He who worships God with wholehearted devotion, and takes refuge in Him as the only help of the helpless, is released by His grace from *maya.*

Mere intellectual study of the scriptures will not bring Self-realization. But merging with God through complete, devotional surrender *(bhakti yoga),* the devotee attains *niralamba samadhi* (detachment of the mind from the external world). When the soul meets God, all ties of *maya* are sundered.

Samskara (Tendencies)

Deep attention on any thought or action creates an impression on the mind. These impressions become tendencies. They manifest effortlessly at any time, and especially so during times of stress or pleasure. With regular repetition, tendencies gain strength in the consciousness and become habits. Much of our everyday behavior is controlled by these tendencies. Since repeated practice creates firm impressions on the mind, it is wise to cultivate good habits. Then, even at the time of death, our good habits will bring thoughts of God and upliftment of our consciousness.

Avataras

By the power of *yoga maya* (delusion), the *Paramartha-tattva* (Supreme Object or Being) dwells unseen in every human being. "The ignorant, oblivious of Me as the Maker of all creatures, are blind to my presence within the human form" (Bhagavad Gita IX:11). To please His pure-minded devotees and to restore righteousness, the unborn, changeless Lord also incarnates on earth as *avataras* (perfected, fully liberated beings), such as Rama or Krishna. The spiritually blind do not recognize the Divinity clothed in the *maya*-garment of an *avatara's* human form, and thus do not rightly regard that divine being. But receptive souls see in that incarnation the transcendent Spirit; and worshipping that form, enjoy supreme Bliss.

Nectar from the Sahasrara

When the *sadhaka* (devotee) is transfixed in *samadhi,* there flows from the *sahasrara,* the thousand-petaled lotus, a divine nectar, *sudha.* Tasting this nectar, the devotee's body is purified and filled with bliss. Throughout this experience, he hears the all-pervasive sound of *Aum* (the creative manifestation of God as cosmic intelligent vibration).

Abhyasa Yoga

The Lord says: "If thou art unable to keep thy mind wholly on Me, then seek Me by yoga practices" (Bhagavad Gita XII:9). If, owing to past tendencies of restlessness *(samskaras),* the devotee's consciousness does not remain fixed on God in meditation, he should think on the worthlessness of those disruptive thoughts and try to detach himself from them by repeatedly bringing his mind back to God. This repeated effort to concentrate the mind on God is called *abhyasa yoga.*

"Wisdom (born) from yoga practice is superior to (mechanical) yoga practice; meditation is more desirable than the possession of theoretical knowledge; the relinquishment of the fruits of actions (is better) than (ineffectual, absentminded) meditation. Such renunciation (of the fruits of actions) is followed immediately by peace" (Bhagavad Gita XII:12). That devotee is untouched by pleasure or pain. He becomes ever merciful, ever contented. This is the perennial attitude of the yogi. He is determined and steadfast, and his mind and discrimination are surrendered to God. He beholds the Self in everything. Attaining this state through his *sadhana,* the yogi becomes dear to God. The scriptures say that knowledge is necessary to understand the things that are to be known. But when realization comes, intellectual knowledge may be discarded as no longer necessary. When God is attained, the devotee no longer requires the paths that lead to Him.

Bhakti (Devotion)

Without devotion, no *sadhana* can take you to God. To the man whose heart is dry of devotion, God remains farther than the farthest. But to the devoted soul, He is nearer than the nearest. All-pervasive, He dwells in the heart of every being. He is the stillness of the Absolute, and the motion of creation; so far, and yet so near.

Aloof from Influences

If you are seated in a place that is high enough, nobody can touch you from below. He who remains nonattached, aloof from the activities of the *gunas* (the three qualities of nature), will not be disturbed by the flux of duality. A man may be said to have attained the state of *gunatita* (freed from or beyond the *gunas*) if he is unmovably settled in the Self. He is unaffected by pleasure or pain, makes no distinction between a stone or gold, is not moved by praise or blame, maintains equanimity in success or failure, and treats friend and foe alike. He is like a *pankal* fish; though it lives in mud, it is not tainted by that mire.

The Soul

The *jiva* is an individualized image of Brahman, as a spark is of the fire, and a wave is of the sea. When the *jiva* can overcome *maya* by Self-realization, it will reattain the Brahman-state. But without Self-realization, it must reincarnate under the influence of *maya* to bear the fruits of its *karma*.

"When the Lord (as the *jiva*) acquires a body, He brings with Him the mind and the senses. When He leaves that body, He takes them and goes, even as the wind wafts away scents from their seats (in flowers)" (Bhagavad Gita XV:8).

When the soul leaves the body at death, it remains for a time in the astral world, in an astral form. When the soul enters a mother's womb for rebirth on earth, its new physical body in that womb does not breathe on its own, but through the oxygenated blood of the mother. But as soon as the baby is born, and it breathes through the nostrils, the internal pranic current becomes linked with the outside world through the cord of breath. The consciousness is drawn outward by the enchantment of the world of matter. The sentient soul then enjoys experiences of matter through touch, taste, sight, sound, and smell.

Just as a snake is covered with a strong new skin after shedding its old one, so the infant body of the reborn *jiva* is infused with energy for its new life. Thereafter, every moment from birth throughout life, the nervous system of that body is receiving impulses from the senses. Through them, the *jiva* experiences pleasure or pain.

Astral Sounds of the Chakras

When the mind is fixed at the *Kutastha,* a strong current of *prana* rises through the *chakras* in the spine producing at the *ajna chakra* a wondrous sound called *nada.* It is also known as *Panchajanya,** because it is a blend of the sounds produced by the five cerebrospinal *chakras* (*muladhara, svadhishthana, manipura, anahata,* and *vishuddha*). It is called the conch shell of Sri Krishna because it is heard at the *ajna chakra,* seat of *Kutastha* or

* *Pancha* means five; *janya,* born of or produced by.

Krishna (or Christ) Consciousness. With this sound, a light appears at the *ajna chakra.*

When the singular sound of the *manipura chakra* is heard, it is like that of a *vina* (a stringed instrument) and is called the *Devadatta* (God-given) conch shell of Arjuna. This is the center of *teja-tattva* (vibratory fire element), called *Vaishvanara.*

"As *Vaishvanara* (fiery power) I exist in the body of living creatures; and, acting through *prana* and *apana,* I digest food that is eaten in four ways" (Bhagavad Gita XV:14). Mentally offering one's food to God, who resides in this center under the name of *Vaishvanara,* will prevent indigestion. (I.e., attunement with the power of God, who alone sustains all functions in the body and in the universe, will keep the bodily instrument functioning in a perfect harmony.)

The Gateway to Hell

Lust, anger, greed—these constitute the threefold door to hell, and are by all means to be avoided.

The Body Is a Temple

The body should be kept pure because it is the dwelling, the temple, of the soul which is a part of God. Once this is realized, you will do no evil in body or mind.

What Is Ishvara?

Patanjali, the great exponent of Yoga, has defined Ishvara, the Lord as Ruler of the Universe, in the following way: He is a personal Being, and yet distinct from man; and more, even, than a liberated soul. Though He creates, enjoys, and is immanent in all things, He is untouched by *maya,* and unmoved by the objects of *maya.*

He is not subject to *karma* or *samskara.* A carpenter crafts wooden horses, elephants, and tigers, and mounts them on a wheel (merry-go-round). They move round in a circle when the carpenter gives them a twist. In the same manner, *jivas* revolve on the cycles of reincarnation, under the influence of Ishvara's *maya,* and drawn by their *pravritti* and *nivritti* (material and spiritual actions). However free you consider yourself to be, you are always under the influence of *maha maya,* and will remain so until liberated.

The Gunas: Sattva, Rajas, Tamas

All creation—man and nature—is under the influence of the three *gunas: sattva,* elevating; *rajas,* activating; *tamas,* obstructing, inertia. Under the influence of *tamas* (the obstructive quality of nature), man descends to lower and lower levels of ignorance and suffers the pain of his self-created hell. If the consciousness is not elevated from the tamasic force by self-redeeming actions, that man, when reborn, will have demonic tendencies—or may even take birth in an animal form.*

Rajas draws man into family life and social duties. He experiences the alternating flux of good and bad, pain and pleasure, success and failure according to his actions and thoughts.

The influence of the *sattva guna* raises man's consciousness: he is drawn into religious activity, spiritual discipline, and thereby approaches *moksha* (liberation).

* Retrogression to birth in an animal form provides the wrongdoer with an opportunity to work out some of his bad *karma* without accruing more in that lifetime; because an animal, acting on instinct and having no free will, is not responsible for its actions and thus acquires no *karma.*

By observing our behavior and different qualities, we can tell which *guna* predominates in our life. At death the predominant *guna* determines the quality of rebirth. If a person dies with a sattvic nature, he ascends to the heavens or reincarnates on earth in a spiritual environment. If *rajas* is predominant, he is reborn as an ordinary human being. If *tamas* prevails, he reincarnates in a very low type of human life, with animalistic tendencies, and may be born in a family with predominantly bestial qualities. If he has been very evil, he may even have to take birth for one life in an animal form.

Only when one rises above the influence of the *gunas* is he freed from the cycles of rebirth. As pure water mixes with pure water with no taint of separation; or as the idol made of salt, when it went into the sea to measure the depth, became one with it, so does the soul that has transcended the *gunas* commingle with God.

The mind, filled with desires born of the threefold *gunas,* must be mastered by lifting the consciousness into *nirvikalpa samadhi.** If the devotee were to exercise rigorous *tapasya* (religious austerity and penance) for a thousand years, if he were to crush his body with a rock, or enter a burning pyre, or throw himself into a hole full of nails, or sever his limbs with a sword; or if he were to memorize all the *mantras* and rites of Shiva and Vishnu; or if the King of Heaven, Mahendra, is moved by his sorrow — yet he would not attain salvation unless he frees himself from desires. So long as he clings to desires, he will move to hell or heaven and back to earth. The *jiva* will not attain the everlasting Good without

* In *nirvikalpa samadhi* the yogi dissolves the last vestiges of his material or earthly *karma.* This is the superior state of *samadhi* in which the yogi moves freely in the world without any loss of God-perception.

desireless nonattachment toward all things mortal. To become free from desires, you have to make the spiritual effort to attain God-realization, and to secure yourself in the state of *yogarudha* (at one with the transcendent soul).

All material attractions are strung on a cord of our desires, and we are entangled in that cord. Sever it, and all attraction will drop away.

After *Kriya* practice, sit long in meditation with the attention fixed at the *Kutastha.* The soul-consciousness that usually flows outward into body-consciousness is turned inward by *Kriya.* Then the mind, freed from its attraction to external objects, will experience the wondrous inner world of Spirit. As the attention remains riveted at *Kutastha,* all dualities born of the *gunas*—pleasure and pain, heat and cold, and so forth—cease automatically.

Aum

The single-syllable word *Aum* is the designator or symbol of Brahman. It is the most suitable word for chanting the Lord's name, for it is not just a word to describe Him; it is His outward manifestation in creation.* Through *Aum,* Brahman may be realized. *Aum* is also called *pranava* (the sacred syllable that has a reverberating or humming sound). It is that which removes all doubts, for communion with *Aum* gives proof of God's presence.

The correct method of *pranava-japa,* the vocal or mental chanting of *Aum,* must be understood and prac-

* The vibratory manifestation of God in creation; the Word, or Holy Ghost, or Amen: invisible divine power, the only doer, the sole causative and activating force that upholds all creation through vibration. *(Publisher's Note)*

ticed in order to be spiritually fruitful. Mere repetition of the word without understanding or concentration will yield no result. The correct method of *pranava-japa* is to actually hear the *nada* (sound) and become one with it through concentration. This will fill the heart of the *sadhaka* with divine ecstasy.

The three aspects of God—Creator, Preserver, Destroyer—and all His qualities are contained in the *Aum* vibration. To concentrate on *Aum* is the surest way to realization of Brahman. The sacred scriptures—the Vedas, *Upanishads,* Gita, *Bhagavata*—all declare that God may be known through *Aum.*

Aum is the best symbol for those who want to worship a personal God. It is a better symbol than images, such as those of Kali, Krishna, and others; because in worshipping God as an image, the mind limits the Infinite to that form. It becomes difficult for the *sadhaka* to think of God beyond that *ishta,* when in fact God is Spirit. While meditating on *Aum,* the mind expands with the omnipresence of that vibration, and the Spirit-nature of Brahman inherent therein is realized as *Sat-chit-ananda*—ever-existing, ever-conscious, ever-new Bliss.

Kriya Yoga

Only those who have acquired great good *karma* through the good works of many incarnations are drawn to the path of *Kriya Yoga.* They are blessed who have learned this technique. It requires eight million incarnations in lower life-forms before the soul gains birth in the unique human body. Even after attaining human form, if the consciousness becomes very animalistic and filled with evil, it will surely retrogress to an animal form again for an incarnation. From where do the souls come to incarnate in human form? They have evolved through mineral, plant, and the lower to higher forms of animal life. The population of humankind is continually replenished from this upward evolution of souls. Only the human being is endowed with the capacity to express the innate Divinity. It is a sacrilege, therefore, to misuse this human instrument of the soul. *Kriya* hastens the spiritual awakening of the soul in man.

Kriya Yoga is to be learned from a true guru, one who has realized God through *Kriya.* When practiced according to the guru's instructions and with his blessings, the technique lifts the consciousness of the devotee through the subtle cerebrospinal *chakras* into God-realization. If the *sadhaka* does not realize God in one lifetime through *Kriya Yoga,* he carries the good effect of his practice into the next incarnation and is drawn again to the *Kriya* path. The *karma* with which a being is born is called *sahaja karma.* Thus, the *sahaja karma* of *Kriya Yogis* is the spiritual advancement they have acquired from the practice of the sacred *Kriya* technique in their previous life, and a natural tendency to make rapid progress in *Kriya* in this new incarnation.

Mejda once asked me: "Do you read the Bhagavad Gita?"

"Occasionally I do," I replied, "but I do not understand it fully."

He told me, "Whatever you do not understand, ask my Gurudeva; or come to me."

In the Bhagavad Gita Krishna says: "O Arjuna! in whatever way people are devoted to Me, in that measure (according to their desire, their degree of understanding, and their manner of worship) I manifest Myself to them. All men, regardless of their mode of seeking, pursue a path to Me" (IV:11). The ways of worshipping God are many: *nama kirtana* (chanting His name); *mala japa* (reciting prayers on beads); *abhyasa yoga* (repeatedly bringing the mind back to its point of concentration in meditation); *Kriya Yoga,* and so on. Sri Ramakrishna said that all religions, all true paths, lead to God. This is indeed so; but some roads are long, some are short. If you wish to go to Kashmir, you could take a bullock cart, a horse carriage, a car, a train, or a plane. The plane is the fastest. This is why I call *Kriya Yoga* the "airplane route" to God.

No matter how full of worldly restlessness the ungoverned mind has become, through *Kriya Yoga* practice it can be purified and brought under control. Why is this control necessary? God does not accept the remains of an offering that has already been tasted. When the devotee indulges in desires and then offers to God the little devotion that is left, God will not respond. How then does *Kriya Yoga* purify the mind that is filled with the desires of incarnations? Centered within the cerebrospinal axis is the subtle *sushumna* passage from the *muladhara* to the *sahasrara*. On either side of the *sushumna* are the *nadis* (subtle channels) called *ida* and *pingala.* In waking consciousness, during which the mind and energy are directed outward into the world of matter, the life current flows down the spine and out through the *chakras* to the senses and all the organs and nerves of the body. This outflowing causes attraction to and desire for material things. During the practice of the guru-given technique of *Kriya Yoga,* the spine becomes magnetized and draws the life current inward along the *ida* and *pingala* and into the *sushumna* to ascend this subtle channel through each of the *chakras,* awakening spiritual consciousness in man. All thoughts, consciousness itself, become interiorized and centered in God. The devotee experiences joy and knowledge beyond all expression.

Sadhus in the Himalayas meditate bare-bodied, sitting on the ice. How can they do this? They are able to withdraw their consciousness from the sensations of the body. (Our father underwent surgery for a hernia when he was eighty years old. He refused a general anesthetic. He was able to interiorize his consciousness and disconnect it from the body because of his many years of *Kriya* practice.—*Author's Note*)

The Gita passage that states, "Indeed, neither the *devas* (gods) nor the *danavas* (titans) know the infinite modes of Thine appearances"* is usually erroneously interpreted to mean that knowledge or perception of God is beyond our capacity. It *is* possible to become one with Brahman, and then one shall know what Brahman knows.

All things finite have a limit, but Divine Love is never-ending. The more you feel this Love, the more you will be intoxicated with its Joy. This Joy knows no bounds. It is ever new, ever increasing. Slowly, gradually, the realization of this Bliss comes, until at last the God-realized soul totally merges with Him in the ecstasy of *Sat-chit-ananda:* ever-existing, ever-conscious, ever-new Bliss. Such souls need never again incarnate in this troublesome world. They remain for eternity immersed in the Supreme Bliss.

* X:14.

Paramahansaji's Answers to Questions

From notes I made of Mejda's responses to various queries

Do prayers bring results? If so, then why is it that so many persons do not receive answers to their prayers? What is the best way to pray to bring God's response?

God does not like a tainted offering; praying with a mind filled with restless desires is like giving to God the leftovers of your devotion. Prayer should be offered after the practice of *Kriya,* when the devotion of the heart and the stillness of the mind are united, and free from desire. Talk to God in the language of your soul; cry for Him. Then you will find Him and receive His response. Such joy will be yours! Endless realizations come to the soul.

AKHANDA MANDALA KARAM
VYAPTAM YENA CHARACHARAM
TATPADAM DARSHITAM YENA
TASMAI SRI GURAVE NAMAH

"O God, Thou art the Supreme Cause; Thou art Truth; Thou art present everywhere and in everything. Thou art the Creator and Sustainer of all life, and the One into Whom all things finally merge again."

["Uttara Khanda," *Skanda Purana* ("Guru Gita"), *slokas* 148 and 182]

Indeed it is difficult to follow the *sadhana* that leads to God — renunciation, *brahmacharya* (self-control), *pranayama,* meditation, and God-realization through *samadhi* — because the human tendency is to gravitate toward worldly experiences. But if one perseveres wholeheartedly, he will gain in the end the greatest satisfaction and supreme joy.

The man of Self-realization knows a bliss that cannot be compared to anything in this world. His joy is independent of any object or sensory experience. It is an incomparable happiness that cannot be described in words. Such joy is known as *sattvik-ananda* (pure bliss).

Rabindranath Tagore has written: "In the deep seclusion of my heart where I came to know Thee, everything is silent, motionless—words cannot express it."

This world, and everything in it, is *asat,* not true, unreal. At every moment, we are being shown its transitory nature: a father loses his only son, a wife loses her husband. Still our eyes are not opened. Our minds remain busy with the most trivial things, revealing how base is human nature.

"O Bhagavan, remove our ignorance. Destroy all mortal desires. Show us the way (the yoga route of *sushumna*) to salvation. Awaken us from delusion by the transforming touch of Your golden scepter. Draw us to Your lotus feet in everlasting devotion. Above all, free us from all obstacles of delusion: remove Your enchanting power of illusion.

"'Heaven, earth, and all creation have come from Thee; and into Thy Being they dissolve again. Awaken within us the knowledge that Thou art the Supreme Being, the only Reality. Let us ever remember this.' [*Taittiriya Upanishad* 3:1.]

"'All beings live by Thy grace; and by that grace even the blind can see, the mute can speak, the lame can climb a mountain. I bow to Thee, and remember Thee always.' [*Bhavishya Purana.*]

"'Sun, moon, stars, lightning, fire — all are made bright by Thine effulgence. It is Thy light that illumines the whole universe, and that remains awake in us forever.' [*Katha Upanishad* 2:2:15.]

"Electricity runs trams, trains, and fans, and lights the bulb of the lamp. But if the current is disconnected, these mechanisms cease to operate. Similarly, we are enlivened by Thee, a Power unseen by the ordinary man. Without Thee, naught could exist; but because Thou art, I am. Thou art my life. May this supreme knowledge forever remain awake within me. For so long as there is life in this body, let my eyes ever watch Thee; let my mind turn towards Thee as the needle of the compass ever turns toward the North Star.

"Take away all obstacles of delusion, that when I draw the last breath of this life, my wisdom-eye may be fixed upon Thy light within me; my mind anchored in Thee; my soul clinging to Thy feet."

Take to your heart this yoga song of the sages:

So long as there is life in your body,
Do your *sadhana,* worship the Lord;
Otherwise, when death calls you,
You will not be able to cling to the thought of Him.
If you leave this earth
With thoughts of delusion predominant,
They will return with you, to bind you, in a new incarnation.

Do your *sadhana* now,
Or mortal desires will not leave you
On your last day.

The thoughts that predominate at the time of death can bring you either salvation—if your supreme desire is for God—or rebirth. If you are filled with worldly desires, those thoughts impinge themselves on the subtle body and bring the soul back into another earthly incarnation. The sum total of past actions and unfulfilled desires determines what kind of body you will have, and sets the general pattern of your new incarnation. Just as the form of a huge banyan tree lies hidden in a tiny seed, awaiting favorable conditions for germination; or as the sounds of a record are secreted in its grooves, waiting for the touch of the needle to bring them out, so the past-life tendencies carried in the subtle body become manifested through the medium of a new incarnation.

At death, when the body is cremated, the disembodied soul thinks: "Where shall I go? Where are father, mother, brothers, and sisters?"

Remember the words of Tagore:

When we leave the old body dwelling,
We wonder in apprehension: what awaits me?
We forget that Thou art in the new
As Thou wert in the old.

When one knows Thee,
Then alien there is none;
Of barriers and fears there are none.
Let me see Thee always—
Thou who art playing in all.

[From *Gitanjali*]

TVAMEVA MATACHA PITA TVAMEVA
TVAMEVA BANDHUSHCHA SAKHA TVAMEVA
TVAMEVA VIDYA DRAVINAM TVAMEVA
TVAMEVA SARVAM MAMA DEVADEVA

Thou art my Mother,
Thou art my Father,
Thou art my Friend,
Thou art my wisdom and understanding—
Thou art my all.

[From "Pandava Gita," "Anushasana Parva," *Mahabharata.*]

It is said that when the moth sees a cockroach, the moth becomes so full of fear and so absorbed in thinking about the roach that it becomes transformed into a roach itself in its next life. Similarly, by concentrating our thoughts on God, may we become transformed into Brahman Himself.

We should always think:

AHAMATMA NA CHANYOASMI
BRAHMAIVAHAM NA SHOKABHAK
SACHCHIDANANDARUPOAHAM
NITYAMUKTASVABHAVAVAN

"I am Spirit, naught else.
I am ever-existing, ever-conscious, ever-new joy; not suffering and sorrow.
By my nature, I am forever free."

[From *Brahmanuchintanum* (Meditations on Brahman), *sloka* 7, by Adi Shankaracharya]

Tagore says:

Let me take the dust of Thy feet;
Do not keep me away.
I will cling to Thy lotus feet forever: in life, in death, in joy and sorrow.

["Geetabitan," *Puja,* Sloka 104]

"Lord, I have no one except You. You alone are my refuge. You have many devotees, but I have only You. Give me that singlehearted desire and devotion that will keep my mind always at Your feet, You who are the One and Only Begotten in all things. Take away all obstacles of delusion. Make me *jivanmukti,* free from all sin and delusion.

"I want to melt in Thee like the idol made of salt that tried to measure the depth of the sea and became the sea itself."

When I sit to practice Kriya Yoga, *restless thoughts crowd into my mind, making it difficult to concentrate. How do I overcome this?*

Mejda asked me to bring a glass of water and some soil from the garden. He mixed the dirt into the water and placed the glass of muddy water in front of me.

"You see that the water is muddy," he said, "but can you see the individual particles of dirt?"

"No," I replied.

"Now wait for a while."

Soon I could see the particles of dirt settle to the bottom of the glass; the water was clearing slowly. After a while, all the dirt had settled and the water had become transparent again.

Then Mejda explained: "Many thoughts are constantly vibrating in our consciousness. When we sit to meditate, we find the mind clouded with this restlessness. Soon individual thoughts stand out, like the particles of dirt settling out of the water. But just because you become aware of these thoughts, don't think you are becoming more restless! Wait patiently. Continue to practice *Kriya* resolutely. In time those thoughts will settle and your consciousness will clear of all restlessness."

You often speak of Parama Jyoti *(the Supreme Light). How can we see that Light?*

When the advanced *sadhaka* withdraws the consciousness and subtle life currents *(prana)* from the senses, and focuses them at the *Kutastha,* the Divine Light may be seen. The color of this Light is like the rising sun; Its brilliance and power are as of a million suns, yet Its luster is cool like the moon. This Light, which reveals the fourth dimension, cannot be circumscribed. Fortunate are those few out of the masses of humanity who have the good *karma* to receive the technique of *Kriya* by which the light of God is revealed.

Metaphysically speaking, what is the function of food in the body?

Food is a gross manifestation of vibratory life force. That portion that is too gross to be used by the body becomes excreta. Vibrations in food that are harmonious with the life processes in the body feed the cells of tissue, blood, and bone. The finer vibrations in food nourish mental activity.

What is sin?

Sin lies in evil thoughts and desires, not solely in wrong actions. If, while practicing *Kriya,* an unholy thought arises in the mind, throw it out immediately. That yogi remains free from sin who performs *atma-dharma* (the duties of the soul) without any desire for the fruits of his actions. Restrain sense inclinations; cast aside dualistic thoughts of pleasure and pain, happiness and sorrow, gain and loss, victory and defeat. Attachment to sense pleasures darkens the mind and obscures the light of the true Self, the soul. In the Bhagavad Gita, Bhagavan Krishna admonished Arjuna to become *nirdvandva* (free from dualities); *nityasattvastha* (ever-balanced; settled in *sattva,* goodness, spirituality); *nir-yogakshema* (not caring for the acquisition of or holding on to possessions); and *atmavan* (fixed in the Self).*

Within the *sushumna* is the *Brahmanadi,* the innermost channel through which the consciousness ascends to Spirit. The *akasha,* or subtle "space," of *Brahmanadi* is *nityasattva* (of the purest goodness or spiritual quality that is perpetual and unchanging). When the consciousness reaches this state, the ultimate blessing of God is within sight. The dualistic forces, such as heat and cold, pleasure and pain, are neutralized and the *jivatman* or *hansa* (soul) becomes *nityasattvastha,* settled in the supreme goodness. Penetrate *kuta* and become ensconced in *sahasrara,* and thus be *atmavan,* ever settled in the Self.

Yoga means the attainment of the Unattainable; and *kshema,* to retain that which has been attained. So in this Gita verse (II:45) *niryogakshema* means one should not be keen to get that which should not be gained, nor to hold on to such acquisitions that have already been acquired.

Krishna further says: "Be *nistraigunya,* free from the triple qualities of nature that bind the soul to delusion." This means you must irrevocably settle your mind and consciousness in Brahman. When you have drawn your consciousness to the *ajna chakra* and (through the spiri-

* *Traigunyavishaya veda / Nistraigunyo bhava 'rjuna / Nirdvandvo nityasattvastho / Niryogakshema atmavan:* "The Vedas expound the three universal qualities or *gunas.* O Arjuna, free thyself from the triple qualities and from the pairs of opposites! Ever calm, harboring no thoughts of receiving and keeping, become thou settled in the Self" —Bhagavad Gita II:45.

tual eye) penetrated *kuta,* the entrance to the *sahasrara,* the activating power of the *gunas* can no longer touch you. The heretofore quiescent soul-consciousness in the *sahasrara* opens like a lotus, radiating *jnana-jyoti* (divine illumination). In that wisdom-light, all things—past, present, and future—are known to the soul. The *atman,* having transcended *maya,* becomes one with Maheshvara, the Supreme Lord.

During a long period of meditation the legs and entire body sometimes seem benumbed, owing to lack of blood circulation. What can the yogi do to prevent this?

Maha Mudra (the spine-stretching *asana* that is done before practice of *Kriya* proper) can be performed again during and/or after a long meditation. When performed as taught in *Kriya Yoga, Maha Mudra* is a combination of *asana* and *pranayama.* It stimulates circulation; and by its beneficial effect on the spine, distributes life force evenly throughout the entire body. It thus benefits—in a way that other exercises do not—the nerves, veins, muscles, heart, lungs, and joints, keeping the body in full vigor and health, adapting it to long periods of meditation. Other *asanas* (postures of *Hatha Yoga*) are not as effective for this purpose. Therefore, it is considered the best of *asanas,* and is called *Maha Mudra* (the great posture).

What is the meaning of Sat *and* asat?

Sat is reality, existence; *asat* is that which is unreal, non-existent. All that is subject to time and space is *asat,* non-existent. That is, if something exists here but not elsewhere, it is circumscribed by space; and if something exists now, but did not exist in the past and will not exist in the future, it is measured by time—therefore, it is *asat.* The wave comes out of the ocean and enjoys its temporary existence for a moment, but it is the ocean that is the real substance. Similarly, creation, subject to the relativities of time and space, cannot be omnipresent nor immortal. Therefore, creation is called *asat,* non-existent. Only Spirit—out of which creation manifests—is *Sat,* or real, for only Spirit exists everywhere at all times.

How do you explain the benefits of Kriya *practice?*

The ancient sages, intuiting the link between life and Spirit, evolved the soul science of *Kriya Yoga.* Let me give you a simple explanation: Keeping company with an evil person makes one evil; conversely, the company of a good person makes one good. The *sadhaka* wants to become free of all desires except the desire for God. How to keep the company of desirelessness and the thought of God?

From the moment of our birth until death, nature makes us perform *pran-kriya,* the act of breathing. This process, which maintains life and ties the soul to the body, goes on automatically, without our conscious desire. Through the practice of *Kriya Yoga* we associate ourselves with the life-process rather than the body: breath, life energy, and consciousness become one. Thus, by linking technique to the heretofore automatic act of breathing, through *Kriya* practice, we eventually become free of body-consciousness, and hence free of desires and filled with supreme Bliss. Therefore, why not employ this perfectly natural process to find God?

(How clear and simple is Mejda's explanation; it is one that can never be forgotten.)

What is the meaning of the Aum *mantra that we chant at each of the chakras?*

Aum is known as *Pranava,* the sacred sound that is the name of Ishvara; it is His voice and the symbol of His presence in vibratory creation. The Absolute is unfathomable without some sound, object, or thought process to define Him. *Aum* is the most sacred symbol that can be used to know God. The vibration of *Aum* contains all the concepts of Him and all His manifestations. No other mantra or symbol gives greater calmness and divine attunement of the mind to God. Chanting this sacred Name leads to perception of the Infinite.

What is the soul's nature?

The soul's nature is bliss; but one may ask why then does man have so much sorrow? Owing to *avidya* (individual delusion, or ignorance) the soul seems to be self-contradictory; yet on the other hand, it is seen to be beyond the contrasts of duality. The soul is self-born, yet unmanifested. It is forever free, yet seemingly in bondage. Is the soul not a fascinating paradox?

This *atman* is of white effulgence, but unlike any physical light, it neither gives off heat nor causes a shadow. It is untouched by any experience. It neither sees nor hears, yet is all-knowing and all-perceiving through its omnipresent *Kutastha* consciousness.

The *atman* is *sat-chit-ananda:* ever-existing, ever-conscious, ever-new joy. *Manas,* or the sentient consciousness of the body, is dependent on the instrument of the senses and the stimulus of the environment. The soul is not imposed upon by these. Though the soul is apparently beyond comprehension, there is a way to gain realization of the Self. It is not through reading the scriptures or listening to them, or through intellectually understanding their truths. But to the yogi who worships God with pure devotion, the Lord reveals Himself, and that devotee realizes the little *atman* as a part of *Paramatman.*

In the Gita Krishna teaches: "This soul, in essence the reflection of Spirit, never undergoes the throes of death or the pangs of birth; nor, having once known existence, is it ever non-existent. This soul was never born; it is everlastingly living, untouched by the *maya*-magic of change. The soul is ever constant through all cycles of bodily disintegrations."* The soul lives in the body like the sun shining upon and in the water: when the water dries up, the sun remains unaffected. With the realization of the soul's oneness with Brahman we attain freedom from the dualities that cause pleasure and pain.

All that is created has a beginning; and being under the control of the three *gunas,* is subject to change and death. Since the soul is Spirit essence, it is not influenced by nature's attributes, and is therefore eternal and unchanging. Although it resides in the body, it is untouched by the experiences of the body. The Gita explains: "As the all-pervading ether, because of its subtlety, is beyond taint, similarly the Self, though seated everywhere in the body, is ever taintless."† The *atman* is forever the pure Self; uninvolved in the activities of nature, it is yet the indwelling intelligence and life in matter, creatures, humans, demons and *devas.*

* II:20.

† XIII:33.

What happens to the soul when a human being dies?

Bhagavan Krishna says in the Gita: "Just as a man who forsakes dilapidated raiment dons new clothes, so also the body-encased soul that relinquishes a decaying physical habitation enters a new body."*

How does the soul manifest itself?

In the world of matter there is nothing higher, nobler, purer than the indwelling soul. In the body it is the luminous eternal tree of life (the divine light and consciousness in the subtle cerebrospinal centers). In oneness with Brahman, the *atman* is all-pervading, indescribable, incomprehensible, illimitable and immutable, unchanging, supreme, and infinite.

I have heard that yoga sadhana *gives spiritual powers to the practitioner. What are these powers?*

These are called *siddhis* or *aishvaryas,* and are eight in number:

1) *Anima:* power to make the body (or anything else) smaller, even as small as an atom.
2) *Mahima:* power to enlarge the body to any size.
3) *Laghima:* power to make the body lighter in weight, even weightless.
4) *Garima:* power to make the body heavy.
5) *Prapti:* power to obtain anything desired.

* II:22.

6) *Prakamya:* power to satisfy all desires by will force.

7) *Ishitva:* power of becoming lord over everything.

8) *Vashitva:* power to control anything in creation.

These eight *siddhis* are achieved through the practice of Yoga. The yogi who attains enlightenment acquires these powers and becomes a *jivanmukta,* one who is liberated while living. As a freed soul, conqueror of death, he dedicates his life to the upliftment of mankind. An example of such an enlightened being is the deathless Mahavatar Babaji, who has given *Kriya Yoga sadhana* for the liberation of souls from mortal bondage. Trailanga Swami, and my own beloved guru and paramguru, Swami Sri Yukteswar and Lahiri Mahasaya, also demonstrated their mastery of these *siddhis.* Patanjali speaks of powers as the result, not the goal, of Yoga.

Will you speak on the glory of the Bhagavad Gita and how its study will help us?

The great sage Vyasadeva [author of the *Mahabharata,* of which the Gita is a part] has explained: "All the Upanishads are the cows; Krishna is the milker; Arjuna is the calf; and the supreme nectar of the Gita is the milk. Wise men drink this nectar." I bow to Lord Krishna, who agreed to become the charioteer of Arjuna, and delivered to him and to all mankind the immortal message of the Gita. Those who want to cross the ocean of delusion can do so safely in the wisdom-ark of the Gita. Containing the ultimate concepts of *jnana, bhakti,* and *karma* — wisdom, devotion, and right action — and of *Parabrahman* as both immanent and transcendent, the

Gita is the essence of all scriptures, and the path to salvation for all men.

The Gita is extolled in various ways in the [Hindu] scriptures:

> Bathing in the waters of the Gita removes worldly impurities....One who reads the Gita in a holy temple, in a place of pilgrimage, or by the shore of a sacred river will receive good fortune....No evil will befall a house wherein the Gita is worshipped....Sins wilfully or ignorantly committed are forgiven him who reads the Gita....The yogis, *rishis,* and gods protect in this life and in the hereafter the man who follows the Gita....Chanting the sacred names of the Gita will destroy one's sins and bestow wisdom and *siddhis* (powers)....At the time of death: If one recites a chapter or even a *sloka* of the Gita, he will gain *para-pada* (the highest place; final emancipation); even a great sinner, if he reads or listens to the Gita, will be saved; a touch of the Gita will earn the dying man a place in Vaikuntha (Vishnu's heaven) in Vishnu's joyous company; a Gita placed near a dying man will ensure him a good rebirth and predisposition in that new life to follow the Gita teachings and find salvation; the mere utterance of the word "Gita" will make the dying man virtuous ....Reading Gita during the *shraddha* (memorial funeral ceremony) brings joy to the departed soul and lifts that soul to heaven....Before starting any endeavor, if one reads the Gita his efforts will be fruitful and protected from evil....The Lord says, "The Gita is My heart and essence, My immutable knowledge, My dwelling place, My

> utmost secrets, and the *dharma* with which I uphold the three worlds"....Study of the Vedas, gift-giving, pilgrimages, ritual worship, or the observance of vows is not as pleasing to Bhagavan as the reading of the Gita....Knowledge gathered from the Vedas and *Puranas* becomes fruitful only by reading the Gita with devotion.

All the foregoing from the scriptures is a statement of the power of truth in the Gita. But to realize these blessings one must be united to that truth through devotion, faith, and inner attunement. Merely to read or hear or worship the Gita without the corresponding inner experience is fruitless. These scriptural promises of blessings from the Gita are metaphorical exhortations to the devotee to reenact within himself the Gita dialogue between the soul and Spirit. Thus does the *sadhaka* offer true worship to God, receive enlightenment, and thereby attain salvation.

Kamdeb
Gopiraman
Kalicharan
Dayaram[5]

Bhabani Charan · Nandadulal · Ramprasad · Shibchandra · Balaram · Ramkanai

Radhamohan (son of Ramprasad)

Ishan Chandra · Bhoirab Chandra · Kailash Chandra (sons of Radhamohan)

Bhagabati Charan · Sarada Prasad · Satish Chandra (sons of Ishan Chandra)

Prasad Das · Prabhas Chandra · Prakash Chandra (sons of Sarada Prasad)

Sibdas · Krishnadas (sons of Satish Chandra)

Balai · Prasanta (sons of Prasad Das)

Kanaidas (son of Prakash Chandra)

Saroj Das (son of Sibdas)

Ananta Lal · Roma Shashi (daughter) · Uma Shashi (daughter) · Mukunda Lal (Paramahansa Yogananda) · Nalini Sundari (daughter) · Sananda Lal · Purnamoyee (daughter) · Bishnu Charan (children of Bhagabati Charan)

Ramkrishna (son of Ananta Lal)
Durlabh (son of Ramkrishna)

Harekrishna · Shyamsundar (sons of Sananda Lal)
Somnath (son of Harekrishna)

Srikrishna · Biswanath (sons of Bishnu Charan)

Note: Chart shows direct lineage to Paramahansa Yogananda, omitting other branches of the family up to our father's time. Also omitted are the daughters, except for those in Paramahansaji's immediate family, since their offspring do not carry the Ghosh family name.

Notes for the above-numbered references are printed overleaf.

GENEALOGICAL CHART

The Family of Paramahansa Yogananda (Mukunda Lal Ghosh)

Dakshin Rarhi[1]

The Ghosh Family of South Rarh

Makaranda[2]
- Purushottam
  - Bhabanath
    - Mahadeb
      - Gabo[3]
        - Prabhakar
        - Nishapati[4]
          - Ushapati
            - Prajapati
              - Bibhakar
              - Mandhir
              - Bhanu
              - Hangsa
                - Purandar
                  - Padmanabha
                    - Krishna
                    - Heramba
                      - Durjyodhan
                    - Jagannath
                    - Sarbananda
                    - Sridhar
                    - Bhoirab
                    - Madhab
                  - Alangkar
                  - Krittibas
                  - Kulapati
                - Balaram
                - Anirudra
                - Raghunath
              - Tapan
              - Madhu
              - Bir
- Subhasita

[1] *Dakshin Rarhi* is a title of the Ghosh family as well as a designation of their ancestral native land. Purushottam Ghosh, son of Makaranda Ghosh, settled in the South Rarh (southwest Bengal) by order of the son of King Adisur. He was thereafter known as a *Dakshin Rarhi* (South Rarhian), and his descendants were designated as a Ghosh family of the South Rarh.

[2] Makaranda Ghosh was a *Kshatriya* of the aristocratic *Saukalin Gotra* (clan) of Kannauj, Uttar Pradesh, in north India. He was a descendant of Maharshi (great sage) Saukalin, founder of the *Saukalin* Clan, and was himself an esteemed scholar of the eleventh century. At the request of King Adisur of Bengal, Makaranda settled in Bengal to help the king in reforming and properly governing the people in the area.

[3] Gabo Ghosh was employed in the service of the king at Saptagram in the district of Hooghly, Bengal, during the reign of King Vijay Sen at the end of the eleventh century.

[4] The exalted social status of "*Kulin*" (the highest rank within a caste) in the *Kshatriya* caste was conferred upon Nishapati Ghosh by King Ballal Sen. By appointment of the king, Nishapati settled in Bali village of Arambagh in the district of Hooghly, Bengal—some time between A.D. 1122 and 1139—with the mission of social service on behalf of the king. The community established by Nishapati Ghosh is known as Bali Samaj (Bali Community).

[5] Dayaram Ghosh, in the middle of the eighteenth century, settled in Ichapur, Bengal—in District 24-Parganas. This was the ancestral home of the Ghosh family until, in 1918, the British Government took over the land, purchasing it from the family (the great-great-grandsons of Dayaram, including Bhagabati Ghosh, the father of Paramahansa Yogananda) in order to expand the government ordnance factory. Thenceforth, those descendants of Dayaram settled variously at Calcutta, Serampore, and Howrah.

PARAMAHANSA YOGANANDA: A YOGI IN LIFE AND DEATH

Paramahansa Yogananda entered *mahasamadhi* (a yogi's final conscious exit from the body) in Los Angeles, California, on March 7, 1952, after concluding his speech at a banquet held in honor of H.E. Binay R. Sen, Ambassador of India.

The great world teacher demonstrated the value of yoga (scientific techniques for God-realization) not only in life but in death. Weeks after his departure his unchanged face shone with the divine luster of incorruptibility.

Mr. Harry T. Rowe, Los Angeles Mortuary Director, Forest Lawn Memorial-Park (in which the body of the great master is temporarily placed), sent Self-Realization Fellowship a notarized letter from which the following extracts are taken:

"The absence of any visual signs of decay in the dead body of Paramahansa Yogananda offers the most extraordinary case in our experience.... No physical disintegration was visible in his body even twenty days after death.... No indication of mold was visible on his skin, and no visible desiccation (drying up) took place in the bodily tissues. This state of perfect preservation of a body is, so far as we know from mortuary annals, an unparalleled one.... At the time of receiving Yogananda's body, the Mortuary personnel expected to observe, through the glass lid of the casket, the usual progressive signs of bodily decay. Our astonishment increased as day followed day without bringing any visible change in the body under observation. Yogananda's body was apparently in a phenomenal state of immutability....

"No odor of decay emanated from his body at any time.... The physical appearance of Yogananda on March 27th, just before the bronze cover of the casket was put into position, was the same as it had been on March 7th. He looked on March 27th as fresh and as unravaged by decay as he had looked on the night of his death. On March 27th there was no reason to say that his body had suffered any visible physical disintegration at all. For these reasons we state again that the case of Paramahansa Yogananda is unique in our experience."

Books by PARAMAHANSA YOGANANDA

Available at bookstores or directly from the publisher:

Self-Realization Fellowship
3880 San Rafael Avenue
Los Angeles, California 90065

Autobiography of a Yogi
Man's Eternal Quest
The Divine Romance
Where There Is Light: *Insight and Inspiration for Meeting Life's Challenges*
The Science of Religion
Whispers from Eternity
Songs of the Soul
Sayings of Paramahansa Yogananda
Scientific Healing Affirmations
How You Can Talk With God
Metaphysical Meditations
The Law of Success
Cosmic Chants

Audio Recordings of Informal Talks by Paramahansa Yogananda

Beholding the One in All
Awake in the Cosmic Dream

Other books from the same publisher:

The Holy Science *by Swami Sri Yukteswar*

"Only Love" *by Sri Daya Mata*

Finding the Joy Within You: Personal Counsel for God-Centered Living *by Sri Daya Mata*

God Alone: The Life and Letters of a Saint *by Sri Gyanamata*

Please request current catalog of books and audio/video recordings before ordering.

Free Introductory Booklet: *Undreamed-of Possibilities*

The scientific techniques of meditation referred to in *"Mejda,"* including Kriya Yoga, are taught in the *Self-Realization Fellowship Lessons.* For further information please write for the free introductory booklet *Undreamed-of Possibilities.*